Jim Wofford

Still Horse Crazy
After All These Years

(IF IT DIDN'T HAPPEN THIS WAY...IT SHOULD HAVE)

T
TRAFALGAR SQUARE
North Pomfret, Vermont

First published in 2021 by
Trafalgar Square Books
North Pomfret, Vermont 05053

Library of Congress Cataloging-in-Publication Data
Names: Wofford, James C., 1944- author.
Title: Still horse crazy after all these years : (if it didn't happen this
    way...it should have) / Jim Wofford.
Description: North Pomfret, Vermont : Trafalgar Square Books, 2021. |
    Includes index. | Summary: "Three-time Olympian Jim Wofford grew up with
    horses, beginning with his childhood on a Kansas farm in the forties.
    The son of an Olympic show jumper, Wofford and his siblings all found
    themselves pursuing a "riding life"-one of reward and growth, of
    challenge and disappointment, but mostly of learning to understand and
    work with a complex animal as an athletic partner and friend. Over the
    years Wofford developed as an international competitor, successful
    coach, and sought-after commentator. Known for his wit, irreverence, and
    whip-smart observations on the sport and its participants, as well as
    the state of the "outside" world, his magazine columns were as legendary
    as his performances in the saddle. Now Wofford brings his immense talent
    for telling tales-all of them (mostly) true-to the page in this
    incredibly entertaining book"-- Provided by publisher.
Identifiers: LCCN 2021007053 (print) | LCCN 2021007054 (ebook) | ISBN
    9781570769559 (paperback) | ISBN 9781570769559 (epub)
Subjects: LCSH: Wofford, James C., 1944- | Horsemen and horsewomen--United
    States--Biography. | Horse trainers--United States--Biography. | Olympic
    athletes--United States--Biography.
Classification: LCC SF284.52.W64 A3 2021 (print) | LCC SF284.52.W64
    (ebook) | DDC 798.2092 [B]--dc23
LC record available at https://lccn.loc.gov/2021007053
LC ebook record available at https://lccn.loc.gov/2021007054

Book design by *Katarzyna Misiukanis–Celińska*
Cover design by *RM Didier*
Index by *Michelle Guiliano (LinebyLineIndexing.com)*
Typefaces: *PT Serif, Noto Serif, Playfair Display, Roboto* and *Lato*

Printed in the United States of America

10 9 8 7 6 5 4 3 2 1

This is dedicated to my father,
Colonel John W. ("Gyp") Wofford,
whom I never knew, in hopes
he would approve—and to my grandsons,
who I hope will come to know me better.

CONTENTS

▪

CONTENTS

▪

CONTENTS

_In the Shadow of the Rainbow

3
—

Jim Wofford

I have spent my life with horses, and I want to tell you about some of the things I have done and seen, the people I have met and—especially—the horses who have made my long life so wonderful.

Native Americans have an expression I often think about. They say a person who experiences an extraordinary connection with animals and the natural world is "standing in the shadow of the rainbow." I have spent my life standing in the shadow of a rainbow, but I am essentially a private person, always reluctant to talk about myself. When I started writing books, articles, and blogs, I was startled by how much personal information I inadvertently revealed. I have gotten a little more comfortable with this process over the years. Since much of what I have written is already a part of the public record, I thought I might as well share in more detail what I saw along the way.

Keep in mind that this book is written by someone who grew up in a different world—one of riding without helmets, of playing outside without television and without computers, of communicating via a party-line telephone that got fainter when more neighbors picked up in order to eavesdrop. There was no man on the moon, no DVDs, no virtual reality, no cell phones. For years, my reality was outdoors, with a rifle for shooting snakes, a cane pole for the sunfish and catfish that lived in Four Mile Creek, and a bird dog for a confidante.

Speaking of years, I have seen a lot of them—considering that Franklin Delano Roosevelt was president when I was born—and I have been "horse crazy" during all that time. By horse crazy, I mean I am obsessed with horses, and always have been—obsessed with how to ride them, how to train them, how to care for them, how they think, and how we should think about them. However, I have always had interests other than just horses. I have several other passions that I plan to talk about as well.

While this book is about me, it is also about people who love horses, the horses themselves, and the changes I have witnessed in their world. These changes are not confined to the techniques we use to ride and train horses; our competitive requirements have also changed and expanded greatly over the past half-century. Veterinary medicine has evolved (with both beneficial and malign effects), technology has impacted our equestrian world just as it has our culture at large, the rise of equestrian professionals has changed our interaction with horses, and the growth of administrative bodies necessary to promote and regulate horse sports has changed the horse world—*mostly* for the better. The changing attitudes of society toward the use of animals for sport are also both good and bad.

Obviously, we have a lot to talk about.

Growing Up with the Sport

——In retrospect, I literally grew up with horse sports in the United States, and I hope to provide the insight of someone who was there almost from the beginning. Certainly, there were horse sports before I started watching and taking part, but at the Olympic level they were completely military. From the first equestrian Olympics in 1912 until 1948, participants were exclusively men in uniform. My father was in uniform when he rode in the 1932 Los Angeles Olympics, which began my family's 75-year connection with the Olympic movement.

Once World War II finally convinced generals that charging barbed wire and machine guns on horseback was murder, not warfare, defense departments mechanized their cavalry units. Horse sport administrators around the world suddenly realized they needed to replace the military with civilian organizations, and I'll share my experiences in the world of "horse politics" as those organizations expanded. My role expanded along with the various civilian organizations: at one point I was an officer of the USET, the AHSA, and the USCTA, acronyms that mean little to the modern reader. The various functions of those organizations remain, but their names are mostly different now—another illustration of the changes I have witnessed.

While involved in horse politics, I began to see both the good and the bad side of the evolution of veterinary medicine. My participation in efforts to regulate its abuse involved me in some interesting experiences; I'll share the circumstances and their present-day ramifications. Horse abuse is always a pertinent topic.

When I entered the horse world, the majority of participants were amateurs in both senses of the word as defined in the dictionary: we were not paid for our efforts, and in large part our riding was "incompetent or inept." There were notable exceptions to this characterization, and I was fortunate to be able to ride with, and learn from, those future Hall of Famers. There is still much to learn from them—both in how they rode and trained horses, and in how they lived their lives.

My adult life with horses at first revolved around preparing for, and participating in, international competitions. Thus, the Olympic movement had a major effect on my efforts, especially the International Olympic Committee's (IOC) rule at the time that all Olympic athletes must be amateurs. During my competitive career I lived as an Olympic "shamateur" in order to comply with this onerous and outdated requirement. Like most shamateurs of the day, I got away with bending the rules, and I'll tell you how.

My efforts to sidestep the IOC rules on amateurism then led me into my first business venture in the horse world as a coach and trainer, which became an enduring pursuit. From this career arose a lifelong interest in training horses and riders that sparked my fascination with the development and application of equestrian theory, from Xenophon in 350 BCE right up to the present day. I have made more mistakes in my riding and training than I want to think about, but I avoided countless others because horsemen who have gone before me shared their wisdom. I am a better rider and trainer for my exposure to the giants of our sport.

You can see that I have a lot of things on my mind, and a lot to say, so I had better get started. The best place to start is usually at the beginning; thus, I am going to open my story in Kansas. I hope you enjoy the ride. ■

_It Started in Kansas

The White Rabbit put on his spectacles.
Where shall I begin, please your Majesty? he asked.
Begin at the beginning, the King said gravely,
and go on till you come to the end; then stop.

Lewis Carroll
Alice In Wonderland

We are not in Kansas anymore, but I need to start at the beginning, in my own personal Wonderland. I was born and raised on Rimrock Farm, a horse farm located in the east central part of the state near Milford, Kansas. My father and mother bought it in the late 1930s in anticipation of Daddy's retirement from the Army. The farm shared a boundary with Fort Riley, which was the home of the U.S. Cavalry School between 1887 and 1949.

Founded in 1853 to protect settlers from Native Americans, the cavalry served that purpose for the next 50 years. The "post" (military installation) remains to this day, and you can drive by the lovely cream-colored native limestone quarters where General George A. Custer lived when he was stationed there, after the Civil War and before the Battle of the Little Bighorn. Fort Riley must have been a bit wild and woolly in its early days. Legendary World War II General George Patton was stationed there several times throughout his career, and his daughter, Ruth Ellen, recalled a sign on the parade ground: "Officers will not shoot buffalo on the parade ground from the windows of their quarters. By Order of the Commanding Officer." (Note that the sign did not tell the officers not to shoot buffalo, just to get out of the house to do it.)

The "School" designation meant that Fort Riley was where all officers were taught to ride (and to teach riding) the "Army Way." (The old saying persists—"There's a right way, a wrong way, and the Army Way.") My father, a 1920 graduate of West Point, would return there as "Master of the Sword," the archaic title for what we would now call the head of the P.E. department. Part of his job was to supervise the riding instruction given to the incoming freshmen, the "plebes" (slang for plebians). As soon as they arrived at West Point, the plebes were marched to the riding hall and told to raise their hand if they had ever ridden a horse. The two groups thus formed were marched off separately to begin their riding instruction. What they did not know was that those who had ridden a horse before had just been placed in remedial riding because they would have developed habits the Army did not approve of, and would not progress as quickly as the plebes who had no bad habits to unlearn.

After graduation, the new lieutenants were usually sent to a regiment for a couple of years, and then reassigned back to Fort Riley for the Advanced Officers Class. This was a program that taught officers how to teach recruits to ride, and from here they would be reassigned to various cavalry regiments around the country.

In addition to the riding instruction at Fort Riley, the Army trained its farriers there, and officers and men were also supposed to know how to trim hooves and nail shoes on their chargers. Part of the graduation exercise for officers in the Advanced Class was to be given a bundle of baling wire. The officer candidate had to heat the wire, forge it into a bar of steel, make it into a horseshoe, and then nail the shoe on correctly after shaping the horse's hoof. When they graduated from Fort Riley, these guys knew every aspect of the horse.

The Army horse show team was based at Fort Riley, which meant there were training arenas, show jumps, and cross-country obstacles suitable for the preparation of international teams. This also meant it was ground zero for horse sports in the United States, because the Army horse show team formed the basis of the U.S. Olympic Equestrian Teams in those days.

An older friend of mine had an after-dinner parlor game he called "Who would you be?"—who would you be, if you could be any person at any time in history? My invariable answer was that I wanted to be a young cavalry officer at Fort Riley between 1920 and 1940. There, I would have been surrounded by thousands of horses, and supported by non-commissioned officers with 30 years' experience supervising men and horses (and secretly advising young officers who were still learning their trade). I would have been paid to ride, show, steeplechase, play polo, and generally live a horseman's dream. Not a bad life, if you are horse crazy.

Growing Up (Almost) Feral

——Although the life of a young cavalry officer was not in my future, I was able to live out a pretty fair imitation while growing up at Rimrock Farm. My backyard was the military reservation, where cavalry maneuvers had plenty of space. My own maneuvers on our Shetland pony, Merrylegs, didn't take up too much space, but she gave me the same start in my riding career as she had given my three older siblings. For transport to local horse shows, she walked into the back seat of our station wagon and stood there happily until we arrived. To unload her, we simply opened the other door and she stepped out.

Merrylegs was a treasure. When Daddy was stationed in Denver, Colorado, before I was born, my siblings hitched her to a cart and drove her to school every day. One of my earliest memories is of my brothers deciding it was time for me (then age two or three) to start jumping. They led Merrylegs over a cross-rail at a trot, with me hanging on to the horn of the little Western saddle like grim death. One of my brothers led her while the other laughed, shouted instructions, and waved his arms and clucked to encourage her. She lurched over the cross-rail (which was probably all of 12 inches high), and as she landed at a walk on the other side, I popped forward, planted my nose on the saddle horn, and immediately started a nosebleed. My squalls of pain and indignation were met with more laughter and helpful comments. Probably the best advice I got was that I was to stop sniveling, because it was just a little nosebleed. Fortunately, my father took over my instruction and I made better—and safer—progress after that.

From birth I was a clone of my father, red hair and all. As I grew older, I was his faithful shadow. Because I arrived by mistake nine years after my nearest sibling, Daddy had a more grandfatherly than paternal attitude toward me. He enjoyed my company as much as I enjoyed his, and we were inseparable. We walked to the stables every morning, discussing our plans for the day, looking for snakes along the creek and spotting fish suitable for catching later on. The stables would have been mucked out by the time we got there, and I saddled up and rode with him when we took the horses out for exercise. I don't remember specific instruction from him, but my few photos from the period of myself on horseback show a fair imitation of the military seat that was in use at the time. (It's a system that perseveres to this day; good horsemanship has never gone out of date.)

Once I was comfortable in the saddle, I graduated up to a 14.2-hand pony, Tiny Blair. With him as my companion from the time I was eight until I was ten, the broad expanse of Fort Riley opened up for me. I explored most of it and had some hair-raising experiences there with my four-legged friend. About 70 years before this, James B. ("Wild Bill") Hickok wrote, "Many a wild ride I had and many a boyish prank was perpetrated after getting well away from and out of sight of home with the horse." I knew how he felt.

I remember riding out onto the reservation early in the morning dressed in blue jeans, ragged tee shirt, high-topped tennis shoes, and no helmet, carrying a fishing pole, with a shotgun tied to one side of the saddle and a gunny sack full of PBJ sandwiches and Dr. Pepper tied to the other. Basically, I was a one-man (-boy) crime wave on horseback. Tiny would have a halter underneath his bridle, and a lead shank looped around his neck; he was a devil to slip off toward home if he was not tied up during my naps after lunch. That was just one of many lessons about horses that I learned the hard way.

Life in the Menagerie

_____I was learning about other animals at the same time. My father had a bird dog named Jack—a Weimaraner with golden eyes, silky gray fur, and no work ethic. He became the canine companion of my early years, dogging my footsteps during the day and sleeping on my bed at night. One sunny afternoon when I was about six, he and I decided to go walkabout. I had nothing specific in mind, just feeling fiddle-footed. We wandered out into the Fort Riley reservation for a while, Jack marking every bush we passed and me throwing rocks at squirrels. Suddenly I noticed the shadows were getting long, I was getting hungry...and I had no idea where home was. As the enormity of this sank in, I sat down to consider my situation, and Jack joined me in the long grass.

My conclusion was that I for sure was going to miss dinner and was going to get a spanking. My father had only ever spanked me once, about a year earlier. I hadn't done what he'd told me to do (stay in our box of seats at the Royal Winter Fair in Toronto while my parents went to present a trophy). I had wandered off—yes, I see the pattern develop-ing—and returned to find both parents panicked, relieved to see me, and then furious at the concern I had caused. Daddy gave me a sharp slap on my backside and growled that in future I was to do what I was told. I did not cry or feel abused, as I realized that I was in the wrong and would have to mend my ways.

I've been partially successful in that effort.

But now, as the shadows took on an ominous feeling, *I* was the one panicking, with no idea what to do next. Jack, having had enough of this business, suddenly leapt to his feet and looked me in the eye. I could al-most hear him say, "If you are tired of sitting here in the tall grass, I'll show you the way home." I was, and he did. Animals talk, if only we will listen.

My expeditions onto the reservation continued and expanded as I grew older; usually I would have Jack, in case we bumped a covey of quail, and a couple of Irish Wolfhounds would lope beside me, ready to pursue any unwary coyote. That's right, Irish Wolfhounds, largest of the canines.

My mother loved them, bred them in large numbers, and showed them every year. At one point we had 26 living on the farm. (I will tell you more about the menagerie I grew up with in a moment, but you are already starting to get a feel for it.)

My father often grumbled that the only reason we didn't have an elephant on the farm was because my mother had never been to an elephant auction. Daddy had decided opinions and wasn't shy about sharing them. Mom's involvement with Irish Wolfhounds eventually led her to become president of the Irish Wolfhound Club, which meant that one year we hosted the "Breed Specialty" show at the farm. This was a big deal in the dog show world. It was a tremendous honor to win a class at a Specialty Show and Wolfhounds—and the people attached to them—came from all over the country. Daddy tolerated this, but he exploded on Sunday night after the last competitor had left: "Goddamnit, Dot, horse show people are crazy, but dog show people are the lunatic fringe of humanity." We never hosted the Specialty Show again.

This suited me, as I was more interested in horses and rode out almost every day. I had plenty of room for these expeditions; Fort Riley contained over 100,000 acres, in those days mostly rolling grasslands. When people think of Kansas, they think of endless prairies of flat wheat fields golden in the sun and billowing in a gentle breeze, stretching on toward the western horizon. That part of Kansas exists, but it starts about an hour's drive west of our farm. The Kansas I grew up in consisted of long, open plateaus of tall grass prairie, cut by ravines with steep sides that were filled with hardwoods, oaks, and hickory. There is an unusual geological formation in the area called the rimrock, which shows as a cream-colored band of limestone; when you see the rimrock, you know you are close to Fort Riley—and Rimrock Farm.

If my account sounds as if there was only one kid left around the farm, it's because the Wofford family master plan didn't exactly include me. In early 1944, my mother (then age 40) told our doctor, Dr. Fred O'Donnell, that she didn't feel well, but that she was "too young for the change of life." When he examined her, he started laughing, and said, "Oh, yes, Dot, this is going to change your life."

Upon hearing the news, my father bragged that after a nine-year hiatus he "was getting his second wind." My mother replied, "No, Gyp, this is your last gasp." She had already raised two energetic sons and one lovely daughter by this time; looking back, I don't think she was too interested in doing it all over again nine years later, especially considering what a wild child the newest red-headed arrival turned out to be. Despite my older sister's best efforts, I was raised feral.

Funny Old World

_____ I'd like to digress from Rimrock Farm for a moment to talk about Doctor Fred (known as "Gaga") O'Donnell, who delivered me. He was born in Ireland in 1869 and never lost his charming brogue. He emigrated to the United States with his parents, went to medical school, and established his medical practice in Junction City, the town next to Fort Riley. He seemed to know every inhabitant of Geary County—no surprise, as by the time I became aware of him he had delivered the vast majority of them. Like many practitioners during that period who worked in a largely agrarian community, he was accustomed to being paid for his services with eggs, roast chicken, and the occasional slab of bacon.

Hugely popular, he was elected mayor of Junction City for decades. He made headlines during the "Temperance Era" of the early 1900s when the

Junction City *Daily Union* reported that word had arrived by telegraph from Abilene (telegraph was the social media of the early twentieth century) that Carrie Nation and her band of do-gooders had wrecked every saloon in Abilene and then boarded a train heading for Junction City. Gaga, who enjoyed a glass of Bushmills as much as the next man, sprang into action. When the temperance ladies arrived at the train depot, they were met by a large band of armed and suitably exercised citizens of Junction City. Gaga explained in no uncertain terms that their saloon-wrecking sort were not welcome in his town, and they should continue their depredations farther down the line.

The *Daily Union* reported that the episode ended peacefully. The only casualty was the town blacksmith, who imbibed an excess of what Carrie Nation termed "devil's brew," tripped over a wagon tongue, and broke his leg. Fortunately, the town physician was on the spot.

All this is to make the point that the residents of my area wanted to be left in peace to pursue their activities, which in my case meant life at Rimrock Farm.

This was a real honest-to-goodness farm, with dairy cows and Angus beef cattle, chickens, geese, hogs, guinea fowl, and—of course—horses. Daddy had purchased a Thoroughbred mare, Perk Up, from the Army. She wasn't a very good polo pony, but she jumped the side boards that marked the polo field boundaries like a made jumper, so she became the foundation for my mother's breeding program. She produced a string of good Thoroughbred sport horses, bred for the Olympic disciplines. At the Helsinki Olympics, my mother had bred three of the four horses on the eventing team—and one of the riders, my brother Jeb.

We grew our own alfalfa and oats for the horses, milked the dairy cows, and I never gave names to the beef cattle or hogs; that made their presence on our table more acceptable to me. Our breakfast room contained several cages of parakeets, budgerigars, and mynah birds. The mynahs had learned to mimic a fairly inclusive list of expletives, profanities, and obscenities, which they displayed at inopportune moments within earshot of polite company. I was not the culprit, although I already knew most of the words. I also knew who had taught them to both the mynahs and me, but I never ratted them out.

My mother thought it would be a good idea for me to join the local 4-H chapter, even though it did not include horses. I am sure she wanted me to interact with children my age, as I was surrounded by grown-ups at Rimrock Farm. If asked, I would have met with scorn the idea of any organized activity involving other boys and girls— why should I go play with other children when I had all the horses and dogs a boy could want? Regardless, Betsy, the Guernsey dairy cow, came into my life as a 4-H project. I was too small to actually milk her every day but I could catch her and lead her into the milking parlor, where our farm manager, George Martin, had a deft touch while milking. The cat and I would squat on Betsy's off side, waiting for the occasional squirt of milk aimed our way. George had a sneaky sense of humor, and it was several years before I figured out he was pulling my leg when he told me the long teats were for milk and the short ones were for cream.

George had been a tail-gunner on a B-17 in Europe during WWII, one of the loneliest and most deadly of occupations during aerial combat. Unlike many of his compatriots, he survived and returned to start a family. Ironically, after all he had been through, a couple of years later a drunk driver killed him. Funny, sad old world, isn't it?

The End of the Cavalry

——By 1950, my family had been involved in horse sports for more than 30 years. My father had ridden on the U.S. show-jumping team at the 1932 Olympics in Los Angeles and was non-riding reserve rider at the 1936 Olympics in Berlin. (This connection would come full circle almost 50 years later at the 1984 Los Angeles Olympics, where I would be the non-riding reserve on our eventing team—but I'm getting ahead of myself.)

Then in 1950 my world turned over with some bad news: the U.S. Army had decided to "mechanize," meaning there would be no more cavalry, no more horses, and no more Fort Riley as the epicenter of horse sports. If tanks were the future of warfare, then horses had no place in the Army, and they were sold—just like that. The final auction was held at Fort Riley in 1953, and when the last hammer dropped there were still 73 horses unsold and declared surplus. Rather than see them humanely destroyed, my father and mother gave them life tenancy at Rimrock Farm.

All the trucks suitable for horse transport had already been sold, so the horses were led by hand from Fort Riley, across the boundary between the military reservation and civilian life. I remember that the men leading the horses were all senior non-commissioned officers, with service stripes and ribbons on their shirts speaking of their long careers. Without fail, as each of them in the long line of horses and men quietly and patiently walking toward a new life crossed the boundary, they covered their eyes so the world would not see their tears cried at the end of an era. I didn't understand it at the time. Later on, I did, and I joined them.

Those retired horses had a pretty good life. They lived outside year-round, but they had shelters and running water, were fed hay, and had sufficient acreage to graze over. The students from the Kansas School of Veterinary Medicine came over to practice on these old-timers, and Master Sergeant Charles Brown ("Brownie") had forgotten more about shoeing horses than most will ever know. He had trimmed these horses' feet before; he was just working on them in a new location. (One of the previous locations was London in 1948, when he was the farrier for the U.S. Army team at the Olympics.)

Daddy inspected them on a regular basis, and whenever one of our Army friends stopped by for the night they accompanied Daddy on his rounds the next morning. General John "Tupper" Cole was along one day, and as we drove across the pasture he either identified various members of the herd, or asked after the health of one who was not present. I took it for granted that these men would remember all the horses that had been in their care. Years later, my mother told me that when they were stationed at Fort Riley, she could always tell and still remembered the sound of Daddy's footsteps on the sidewalk coming home from work. We don't forget the people and things we love.

I have often been struck by the phenomenon of families who produce several generations of horsemen. I suppose part of it is genetic—that one is genetically predisposed to have a strong affinity for animals. But a more important part might be the advantage one gains by growing up surrounded, not just by horses, but by people who are unusually adept at training, riding, understanding, and taking care of horses. I think there is a process of osmosis, whereby one absorbs knowledge about horses without actively thinking about it. For someone born into that sort of environment, it is instinctive to know how horses react, and how to relate to them. Growing up in a horse-crazy family is not an absolute necessity, but it helps. The fact that horses are not machines, but living, thinking, breathing creatures is second nature to me.

Icons at the Breakfast Table

———As a result of "mechanization," the U.S. Olympic Equestrian Team would no longer be military, and my father in 1951 became a founder and the first president of the newly formed civilian U.S. Equestrian Team. In addition, he was the coach of the 1952 Olympic show jumping and eventing teams. This is central to my story, because Rimrock Farm became the training center for those teams as a result. I had grown up surrounded by horses until now, but this turn of events took the horses and riders surrounding me to a new level. It also explains why so many of the names on our various Halls of Fame are part of my life. I grew up with them around our table.

One of those icons who was at Rimrock Farm during that period, General Jonathon R. (Jack) Burton, loved to tell the story of coming down to our breakfast room, which had a large glass-topped table capable of seating ten people. He would sit down to his bacon and eggs, look through the glass tabletop, and there I would be, looking back up at him with my favorite Irish wolfhound, Lassie (spelled like the television program of the same name, but given the Scottish pronunciation, "Lossie"). He said it almost put him off his eggs.

The spring of the year I turned nine, Tiny Blair and I did our first combined test (dressage and show jumping) at Fort Leavenworth. I didn't know the test, so Jack Burton got me through it by running around the dressage ring, yelling, "Okay, Jimmy, now trot over here to me, and walk when you get here." Later on that summer, I went to my very first event at Percy Warner Park in Nashville, Tennessee, where I had the unusual distinction of being eliminated in all three phases. I eventually got better; I just wish I hadn't set the bar so low at first.

Several of our family friends had vivid memories of me as a small boy. Whitney Stone, one of the small group who founded the USET (and later my father's successor as president), once wrote me to say that he remembered how as a very young child I had bitten him in the ankle. He said that as I grew older the only thing that changed was that the pain moved a little higher.

If it didn't happen that way, it should have.

Looking back, I realize it was an unusual upbringing, but at the time it seemed perfectly natural. I mean, who didn't pass the peanuts while my father and Bill Steinkraus were having another cocktail before dinner? I took all of this as natural, as I did the growing sense of a large, inter-connected horse-world family that I was starting to be aware of, and to benefit from. In the years to come this extended family would guide me at critical times, and possibly even save my life. Their presence and influence will reappear throughout my story.

More about that in a minute, but first—what do I mean by "intercon-nected"? Consider this: my father graduated from West Point in 1920 and joined the cavalry. (Yes, the cavalry!) At that time, the entire U.S. Army had roughly 1,700 officers and 20,000 men. Given those numbers, it was probable that officers knew each other throughout the Army. Young officers were known; senior officers took an interest in their careers and made sure the young officers had the sort of educational opportunities that would lead to high command. The Old Army took care of its own.

Jack Burton is a good example. Although he was a good rider, it was his performance in combat that brought him to the notice of senior officers. By the time I first knew him, Jack had already been wounded in two wars (World War II and Korea); he would later go on to be wounded in Vietnam while commanding the 1st AirCav Division in combat. One of the most

1. ___ At the age of four, I was ready to throw my leg over anything. "Lassie" (pronounced Loss-ie) came home from England with us on the *SS America* after the 1948 Olympics. My mother was about to start breeding Irish Wolfhounds, and Lassie was only the first of many Wolfhounds I grew up with; however, I soon turned my interest to horses. ■

2. ___ Every family should have a friend like Merrylegs. She taught my three siblings how to ride and got me started in the saddle. People were not as safety-conscious in 1946 as we are today. At her age, Merrylegs was safe enough, as she could not move fast enough to escape an adult at a fast walk. ■

3. ___ I got my first jumping lessons from my father, seen here in the background while I jumped a formidable 3-foot obstacle. From the pained expressions on both my father's and Tiny Blair's faces, they can tell they have their work cut out for them to turn me into a rider. ■

4. ___ I spent eight years of my life incarcerated here. Heated by a Ben Franklin stove, Pleasant View was a one-room school, with all eight grades taught by the same teacher. The cream-colored stone used in the construction of the schoolhouse is from the "rimrock" geological formation indigenous to the area and lent its name to our nearby Rimrock Farm. ■

5. __ While my father died when I was quite young, and I have very few memories of him, I did inherit his sense of humor. He broke his little finger in a riding accident, and it was permanently straightened. His response was that he was now ready to have tea with the Queen. ■

6. __ The rest of the Wofford family—my sister "Dodie," my mother "Dot," and my brothers Warren and Jeb—all got here before I did. Mom had her hands full, raising one daughter who would have a family of five, plus three boys who would all ride for their country. ■

7. __ My father "Gyp" Wofford before a polo match. In the 1930s, cavalry officers did not specialize; they all played polo, rode show jumpers, evented, and did dressage. Several of my father's compatriots won Olympic medals in more than one discipline. ■

8. ___ I was introduced to firearms at an early age, and instructed in the concepts of firearm safety and legal game laws. Songbirds were off limits, but I transgressed, which explains why I can tell you to avoid pan-fried robin's breast. It was a family tradition to eat what you harvested. ■

9. ___ I would love to have been a fly on the wall when Tommy Thompson (at left) and my father threw a party. Obviously, these two have had a relaxed dinner and now, in the Cavalry tradition, are getting "stuck in." One suspects that adult beverages played a part, and the conversations were lively and far-ranging. ■

10. ___ This was my mother's favorite picture. She said it was the only time she knew of when at least two of us weren't fighting. Left to right: Me, Warren, and my oldest brother, Jeb, taken at the 1954 National Championships, Percy Warner Park, Nashville, Tennessee. ■

11. ___ A student of my father's, Captain (later Colonel and my coach) John Russell, winning the 1952 Hamburg Derby riding Rattler. Six years later, Rattler would be my first open jumper. I'm sure Rattler was puzzled, if not surprised, by some of my stride selections. I was successful with him at local shows, but not so much when I got to the "A" shows level.

■ © Courtesy of the Russell Family

12. ___ When I grew up at Fort Riley, a cavalry post, thousands of horses lived there. Each trooper cared for his horse as if his life depended on it, which it did. Every horse on the post was exercised and groomed daily. Like most of the stables at the west end of the post, these were made of the limestone rimrock indigenous to the area. ■ © U.S. Army

13. ___ Our family life centered around horses, as shown here in our 1949 Christmas card. My siblings—Warren, Dodie, and Jeb—are mounted in the background, Mom and Dad are in the cart, while I am on my faithful Merrylegs. Out of the six members of the family, four of us would be on an Olympic team between 1932 and 1984. ■

14. —— The Army Olympic Team had not won an Olympic medal since 1912.
After Major Harry D. Chamberlin joined it, the 1932 Team broke that drought:
Chamberlin won an individual silver medal in show jumping and joined
the gold-medal-winning Eventing Team, with Tommy Thompson
winning the eventing individual silver medal. ■ © U.S. Army

15. ___ One of the many things I wish I could have asked my father, Lieutenant John W. Wofford, was how it felt to ride into the 1932 Los Angeles Coliseum in front of 105,000 spectators, on a horse of dubious character. While Daddy finished covered with more dust than glory, he started a family Olympic tradition that lasted 75 years. ■ *© U.S. Army*

16. ___ My father riding Nigra, probably about 1930. Nigra had quite a career: on the back of this photo in my mother's handwriting is a note that Nigra was wounded in World War I and carried in her body shrapnel from that period. She was General Harry D. Chamberlin's ride at the 1920 Inter-Allied Games and would have been about 20 years old at the time of this photo. ■ *© U.S. Army*

17. ___ By 1939 my father was a major and serving in Ireland as Military Attaché. It was a serious military post, but Daddy found time to go racing with Fred Ahern, a member of Ireland's horse-show team and a legendary Irish horseman. From the intent look in their eyes, I suspect the bookies took a beating that afternoon. ■

18. ___ A friend of my father's remarked that Babe Wartham was one of the best jumpers the Army had, but she was one of the least dependable. Although her evil twin sister showed up when my father rode her in the 1932 Olympics, her considerable jumping abilities were on display there. More trustworthy horses came down with soundness problems before the competition, and Babe was the last one "on the bench." ■ © U.S. Army

19. ___ In 1946, my godfather, Major General I.D. White (on the left in this photo), was in charge of the constabulary in Berlin, Germany. His aide and our close family friend was Captain Jonathon R. ("Jack") Burton. This is such a symbolic and poignant photo: two cavalrymen out for a ride with a Sherman tank in the background. Horse-mounted cavalry was now a thing of the past. ■ *© George Patton Museum*

20. ___ I knew Gail was "the one" the moment I first saw her on July 7, 1958, but it took me a week to gather my courage enough to ask her out for our first date. This photo was taken at one of the nightly dances held on the patio of the Broadmoor Hotel in Colorado Springs. Now 63 years later, we are still dating. ■

21. ___ Not bad, for a 14-year-old Lance Corporal. At the 1959 Round Barn Horse Show in Barrington, Illinois, I'm doing a pretty good imitation of the U.S. Cavalry seat as a member of the Culver horse-show team. Going to a show was a real treat as we had few opportunities to get "off campus." ■ © *Culver Academies*

22. ___ In 1961, I followed the Black Horse as the last cadet to pass in review in President Kennedy's inaugural parade. In 1962, I occasionally led the entire squadron in our weekly Sunday parade. Even the horses stood at attention when they were on parade. ■ *© Culver Academies*

23. ___ When the parade ground was too wet, the Black Horse Troop would parade dismounted in order to save the turf. The administration didn't care if we got mud on our boots; cleaning them would give us something to do on Sunday afternoons. ■ *© Culver Academies*

24. ___ When you are dancing while wearing white gloves, a sabre, and a high starched collar, you are no Fred Astaire on the dance floor. However, I'd say those were the furthest things from my mind at the time of the Class of 1962 Graduation Ball. ■ © *Culver Academies*

25. ___ Culver frowned on "PDA," public displays of affection, but I thought I'd steal a kiss anyway and risk getting put on report. By the time the demerits caught up with me, I'd be a civilian. The shako got in the way, but we managed. ■ © *Culver Academies*

26. ___ Gail and I were both riding in point-to-points by the spring of 1967. Here, Gail has just finished her race, and I will saddle up in a minute. You can tell from the look on our faces that we were both intoxicated at the prospect of riding at speed over fixed fences. ■ *© Freudy Photos*

27. ___ You can tell we were going at speed, when you look at how far beyond the fence Mr. Lewis Murdock's Phaeton is landing in the 1967 Essex Point-to-Point. My point-to-point career was never spectacular, but I enjoyed it immensely, and learned a great deal about conditioning horses to compete at speed. ■ *© Freudy Photos*

28. ___ It's hard to make the U.S. Team when you are on crutches. Mike Plumb, on our homebred, Malakasia ("Mac"), had sprained his ankle in a motorcycle mishap. Our stable manager, Alex Edmonds, waits patiently with Kilkenny ("Henry") while I try to figure out how to get on with a broken left leg. ■

29. ___ We did some unusual things in the early days of eventing. At Ledyard in 1967, the Ipswich River, which ran through the cross-country course, flooded. The competitors all agreed to swim the river in order to take advantage of the whole course. Atos was only 15.3 hands but had been a cow pony, and it was just another day at the office for him. ■ © Jane McClary

30. ___ Gail and Henry are walking up to the gallops at Waterstock House, with Gail four months pregnant at the time. Henry sensed this, took advantage of her compromised condition, and ran away, scattering a flock of sheep in the process. She was supposed to keep him in work while I recovered from a broken leg, but we changed our plans after that experience. ■

31. ___ Riding in the Olympics is a thrill, and even more so when you finish with a silver medal. I was the "rookie" on the squad, standing with riders I had looked up to for years. Kevin Freeman, Michael Page, and Mike Plumb had been my role models ever since I set my sights on riding for the United States. Winning an Olympic medal with them was beyond my wildest dreams. ■ © *Ray Firestone*

32. ___ Course designers at the 1968 Mexico Olympics were still learning. Michael Page and Foster are jumping a dangerous triple bar—dangerous because the third rail is hidden by the brush. Mike's position is such that no matter what, he will still be aboard on the other side. When you go to a Team event, you want Michael by your side. ■ © *Page Family*

mild-mannered of men, Jack might have been overlooked in a civilian setting. However, the ability to lead other men in combat is a rare skill, and he found a home for his talents in the Army. By the time I knew him, Jack was the "aide" to General I.D. White. A general's aide is a young officer who is a combination of personal assistant, troubleshooter, dog robber (one who would steal from a dog, in order to get the job done), and senior-officer-in-training. I have a soft spot in my heart for I.D. and his lovely wife, Judy, as they were my godparents.

Like most cavalrymen, I.D. was horse crazy, which probably explains why our families were so close. He was chef d'équipe for the U.S. team at the 1948 London Olympics, so you know he understood horses and horsemanship.

Another aside: I.D. was a life-long cavalryman and a brilliant combat commander, but he had a famous temper. When he heard that the Army was going to change the uniform lapel insignia and remove the historically significant "crossed sabers" that signified a cavalryman, he caught a plane for the Pentagon. Witnesses say that when he got there, two-star generals jumped out a window rather than face his considerable wrath at this insult to the generations of cavalrymen who had gone before him. Only about three men in the whole Army outranked him at this point in his career, and it took an ironclad promise from a superior officer to assuage him. The next time you see the branch insignia for armored divisions that succeeded the cavalry, you will notice the crossed sabers around the insignia of a tank. This is in homage to the long line of cavalrymen, and their horses, who served so bravely and honorably. We can thank I.D. for that.

The point of this reminiscence? It's that horses were at the heart of all our family connections.

There was a lot for me to love, growing up at Rimrock Farm: horses, dogs, people, things to do—I had it going on. Then, like a thunderbolt out of the blue, I was incarcerated. There is no other word for it. I was put in jail. I would remain there for the next 19 years of my life, and I would gaze longingly out the window every day of my captivity. That's the short story; the long story is that just short of my sixth birthday I was sent to Pleasant View School, to begin my education.

Pleasant View

____Most of Kansas was still agrarian in the 1950s. Children in farming areas were educated close to their communities, often with all eight grades taught by one teacher in a one-room schoolhouse. We started school a week later than city children in the fall, due to helping with the harvest; in the spring, we got out of school earlier in order to help with the spring planting.

During my eight years at Pleasant View, there were never more than 14 children, total, in all eight grades, and I never had more than one other student in my grade. For the first six years I had the same teacher, Mrs. Perry, a large woman who easily commanded the entire room. I assure you there were very few disciplinary problems; Mrs. Perry wielded a wicked steel-edged straight ruler. In addition, telephone service for all the farms in the area was on the "party line" system. You answered when the phone rang a certain number of times, but as you talked, you would hear a click and the volume would drop. This meant more and more people were listening in on the line. A "bush telegraph" had nothing on the Geary County telephone system; if you had misbehaved at school, news of your transgression preceded you, and by the time you got home your protestations of innocence fell on deaf ears.

Our curriculum was typical of the era: the three "Rs," meaning "readin'," 'ritin', and 'rithmetic." Fortunately, during my early years at school, the county participated in an experimental program to teach young children to speed read. In my case it worked, and my ability to read quickly was of inestimable value throughout my educational career.

Although the entire area had electricity, the same was not true of central heating and until the mid-1950s the schoolhouse was heated with a coal-burning Ben Franklin stove. The boys carried the coal in from a separate building next to the schoolhouse every morning, and it was a source of great pride for a boy to get strong enough to be able to carry the coal scuttle without help.

In the meantime, the girls were helping Mrs. Perry tidy the schoolroom, getting ready for their class in home economics. Gender discrimination was alive and well in Kansas in the 1950s. This extended to the bathrooms; it was a cold and lonely walk to the outdoor toilets at the far end of the property, with boys and girls at opposite corners. Anyway, I don't recall a lot of curiosity about the opposite sex while growing up; farm children don't need the "birds and bees" lecture from their parents. Tardy arrival was excused if one had been assisting a stallion to cover a mare or supervising the family's sow while she delivered a large litter of piglets.

One of the advantages to growing up in Kansas back then was that you could get a driver's license when you turned thirteen. Yup, thirteen. The reasoning was that farm kids were already driving trucks and tractors from the time they were tall enough to reach the pedals, so driver education was a waste of time. The license allowed us to drive alone between sunrise and sunset, which meant that the youngest on the farm could drive to town for tractor parts and groceries. There was very little traffic on the road to town, and usually the only vehicle I saw was a combine on its way from one field to another.

These licenses were a good idea at the time, but probably wouldn't work today.

All in all, it was an educational system designed to produce good citizens of the Eisenhower era. We said the Pledge of Allegiance every morning to start our school day, and the daily ceremony of raising, lowering, and correctly folding the U.S. flag was fraught with significance. We instinctively knew we were dealing with the symbol of the greatest country the world had ever seen, and we treated that symbol with appropriate reverence. At that time, patriotism was not taught; it was assumed. Not a bad way to grow up, looking back at it.

Eventing in Transition: Military to Civilian

___While I was incarcerated at school, the activity at the farm continued. Our local church organized an annual spring charity horse show, which had served as a sort of homecoming for graduates of the Cavalry School. This tradition continued even after mechanization of the cavalry. I promise you that when you hear old-timers going on about the good old days, "when we all did everything with our horses," they are telling the truth. Horses would jump around the outside hunter course at the charity horse show, catch their breath, go back into the open jumper class, stand hitched to the trailer in the shade for a while, and then come back for the family class. Most of these horses were Thoroughbreds or Army remounts, but they were able to adapt to the class specifications. What people lacked in expertise they made up for with enthusiasm. We weren't much for polish, but we were hell for fun.

During the 1950s, the competitors' party noise level in our basement bar would have registered on the Richter scale, and continued past midnight. (We did not have much in the way of professional entertainment in those days; people tended to entertain themselves.) It didn't take long after dinner before a group gathered around the piano to belt out old ballads, Army songs, and the latest Broadway hits. Some of the group had good voices and always sang one or two of their favorites to loud applause. Given enough bourbon, Daddy would recite endless verses of "Abdul, the Bulbul Emir." He claimed to know 99 verses, but usually got shouted down after a dozen or so grew more and more ribald, while the nearest grown-up lady covered my ears.

Many of my parents' friends took great glee in telling me their earliest memory of me was at the Officers' Hop, a dance party held once a month at the Fort Riley Officers' Club during World War II. Because gasoline was rationed and we didn't have a babysitter, Mom and Dad would stick me in a wicker basket and bring me along to the party. My Dutch aunts and uncles marveled at my ability to sleep on top of the piano while a well-oiled group of officers belted out "Fiddler's Green." It begins:

—— HALFWAY DOWN THE TRAIL TO HELL
IN A SHADY MEADOW GREEN,
ARE THE SOULS OF ALL DEAD TROOPERS CAMPED
NEAR A GOOD OLD-TIME CANTEEN
AND THIS ETERNAL RESTING PLACE
IS KNOWN AS FIDDLER'S GREEN ——

The song went on for several verses, and usually ended with several whiskey-soaked, gruff old cavalrymen surreptitiously wiping their eyes before launching into "The Caissons Keep Rolling Along."

I'm told this, you understand; even though I was there, I slept through it.

In a way, I wish I had been older when I had the opportunity to observe this particular sub-set of society at a country horse show with dusty rings, rudimentary jumps, no commercial sponsorship, no announcer, and a relaxed atmosphere. Six months later the same group would show up in New York City for the old National Horse Show at Madison Square Garden, with the ladies decked out in long dresses and jewelry and either white tie and tails or full dress uniform for the gentlemen. The only things that stayed the same throughout the year were the people involved, and their love of horses.

Our spring horse show took a bit of organizing, but nothing like the pre-Olympic preparation at the farm. The Eventing National Championships were traditionally held over Labor Day weekend in the 1950s, due to

THE CLASSIC EVENT

The Classic is a multi-discipline competition, where the same horse-and-rider combination has to complete a dressage test on the first day, negotiate a speed and endurance test on the second day, and show jump successfully on the third day; hence, the term "three-day event." The term continues to this day, even though modern events have added a second day of dressage due to a large number of competitors, and modern events have become five-or six-day events, yet are still referred to as "three-day events." Indeed, in its title, the biggest competition in the United States calls itself the Land Rover Kentucky Three-Day Event. This is the still-close connection between the military and the small but growing civilian equestrian community. This was eventing in the Classic format, which is insanely complicated both in scoring and in organization (see sidebar below for more details). (Well into the 1970s, it was not unusual for riders to find out their Speed and Endurance scores at the competitor's party on cross-country night. It took that long to calculate them.)

Part of the organizational complexity was the need for communication on Speed and Endurance Day between the various start and finish lines of Phases A, B, C, D, and E (roads and tracks, steeplechase, a second roads and tracks, cross-country, and the cool-down phase), and also to report on the progress of competitors around the jumps in the steeplechase and cross-country phases. This is where the army came in. Labor Day weekend was traditionally a training weekend for local National Guard units.

a nice "tip of the hat" to the history of the sport.

On the second day of a Classic at the Olympic and World Championship level, the "speed and endurance" test length totaled 22 miles, which included a 2-mile steeplechase phase, and a 5-mile cross-country phase. At that time, there were four phases in a Classic event: Phase A, roads and tracks; Phase B, the steeplechase; Phase C, another roads and tracks; a 10-minute veterinary inspection; and finally a 5-mile Phase D, the cross-country.

Classic riders spoke approvingly of "maxing the course," meaning to finish inside the time allowed in all five phases, thus obtaining the maximum number of bonus points. Bonus points? Don't ask. I would have to write another book to explain the scoring system in place at the time. Classic riders are historically viewed as "hell for leather" riders, but the truth is, we set out with the attitude that although we would ride as close as possible to the perfect time, it was more important to finish. In addition, the show jumping always loomed in the back of our minds; we knew that even after finishing the speed and endurance test, our horse had work to do. ∎

What better training for a unit than to lay out the communications network needed for an event?

There was a great deal of riding going on in the fall of 1951; the selection trials for the 1952 Olympic dressage and show-jumping teams were being held, and both Fort Riley and Rimrock Farm were full of horses and riders in training. Thus, I found myself in the back of a pickup truck in early September of 1951, the week of the selection trials for the 1952 Olympic eventing team, helping to mark the route of the roads and tracks phase. The rules stipulated that directional markers be orange. In the interest of economy, my brothers and I were tying orange crepe paper on trees and branches to mark the path.

All was well, the judges approved our work, and we thought we could relax and enjoy the competition. However, a substantial rain the night before cross-country drained the crepe paper of all its color. You guessed it: rules are rules, and we had to replace all the washed-out markers with new orange ones. We hustled, but the morning of the competition we were barely ahead of the first rider when we hung the last strip of orange crepe paper on the last tree. Ever since then, Halloween has brought back memories of hanging orange crepe paper in the hot Kansas sun.

The eventing cross-country course was laid out along the banks of the Kansas River, with spectator seating on the rimrock above it. This was as fine a natural amphitheater as one could imagine, with our natural vantage point allowing us to watch horses gallop back and forth along the plains and through "Breakneck Canyon." If you ever see a photo of cavalry galloping down precipitous slides, it was probably taken at Fort Riley's Breakneck Canyon. Think of the canyon as a zip-line course for young cavalry officers; once they survived that, they believed they could ride anywhere.

Growing Up with the Team

——Because of my family's unusual connection with the Olympics, I have always remembered things based on the Olympic quadrennial. The first Olympics I remember were in London in 1948. At that time the U.S. Army was still in charge of all three Olympic equestrian disciplines, so the riders were all officers, the horses were for the most part owned by the Army, and the grooms and farriers were all enlisted men. Master Sergeant Harry Cruzan was Major F.F. "Fuddy" Wing's groom then. Harry was only a lowly corporal at that time, but he will resurface in my tale. I remember him telling me 20 years later that they had a heavy wooden trunk for each horse, an additional one for the vet, one for the farrier—and one full of whiskey!

Speaking of whiskey—years later, I commented to my mother that equestrian team selection was getting more and more competitive. "You have no idea," she told me. During Prohibition, the Army horse show team went up to the Royal Winter Fair in Toronto. The horses shipped on special trains, and the team always took a certain horse who wasn't much account when it came to jumping, but he was hell to kick, so no customs official in his right mind would get in the stall with him. The team stored their hay behind Widowmaker on the way up to Toronto, and for the trip back down they built a wall of hay that concealed a year's supply of Prohibition-era whiskey for all concerned. "You just *think* teams are competitive these days," my mother said. "Those young officers would have killed each other for a chance at smuggling home a year's supply of whiskey!"

I was only three years old during the 1948 London Olympics, so I remember very little of that time. I do recall that the damage done by the Blitz was still evident everywhere. Rationing was still in effect, so my mother had brought an extra steamer trunk full of Hershey's chocolate bars, silk stockings, and other delicacies and necessities. She also brought a case of rice, which had been unavailable in England since 1939. These treasures made us popular with our friends in England. (Fortunately, I found a way to jigger the lock on the trunk and break into the chocolate stash; I stayed sugar-buzzed for the entire trip.)

While General Humberto Mariles of Mexico was winning the gold medal in show jumping on Arete, I snuck into the enclosure at the base of the Olympic flame tower in Wembley Stadium to do what little boys do. A horrified English bobby, helmet and all, chased me over the fence, calling me a "horrid little boy." He did not know how right he was.

In the early summer of 1952 we boarded a special train in Junction City, Kansas, and I remember riding the train to a siding at Fort Riley, where the horses and equipment were loaded. The three teams left for a European tour leading up to the Helsinki Olympics. (One thing about training teams that has not changed is the continuing need for European exposure before big competitions.) The horses crossed the Atlantic on a British cargo ship, the *SS Parthia*, and once they got to Europe they traveled by rail, as horse vans were not yet in general usage.

Although Helsinki was a lovely venue for the equestrian part of the 1952 Games, given my age at the time I was more interested in watching the sinister-appearing KGB agents hustle the USSR riders out of a van and into locked stables than I was in the fact that the USET won bronze medals in both eventing and show jumping. This was the first instance I can recall of the trend toward the politicization of the Games, but the Games have never been as pure as Baron de Coubertin would have wanted us to believe. I wasn't around yet in 1936, when Hitler refused to award Jesse Owens his gold medal at the Berlin Olympics, but my parents were in the stands.

Politicization of the Olympic movement has continued in various forms with the Communist riots and Black Power protest in 1968 at Mexico City, the Black September terrorists' murder of the Israeli athletes at Munich in 1972, and the United States and USSR boycotts of 1980 and 1984. You can be sure that human-rights advocates and environmentalists will be making things lively in future Olympics.

As a personal aside, my oldest brother, Jeb Wofford, was on the bronze medal eventing team at Helsinki. The average age of the riders on the U.S. Eventing Team team that year was twenty, and the average age of the horses was seven—quite a contrast with the rider and horse demographics of today.

In addition, my mother owned Hollandia, a lovely chestnut mare on the show-jumping team. Hollandia was by Bonne Nuit, one of the most successful Thoroughbred jumping sires of the 1950s. He jumped in two Olympics: for the United States in 1952 with Bill Steinkraus and for Great Britain in 1960 with my sister-in-law Dawn Palethorpe Wofford aboard. When Dawn's engagement to my brother Warren was announced in 1957, she got a telegram from Jack Talbot-Ponsonby, the British show jumping chef d'équipe: "Marry Wofford and get Hollandia." She did both, which meant that her name was now on the ownership papers, and she had retained her citizenship in the United Kingdom. In those years, international rules required that both the rider and the owner had to be from the same country in order to compete in the Olympics, World Championships, or Pan American Games. In a few years those rules would play a big part in my story.

Dawn rode her wedding present in Rome in 1960, although she didn't have to travel as far as some of the equestrian teams. The U.S. Team horses traveled by air for the first time in 1956. This was considered cutting edge; previously, travel to Europe had always entailed a lengthy sea voyage for the horses. Sea travel continued to be the only option for some horses. In 1972, Sloopy, Neal Shapiro's ride on the U.S. show-jumping team, had to travel by sea. He had been left behind from the 1971 tour because he had a panic attack before the plane took off. The extra trouble was worth it, as Neal and Sloopy won an individual bronze medal in Munich. The USET was understandably reluctant to ship a horse that had a history of traveling badly by air; Markham, Mike Plumb's eventing ride for the 1964 Tokyo Olympics, had thrown a high-altitude fit between JFK and O'Hare, and had to be destroyed en route.

I have mentioned in passing that my father was heavily involved in the U.S. preparations for and participation in the 1952 Olympics, and was the coach for two of the disciplines. In fact, his involvement was even deeper. By this time he had helped establish the U.S. Equestrian Team, and was its first president. He was also on the Bureau of the FEI (Fédération Equestre Internationale), the international member of the IOC. This position naturally led him to be involved in various committees of both the USET and the AHSA (American Horse Shows Association). He was a busy guy.

In addition to my mother's ownership of Olympic horses, much of the training and support of the various teams was undertaken by my family; to a certain extent, the early days of the USET looked like a Wofford family affair. In later years, I encountered people in the horse world who had an aversion to me—without even knowing me. It took me a while to realize that my family's outsized role in the USET's early days created jealousy in certain groups. I had played no part in those early times; I was just along for the ride. My family's efforts brought me name recognition throughout the horse world, and my family's friends, scattered around the globe, gave me a warm welcome wherever I went. However, my family also had its detractors, and I was the recipient of some undeserved hostility as well. When I mentioned this to my mother years later, she smiled grimly and told me, "Don't worry, you'll outlive them."

I did. ∎

2

Seasons of Change

O, that our fathers would applaud our loves,
To seal our happiness with their consents!

William Shakespeare
Two Gentlemen of Verona

My father was a huge presence in my life; I rode out with him, hunted and fished with him, and generally idolized him. Thus, it was a shock to me when he died of cancer in early 1955. This was a sad time for my family and me. My much older siblings were making their own way in the world away from the farm. Because I associated my father with horses, I turned away from them and did not ride for the next three years. I avoided the stables and devoted myself to hunting and fishing—activities I could do alone.

Because I knew my father only when I was a young boy, I'm intensely curious about him. Little written record survives; even his military records are gone, burned in the 1973 National

Personnel Records Center fire near St. Louis, Missouri. But snippets and vignettes have surfaced from time to time. My aunt mentioned that the family got a huge outpouring of mail expressing sympathy at his death. She thought it interesting that two letters arrived on the same day: one was from Prince Bernhardt of the Netherlands, at that time president of the FEI, saying how sorry he would be to miss Daddy's wise counsel on the Bureau. The other letter came from the elevator operators at the Dorset Hotel at 30 West 54th Street in New York City, where we always stayed during the Madison Square Garden Horse Show. They also expressed their sorrow at the Wofford family's loss. I was struck by the breadth of society that remembered Daddy fondly. Bill Steinkraus remarked to me that Daddy "was equally popular with both men and women." These bits of information were some small comfort to me, as I embarked on the project of growing up.

My ability to read at a high rate of speed came to my aid, and I devoured any book that came my way. Sir Lancelot and the Knights of the Round Table, plus Natty Bumpo in the Leatherstocking Tales of James Fenimore Cooper, held my interest for a while, but they did not entrance me as much as the popular Western authors of the day—Zane Gray, Max Brand, Luke Short, and Louis L'Amour. Tom Sawyer and Huck Finn were compatriots, and if some of the larger themes of Mark Twain's books went over my head, they kept me occupied and provided company when I needed it.

Huck's attitudes toward black and white people provided me with food for thought and were pertinent to my situation. I was being raised in an era of casual racism. We had two domestics working in the house, a cook and a maid. They treated me well and started my progress toward a more enlightened attitude. They were doubly important in my life at the time, as my mother had taken refuge in alcohol from the sudden and unexpected loss of her husband. Bessie Smith and Doris Payne got me up in the morning, packed my school lunch, and sent me off to another day in "prison." When I came home in the afternoon I made sure to head outside, or hid with a book where my mother could not find me until dinner. After Daddy died, Mom regularly reminded me that Bessie was the only college graduate in the house. This was obviously a bit of a sore subject for her. My father had nine siblings, of which he was the oldest. Those 10 Wofford children had 12 degrees among them. I suppose by now she had an idea that at age 13, higher education was not high on my list of priorities.

Bessie, who was part Cherokee, had studied at an American Indian teacher's college and gotten a degree before she married Master Sergeant E. "Red" Smith. Red, an African American obviously related to Thomas Jefferson (or someone of similar coloration) had served as one of my father's NCOs. He loved to sit on our breakfast porch, smoking cigars and telling me stories of cavalry days. Some of them might have even been true.

I would learn of Thomas Jefferson's complex relationship with slavery and the slaves in his purview years later. Jefferson kept mockingbirds in a cage in his library because he loved the sound of their songs. In his library at Monticello, surrounded by his books, he would close the doors and open the cage so they could be free to fly around his library and sing, while he wrote his letters and read his books. He wrote words that would set men free around the world, yet he never opened the doors to his human cages. It would take another generation, and the deaths of nearly a million young men, before those caged birds were set free to sing their own songs.

Most of this thinking came to me later, but vague thoughts like this occupied me as a boy. Between my solitary outdoor activities and my reading, I was content. Books have played a major part in my life. I have often thought how lucky I was to read the books that I read, at the time that I read them. One of my numerous aunts, Maude Wofford Elmers, "took me to raise," in Mark Twain's phrase. Aunt Mike (I called her "machine-gun Mike," due to her rapid speech patterns) had noticed my precocious reading habits and gave me a history book, *King's Mountain and Its Heroes*. It told about the October 1780 Battle of King's Mountain in South Carolina, which was a turning point in the Revolutionary War. She remarked that several ancestors of ours had fought in that battle, and that I might be interested in learning more about them. This book achieved several things. I took pride in my family origins, although I already knew that if you look far back enough, every family tree has a horse thief hanging in it. I also learned about the War of the Revolution and, most importantly, discovered my lifelong interest in history.

In order to get me away from an unpleasant family situation and out of the house, Aunt Mike took me on a trip through the South that summer of 1955. We traced General Sherman's Civil War march through Georgia "from Atlanta to the sea," and discussed its effects. The stop I remember best, though, was the subject of my book about the Revolutionary War— King's Mountain, where American colonists who wanted independence defeated American colonists still loyal to Britain. I had also heard of the battle from a different angle. Little boys of my era were expected to be interested in firearms of all sorts, and so I was. What 10-year-old country boy wouldn't be interested in a book about firearms with a title such as *Hand Cannon to Automatic*? My readings had led me to a study of the various weapons in use during the period of the American Revolution, and I knew the difference between rifles and muskets in 1780. I remember explaining to Aunt Mike how the Patriots had defeated the Loyalists, by using better weapons and superior tactics.

Just as with history, my interest in firearms continued. As a public speaking exercise I had to give a presentation to my local 4-H chapter on a topic of my choice. My topic was "How to Clean a Rifle," and I got high marks for it. I laugh now at the thought of a 10-year-old boy carrying a rifle through the halls of the local high school. Different times.

I was raised with firearms in the house, had taken the firearms safety course twice, and was a pretty good shot. When I was eight, Daddy gave me a single-shot 22 caliber rifle; the following spring, an Army friend dropped off a case of ammunition for me. It takes a while, but it is possible for a little boy to shoot his way through 10,000 rounds of ammunition. Although I aimed at a lot of targets, and learned to shoot my initials in a tree trunk, the wildlife around us was safe because of the "eat what you shoot" rule around the house. My mother drew the line at robins, and I soon drew the line at squirrel and rabbit, which I found exceedingly tough. The less said about possum and sweet potatoes the better.

Aunt Mike returned me to Rimrock Farm, but I was speedily transferred to two of my favorite Army "Dutch aunts and uncles," Colonel and Mrs. Earl (Tommy and Lorraine) Thompson, who swept me away for a week of fishing and reading. You may know Tommy Thompson as one of the most famous horsemen of the pre-World War II period, when he won medals in two Olympics, but I knew him as a family friend and role model.

During our 1952 family trip to the Helsinki Olympics, we had stopped in Munich, Germany, where Mom and Dad dropped me off with the Thompsons, probably to get a break from me. Tommy introduced me to two of my lifelong passions. One morning we took off in a brand new 1952 MG two-seater convertible. It was British racing green, with tan leather seats, and just about the most gorgeous car I had ever seen. I eventually got over my love of sports cars, but it took some time. Tommy took me fishing in the mountains of Bavaria, where I caught my first trout. While it was only a tiny eight-inch brown trout, it was not the only thing that got hooked that day. By 1955 my fishing skills had improved. I had a lovely time with Tommy and Lorraine, and was reluctant to return to Rimrock Farm.

With the death of my father, our farm went from being the center of USET activity to somewhat of a backwater. The new USET leadership understandably wanted to establish training sites close to the new civilian centers of activity on the East Coast. As a consequence, both the farm and our house now seemed a dark, empty place. I suddenly was afraid of the coyotes that came down onto the rimrock to howl at the moon, and I began having trouble sleeping. One of our family friends, Colonel Les Carter, heard this, and drove out to see me. He was commander of the 27th Infantry Regiment, whose mascot and unit shoulder patch was a Wolfhound. He gave me a shoulder patch, told me I was now an honorary member of the 27th Infantry Regiment, and casually mentioned that the "Wolfhounds" were not afraid of the dark, and that, as I well knew, coyotes were afraid of Wolfhounds. After this initiation, my Weimaraner pathfinder Jack and I slept through the night.

Life had to go on, and we went to the 1956 Olympics in Stockholm to support my middle brother, Warren. He was the reserve rider for both the U.S. show jumping and eventing teams. (The rules on substitute riders were much different in those days.) The 1956 Olympics were held in Melbourne, Australia, but the equestrian competitions took place in Stockholm due to the equine quarantine regulations in force in Australia at that time. Stockholm had been the site of the 1912 Olympics—the first time that equestrian disciplines had appeared on the Olympic schedule—thus the basic facilities were already in place.

Fortunately, by 1956 I was housebroken, and the police did not have to chase me away from the base of the tower containing the Olympic torch. I was too busy fighting with Warren to get into much trouble otherwise.

The stadium that was originally constructed for the 1912 Games is a very warm, intimate brick structure. When it was once again used for the 1990 World Equestrian Games, I went to the same seats we had held in 1956 and sat there for a moment, thinking about all the wonderful horses and riders I had watched in that stadium. There have been a lot of changes since then, both in my world of horses and society in general.

Kansas was a conservative area in the 1950s. Social changes came slowly. I had to make my own amusement; television did not reach us, which made the local radio station my major source of entertainment. The rock and roll phenomenon had arrived a couple of years before the Stockholm Olympics, but KJCK (1410 on the AM dial) was still playing Patty Page and Doris Day when we left for Sweden. When I came home a month later, the first thing I heard on the radio was "Be Bop a Lula" by Gene Vincent and the Blue Caps, and "Rock Around the Clock" by Bill Haley and the Comets. Rock and roll had arrived in Kansas.

It strikes me that I have been incredibly lucky to have the right people show up in my life at the right time. After my father died, my new brother-in-law, Paul Seymour, stepped in and helped raise me. At first the male authority I needed, he later on became my best friend, best man at my wedding, and life-long fishing and hunting partner. I lost Paul recently, after a friendship that lasted nearly seventy years, and for me the shock was equal to the loss of my father. Age does not lessen the pain of these experiences; it just changes the way we deal with them.

Horses Take Center Stage Again

_____I was released from incarceration at Pleasant View School for time served in May of 1958 and had no plans for the summer. Another figure then appeared to guide my path: our stable manager and Rimrock Farm head rider Jonas Irbinskas. Born in Lithuania, he fled the oncoming Russian army in 1945, and found refuge in Allied Occupied Germany working at the stables of the U.S. Constabulary. My godfather, Major General I.D. White, was in charge of the constabulary in Berlin after World War II, and noticed Jonas's talent. He arranged passage to Rimrock Farm, where Jonas became my first instructor after my father's death.

It was after breakfast on my first day of freedom from school when he came to the house, pulled the book out of my hands, and said, "Get up. I need you at the stables." When I got there, I found a shed row of four stalls, a saddle, four bridles, and four horses. Jonas indicated that I should take over their care and riding, and thus reawakened the interest in horses that has defined my life.

My first serious dressage lessons consisted of Jonas putting me up on my brother's 1952 Olympic horse, Benny Grimes, and telling me, "Put your leg here, and turn his head that way," and similar instructions. I did not realize it at the time, but at the ripe age of thirteen, I was introduced to all the dressage movements I would ever need. Jonas had that happy facility of telling a rider to do something, and if you executed as he instructed, it worked. Benny had been well trained. He went along with the program, and I made rapid progress for a while.

Jonas described these strange new exercises (which I now recognize as shoulder-in, half-pass, and so on) as the tools we use to communicate with our horses, especially when galloping and jumping. It never occurred to me at the time that I might apply these skills to executing the movements at an exact spot on the flat. That would come later.

Jonas was one of the unsung eventing heroes of the 1950s. As well as getting me started, he won the U.S. National Eventing Championships in

1957 and 1958. Later in his career, he made perhaps his greatest contribution to our horse world. One of his young students was the incomparable Kim Severson. Funny old world, isn't it?

My own world didn't look the same by the summer of 1958. Jonas and my brother Jeb had shipped about 20 horses to Colorado Springs to prepare for the Wofford Trophy and the 1958 National Eventing Championships, and I was brought along as an extra rider for the young horses and a couple of jumpers unsuitable for eventing. A little background here: after my father died, the USET gave a trophy in his name for the winner of the championship. It was meant to be a perpetual trophy, but such was the jealousy of some of the USET officers at the time that when Michael Page won it for the third time several years later, they declared it had been a challenge trophy and was thus retired. They hoped that in this way they could remove the Wofford presence from their affairs. Little did they know.

Naturally, in 1958, all this was going on over my head. I had horses to ride, lovely weather at the foot of the Rockies, and the prospect of more horses in my future. I was showing junior jumpers that year, and for the first time in my life I was well mounted. Before this, my brothers had gotten the nice horses, and I was left with the not-so-nice ones. Now, with Warren married and living in England, and Jeb concentrating on eventing, I had some good rides. How good? Well, how about Rattler, a U.S. Army Quarter Horse from the Remount program? He had been Johnny Russell's ride in 1952, when Johnny became the first foreigner to win the Hamburg Derby.

Johnny is another of the Old Army types who would continue to play a big part in my story. I was standing at the in-gate when he won the Derby and can remember the roar from the crowd as he jumped the last. The winner's party that night probably did not help my father's attitude the next morning, when he had to deal with the results of my latest transgressions. The entire Russell family came along on the Team's trip through Europe. Young Johnny and I were about seven at the time, and partners in crime. The U.S. contingent was staying at quite a nice hotel in Hamburg, with a lovely fountain in the center of a large reception area. Little Johnny and I decided that the polliwogs we had found in the water jump in the arena at the Hamburg show grounds needed a new home, with fresh running water. We moved as many as we could capture to the fountain at the hotel, and then forgot about them—until they metamorphosed into young bullfrogs and started to serenade the guests at breakfast. Some public-minded citizen snitched us out to the manager, who spoke with my father. For the next few days I did not have the feeling that I was the pick of the litter.

Anyway, I was talking about my string of horses in the summer of 1958, but I digressed. (As you can tell, I have a tendency to digress—I love digressions, don't you?) Where was I? Oh, yes, in Colorado Springs, riding Rattler, and another good horse named By Day. He was about as loopy as a chestnut Thoroughbred can be, but I was about as loopy as a redheaded kid can be, and we got along just fine. Earlier that summer, I had quite a lot of success with him in the Junior Jumper divisions in Kansas, Missouri, and Nebraska. As I made my circle to the first fence at one show, a lady along the rail was heard to shriek, "Get that child off that horse, or he'll be killed." Fortunately, her prediction hasn't come true—at least not yet. I was never sure before the fence if By Day would leave long or short, and he didn't care. However, when I came out to Colorado, I moved up to the Open Jumpers (we did not yet have all the different levels now available) and my results tailed off. It wasn't until much later that I learned the truth to the saying, "It's not what you win, it's who you beat to win it."

A Time for Big Changes

——I wasn't happy with my horse show results, but the rest of my world was about to change for the better. Jeb had made friends with a nice local couple, Dr. and Mrs. John Karabin. Jean Karabin asked us to dinner, telling Jeb, "There's a cute little girl, Gail Williams, who lives down the street. She's the same age as Jim, and she is horse crazy, too."

About four blocks from the Broadmoor Hotel, on July 7, 1958, at 6:15 in the evening, I turned the corner into the Karabins' living room. There I met a gorgeous young blonde lady, and instantly had the epiphany she was the girl I would marry and spend the rest of my life with. Gail was not smitten to the same degree as I was, but she *was* horse crazy; she soon found out that my mother had a seemingly inexhaustible supply of homebred Thoroughbreds, and my stock started to rise. Eight years later, my epiphany became reality. The epitaph on my tombstone will read, "On June 11, 1966, he was married, and lived happily ever after."

This was life-changing enough, but there was more to come. In addition to meeting my future wife, I had decided to go to Culver Military Academy so I could ride every day there with the Black Horse Troop. I was already comfortable with a military system and had not yet grasped what a culture shock awaited me. I was about to join a Corps of Cadets that totaled eight hundred young men—this after leaving a school where, for eight years, there was one other student in my grade. In addition, Culver's academic standards equaled those at the best private boarding schools on the East Coast. I was moving into a different academic world. Can you say "algebra?" ∎

3

_Indiana, and Still the Old Army

Discipline *is defined by Webster's Dictionary as training to fix incorrect behavior or create better skills.*

I arrived at Culver in the fall of 1958 and the first few months passed in a whirl. I soon learned how to march in formations, to stand at attention, and was introduced to the intricacies of the M-1 rifle—how to carry it, how to care for it and, later on, how to fire it. We marched everywhere: to meals, parades, matins, and vespers. Plebes marched in the barracks, turning "square corners" in the hallways and never, but never running indoors. From my first day at Culver, I learned to refer to everyone I met as either "sir" or "ma'am," a practice that has stayed with me.

Being raised around the Army had prepared me for discipline, and I was comfortable with that aspect of the school. Fortunately for me, Culver had outlawed physical "hazing" the year before I got there. I was subjected to verbal abuse, and plenty of it, but tolerated it as part of the process. I soon was able to loudly declaim that I was indeed a plebe, and a plebe was the lowest form of life on earth—so low, in fact, that whale shit looked like a falling star to me. I was secretly amused by this, and certainly agreed that I was at the bottom of the social pecking order.

Another thing I noticed was that the Old Army's reach was long enough to find me at Culver. I had barely been there a week before the Commandant of Cadets summoned me. This usually meant some serious transgression, and I was in a sweat, thinking, "Hell, I haven't even gotten my first demerit, and I'm already called on the carpet." Regardless, I marched into Colonel Ed Stephenson's office, stood at rigid attention, and saluted. He left me standing at attention while he checked me out. This was a terrifying experience; he had a tall, spare frame, cold blue eyes, red hair in a "high and tight" haircut, and an immaculate uniform covered with badges and ribbons. Colonel Stephenson never relaxed in his office chair, but sat in a "brace" on the edge of his seat—at least when anyone else could see him.

I was well acquainted with the concept of a brace after a week at Culver and was doing a fair imitation of one myself. (When an upperclassman told you to "Sink your chin, mister," you stood at attention, eyes forward, heels together at a forty-five-degree angle, chest up, back erect, arms straight at your sides, thumbs and forefingers touching, the backs of your hands out, and with your chin sunk deeply enough into your neck to produce extra chins.)

After what seemed like an hour, Colonel Stephenson told me, "Stand at ease [relax in place], Mr. Wofford," and explained that he had called me in to have a look at me. Turns out the colonel had been a plebe at West Point when Daddy was stationed there, admired him tremendously, and had followed Daddy's career. In addition, Colonel Stephenson was Commandant of Cadets when my brother Warren attended Culver from 1949 to 1954; he remarked that after a few bumpy spots, Warren had made a fine record at Culver. Colonel Ed gave me another cold, hard stare, and remarked that he was keeping his eye on me, because he expected me to match or exceed the records of my father and my brother. Then he said, "That is all, Mr. Wofford, you're dismissed." I saluted and got out of there as quickly as I could, thinking that I sure could have used a safe space right then, but there was no place to hide. I was going to have to perform.

Warren later admitted to me that he had received a very different treatment from Colonel Stephenson during his first week at Culver. Warren was almost as feral as I was and had left two other very nice boarding schools—once for illness and once just pure AWOL—before arriving at Culver. Stephenson had Warren march into his office and gave him the same welcoming speech about our father that I later received. The variation for Warren, however, was that Colonel Stephenson thought that Warren could not match up to Culver's standards, and that he was going to make it a personal goal to "wash out" Warren as soon as possible. Otherwise, Colonel Ed was afraid that Warren would become a disgrace to Culver, his father, and the entire Wofford family. When Warren was dismissed, seething with anger, he told himself there was no way in the world that horrible man could get rid of him. The reverse psychology must have worked, because Warren made it through all four years, graduating as the Squadron Stable Lieutenant.

There Is Learning...and Learning

____Psychology wasn't what I needed for my first few academic experiences at Culver; it was to develop an aptitude for mathematics. It immediately became clear that algebra and I were not going to get along. Pleasant View was satisfied once I learned my multiplication tables and could divide and multiply. This algebra stuff came as a shock to me, and I was placed in afternoon remedial mathematics. I went along with this, partly because Culver did not ask, it told, and partly because I already had figured out that my ability to spend any time with horses was going to be based on my ability to stay in school. No grades, no horses; the next 10 years of my life would be regulated by this simple rule. I figured out the arcane idiom of algebra after some mental gymnastics and was now free to spend my afternoons at the riding hall, which was the point of the exercise all along.

If you were to examine all my grades and transcripts from this period, you would soon determine that I had an uncanny ability to expend the minimum effort required to pass the course in question. A student I was not. This is not to say that I wasn't interested in learning, just that I was only interested in learning about things that interested *me*, and this meant horses.

A winter reading list from my first couple of years at Culver would have included my father's copies of *Training Hunters, Jumpers, and Hacks* and *Riding and Schooling Horses*, both by Colonel Harry D. Chamberlin; *Horse Training: Outdoor and High School* by Major Emile Beudant; *The Forward Impulse* by Major Piero Santini; and *Riding Logic* by Wilhelm Müseler. Not bad, for a teenager. Not bad, but not usual for a teenager, either.

The riding instruction at Culver was based on the system of my father's coach, Colonel Chamberlin, so I was very familiar with the methodology.

I didn't realize it at the time, but the first ten years of my riding career were all spent with instructors who based their teachings on Colonel Chamberlin. This is a marvelous system of riding and training and I still ride and train according to its principles, nearly a century later.

One of the stable employees at Culver was Jim Jolley, a retired Master Sergeant who had been 30 years in the cavalry and spent several years as Hiram Tuttle's stable sergeant. Following that, he was the stable sergeant for the Army team at the 1948 London Olympics. Sergeant Jolley told me a story about Colonel Tuttle advising him that a new dressage prospect was coming to the dressage team. It was a five-year-old Thoroughbred who was now cleared to resume activity after a tendon injury. Colonel Tuttle told him the horse would arrive and that he wanted Jolley to "walk him," then turned to leave. Jolley asked, "Sir, how long do you want me to walk him?" (thinking an hour a day for a while, and so on). Jolley then laughed, and said to me, "Jim, Colonel Tuttle looked at me like I had crawled out from under a rock, and told me, 'a year!' And that's what I did—for one year I walked him up and down the rimrock at Fort Riley. Here, let me show you the photos."

And Sergeant Jolley produced a set of photographs of this horse, taken a year apart, that showed a miraculous transformation. The first photo, taken outside against the lovely cream-colored limestone walls of the West Riding Hall, shows a young Thoroughbred, lacking in condition and muscle, basically skin and bones. The second photo, taken at the same location a year later, shows a different creature, one obviously in good condition, with muscles rippling under a gleaming coat.

Jim Jolley only stayed at Culver for a year, and I was never able to ask him more questions about his life or about horses. One of the things I have noticed over the years is how, even in old black-and-white photos, the horses glistened with health and condition. And this was in an era before additives, supplements, and grooming aids. We lost a lot, when we lost the cavalry.

Sergeant Jolley was obviously a skilled horseman, and I occasionally watched him working with a very difficult horse, Var, a fabulous jumper who had become unsuitable for the cadets. Colonel Gerald Graham, the head of the riding program, had given up on the horse after trying to re-school him without success. Jolley had quietly made a project out of Var, and would put him in the cross-ties and apply what I now recognize as the techniques of François Baucher. Colonel Tuttle was a big proponent of Baucher, a famous dressage rider and trainer from the previous century. Baucher was a controversial figure who advocated unusual practices, such as galloping backward.

Jack Burton told me of watching a dressage exhibition at the Madison Square Garden Horse Show in the 1940s, in which Colonel Tuttle would appear in a dark arena, lit by a single spotlight on horse and rider. Tuttle would be in his dark blue full-dress uniform, wearing white gloves, with a white double bridle headstall, and seemingly no reins. The secret was that Tuttle had black silk thread for his reins. He would produce various dressage movements, then as a grand finale he would canter to the center of the arena, salute the crowd—then gallop backward out of the arena. Jack Burton chuckled and remarked that while Colonel Tuttle could get his horse to gallop backward, it did not produce a movement of grace and beauty.

I'm digressing (you're used to that by now), but my main points here are—first, like all cavalry officers of that era, Colonel Tuttle had an unusual attitude toward the time necessary to train horses. Not many of us these days would be willing to devote a year of a horse's life to what my father called "pick-and-shovel" work, in order to develop the muscle and condition needed for optimum performance.

My other point is the amount of knowledge that existed in the U.S. Cavalry. Here was a retired NCO, probably with a grade-school education, in a dead-end job at Culver, who was applying sophisticated techniques to the retraining of a spoiled horse. Jim did flexions in hand with Var, practiced turns on the forehand and on the hindquarters from the ground, and worked him in long reins. After a couple of months of this, Colonel Graham suddenly appeared riding Var again, and Jim Jolley left Culver at the end of the school year. I think there was a lot more to the story, but I will never know, and my life at Culver was moving on.

My First Published Work

——The life I had led at Rimrock Farm left me most comfortable on my own or in the company of adults; being surrounded by boys my age was disconcerting, and I kept to myself a great deal. Horses, dogs, and fresh air were more my style. I was already an eager student of riding technique and found that many of the things I read about were possible; with practice I could do them, and I could feel the improvement of my horse. I can remember the exact place in the indoor arena where I felt the effect on my position of the relaxation of the ankles that Colonel Chamberlin wrote about. This small but important step convinced me of several things: that I could learn from books and apply that learning, that my horses went better as I got better, and that I found the whole process endlessly fascinating. Those early experiences awakened a desire to learn about horses that has stayed with me to this day.

Between my sophomore and junior year, the Wofford family went to Rome to watch Dawn Wofford ride Hollandia for the British show-jumping team in the 1960 Olympics. I watched all three disciplines with rapt attention. The most exciting part for me was to see my heroes go cross-country over one of the most difficult courses ever built. Back at Culver that fall, I wrote a letter to the *Chronicle of the Horse*, lamenting the lack of a USET developmental program for young riders. The only way I could have been more obvious would have been to take out an advertisement in the *Chronicle*, saying, "Me, me!" Much to my surprise, the magazine printed it—the first time that something I wrote appeared in print. It wouldn't be the last.

Winston Churchill once remarked that schools are more a place where young people are inculcated with basic rules and customs than a place where education occurs, saying, "Education is quite different and has little place in school." He must have had me in mind, because that was my experience. At the same time, the lessons Culver taught me were very real, and very important. Those lessons entailed developing young men into leaders in their communities.

Although a military school and part of the ROTC (Reserve Officers Training Corps), Culver did not view its role as preparing us for entrance into the service academies. True, cadets went straight from graduation into the Army as second lieutenants during World War II, but the United States was involved in a global conflict at the time; everyone took part, and many Culver graduates died in uniform.

I made it to 1961, the summer before my senior year, and tried out for the USET Talent Search in Denver. I did not make the cut but returned to school with my riding resolve unshaken. I was sure that someday I could make the cut and compete with the best of the best.

Applied Lessons

——Leadership was part of the curriculum at Culver, and I still remember several of the rules: learn to take orders before you can give orders; never ask a man to do something you would not do yourself; and feed your men before yourself. This was drilled into us, and I practiced it during 1961–62, my senior year.

I was a cadet captain by then, and in charge of Troop B. We dined cafeteria style, and during my last year there I quietly made sure that all sixty members of Troop B, plus the troop NCOs (non-commissioned officers) and lieutenants, went through the "chow line" before me. I was serious about applying those lessons. In the fall of 1961, I learned that someone in the troop was stealing money from rooms in our barracks. At our next formation, I called the troop to attention, told them to stand at ease and listen up. Stealing was an honor offense, and I wanted it to cease immediately. If I caught the offender, I would make sure he was summarily expelled from school. If he was still compelled to steal for whatever reason, I had placed a twenty-dollar bill on my desk, and he should steal that, instead of taking it from someone who might need it. All I asked was that he pay it back when he could.

My reasoning was that I wouldn't miss that twenty, and there might be some psychological need that someone had to satisfy by taking it. I left that twenty on my desk all year. Sometimes it would be on top of my pile of mail. Sometimes it would be buried, and might have gone AWOL, but when I cleared out my desk in June of 1962 there was a twenty-dollar bill still there on my pile of mail. I stuffed it in my pocket and didn't think about it again until I started writing this book. I wonder who that kid was, who stole from his friends. I wonder how he turned out. With an attitude like that, he probably came to a bad end and got elected to Congress or something.

SELF-DISCIPLINE

A mong the most important things I learned at Culver was not the military system of discipline, but how to develop a personal system of self-discipline. Another important aspect of my experience there was the honor system. In essence it said, "We will not lie, cheat, or steal, nor tolerate among us those who do." I was comfortable with this, having from an early age been taught I should ride hard, shoot straight, and always tell the truth. (It was assumed that there was a little wiggle room in that last bit about the truth when it came to fishing.) During my four years there, Culver had very few honor code violations that I remember.

However, I do remember vividly one transgression of Culver's code of conduct—and I was one of the perpetrators.

In January of 1961, the Black Horse Troop rode in President Kennedy's Inaugural parade. This was a big deal for us, and about 100 cadets made the trip to Washington with their horses. Washington had been hit with a blizzard the night before the parade; there was snow everywhere, and a cold wind. We were given "Boots and Saddles" (troopers, mount your horses) about 10 in the morning, and started a long, stop-and-go process of joining the parade procession, all in bitter cold. After several hours we stopped at a restaurant; the adult staff had prepared water and a picket line for the horses, while we went inside for lunch. We were not allowed in the bar but watched on a small black-and-white TV in the dining room as JFK gave his inaugural speech: "Ask not what your country can do for you, ask what you can do for your country." We didn't realize at the time how historic this day would be.

This was my junior year and as First Sergeant of Troop B I was now the senior non-commissioned officer in my troop. As such, I would be the last member of the Black Horse Troop past the review stand. Colonel Stephenson gave me a handful of change to use in pay phones, and a number to call if I needed help. If anyone was injured or got disconnected from the main body, I was to stay with that cadet and call for help when I could. This was a fairly sensible plan in an era before cell phones. A few blocks before the reviewing stand, a trooper's horse spooked at something, reared, slipped out behind, and horse and rider crashed down onto the icy pavement. I quickly moved up, but the pair had miraculously escaped injury. They were soon reunited, and we resumed our assigned places in the parade. It was dark by the time we made the turn to finally pass the reviewing stand, and we had been in the saddle several hours non-stop.

The reviewing stand was deserted when we passed by and saluted, which was a bit anticlimactic after all the effort and discomfort we had suffered to get there. But we alternately walked and jogged into the night, and after about half an hour came to our assembly point and were given the command to dismount. As I stepped down, I happened to look ahead just in time to see a cadet dismount and fall backward. I gave my horse to another cadet, went to check him out and immediately saw that he was shivering badly, incoherent, and entering what we now recognize as hypothermia.

I realized we needed to get him warm as soon as possible. A Greyhound bus was parked next to our trailers, its motor running and interior lights on. I knocked on the door, explained the situation to the driver, and we climbed the stairs into a rush of warmth and noise. We were in a bus full of Shriners who had also been part of the parade and were now in full party mode. One of them grabbed my charge, sat him down, and handed him a cup, saying, "Here, drink this." As the cup passed by me, I smelled whiskey and grabbed at it, but too late—down the hatch it went. This was serious trouble for cadets, and we could expect to be expelled for drinking while a student at Culver.

My frozen young friend was a goner, and probably I was as well. All this flashed through my mind, while that whiskey was flashing through my young friend's system. His complexion changed from pale blue to bright red in a few moments, and I figured we had to get back and face the music. Resisting the blandishments of several jovial Shriners, I pulled my fellow cadet to his feet and hustled him down the stairs and out into the cold night air. When the bus door closed, I gave him two orders: "Don't breathe a word of this to anyone, and for God's sake don't breathe on anyone, either."

I got this poor unfortunate, who by now was starting to realize the enormity of his situation, reunited with his horse, while I went in search of Colonel Stephenson. Asking to speak with him in private, I explained the situation as best I could. I remember that he looked off into the distance, thought for a moment, then looked at me and said, "Wofford, you did the right thing. Now I never want to hear of this again. Dismissed." You can bet I waited until I was safely graduated before I shared that little story. ■

College placement was starting to be a more important topic at secondary schools, and in the fall of my senior year I was duly summoned to see Dean Craig, who was in charge of making sure Culver graduates went on to suitable colleges. He asked me if I had thought about college. When I admitted that it was the farthest thing from my mind, he said it was time I made plans, remarking, "Where would you like to go?" "Well, my father went to West Point, so I could get a place there," I responded. West Point at that time graduated officers who were basically engineers, and math played a big part in the curriculum. Dean Craig, who had read my file, scoffed, "Oh, come on, Wofford, get serious." After further negotiation he agreed that a college where I could continue to ride would fit the bill, and thus the University of Colorado should be a good place for me.

The next thing I knew, after four years at Culver I had my diploma, an acceptance letter from the University of Colorado, and a bigger and better world of horses to explore.

First, however, the grass on the other side of the Atlantic was greener: a summer spent riding in Ireland was next on my agenda. ∎

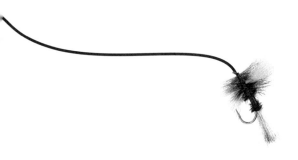

_Irish Interlude: Summertime 1962

My salad days, when I was green in judgment.

William Shakespeare
Anthony and Cleopatra

A long, glorious summer stretched ahead of me—and in Ireland, too, the Emerald Isle. Ireland couldn't have been any greener than I was, but I figured I would substitute speed and enthusiasm for experience. Life was good. As a reward while I was on parole between high school and college, Mom had given me a choice of a summer in Germany doing dressage with Willi Schulteis or riding green horses in Ireland. My choice was to spend the summer working for an old family friend and one of Ireland's most successful horse dealers.

Cyril Harty, "the Captain," had been on the Irish Horse Show Team in the 1930s (along with other famous Irish horsemen such as Captains

Dan Corry and Fred Aherne) at the same time my father was on the U.S. team. They met as young officers and remained friends throughout their lives. Cyril Harty had 10 children, which meant my siblings and I usually had an instant pal our age when we arrived in Ireland. I was fortunate in my Irish alter ego, John Harty, who went on to be a champion steeplechase jockey as well as riding on the Irish eventing team at the 1964 Tokyo Olympics.

My father was also the U.S. military attaché to Ireland in 1939–40 and made many friends during his time there. This was a serious time to be an Army officer, as World War II had just started, and I have seen some of his letters from that period. Early in his assignment, he writes about beachfront fortifications and machine gun emplacements, items of great interest to professional soldiers. Later, his letters describe the racing and hunting side of Irish life, and one can tell his focus is changing. One letter mentioned that Daddy had run into Dan Corry, who was out walking his racing Greyhounds. With typical Irish generosity, Captain Corry invited my father for a day at the races, and Daddy accepted this invitation with alacrity. It was obvious that as time went on, my father fell more and more under the spell of the Irish horses and the people who love them. In his last letter to my mother before he transferred back to the United States, he closed by saying, "You know, I don't think the Irish care if they are invaded or not."

(When I was older, my Irish connection extended to that country's wonderful horses. Take it from me, a good Irish horse can change your life. I rode an Irish horse at all but one of the international events I ever won, which explains my fondness for them.)

My magical 1962 summer started as soon as I landed in Ireland. Imagine getting in a taxi at the old Dublin Airport and immediately falling into a serious debate with the driver as to whether Arkle or Mill House was the greatest steeplechaser that Ireland had ever produced, or "was dere a better in all tha Emerald Isle?" By the time I got to my destination, I had a lead on two of the "greatest young leppers" the world had ever seen, a tip on the 4:30 race at Punchestown Racecourse, and an invitation to an IRA fundraiser that evening at The Grasshopper, in the village of Clonee.

It was a wet summer, even for Ireland. The sun was out the morning I landed in Dublin and shone again the day I left—and it rained every day in between. When I mentioned this, I was told, "Yes, but it's a dry rain." The Irish have a subtle conception of the truth.

Despite the weather, I rode young sales horses every day for the next few weeks. The Captain had a steady stream of clients, and John and I presented likely prospects to them. Whatever technique and polish I had gained at Culver was going to have to suffice; at that time, the Irish were long on horse sense, but short on technique. It took a fair amount of "git 'er done" to ride uneducated young stock over colored poles and up and down the few banks and ditches we had on the place.

I was on a strawberry roan mare one morning and had gotten the bucks out of her by the time The Captain drove up. I showed him her new tricks by circling a few times, riding a couple of figure eights, and changing back and forth from trot to canter. The Captain seemed happy enough with the progress of her flatwork and told me to pop her over the bank at the end of the field. "Okay," I said. "Has she been over it before?" "Ah, no," was the reply, "but her dam was a great lepper." I wouldn't say this one was great, but she had a good attitude, and we eventually scrambled back and forth successfully. I learned a lot about horses that summer, including what happened when horses from a good gene pool crossed paths with enthusiastic ignorance. Horses have an extraordinary desire to please humans; they will put up with our most outlandish requests, if asked in a determined and confident manner. This was the first time I noticed this about horses, but it wouldn't be the last.

I was spending plenty of time in the saddle, but my chances for instruction were limited; when I got the chance to take a clinic with Major Joe Lynch, the coach of the Irish Olympic eventing team, I was ready. Joe had been in the British cavalry most of his life, and during World War II, he was a training officer in Scotland preparing troops for combat in North Africa, Sicily, and then Italy. Like many of his countrymen, he had a marvelous command of the English language, including a career soldier's use of profanity and obscenity, as well as an instinctive understanding of horses, and a deep appreciation of whiskey.

Given some of the more lurid tales he told after hours, we suspected that Joe was either about 105 years old or more than capable of embellishing a story. His age or his nightly intake could affect his coaching, and I have painful memories of him, still under the weather from the night before, standing on top of a cold, wet, wind-swept hill, red-faced and screeching at me in a British accent while obviously forgetting my name, "You theah, come heah, you *[expletive deleted]* imbecile, you, YOU! ...TREATY STONE! Come heah!" (He never forgot your horse's name, but you? Not so much.)

Treaty Stone, the horse Captain Harty had given me to ride at Joe's clinic, was a grey, seven-eighths Thoroughbred gelding, and one of the laziest horses I have ever ridden. I don't know if The Captain was mad at me, or just saw a chance to get his horse off the farm and educated at the clinic with Joe. Whatever the reason, Treaty took all the leg I had to get over the jumps—and then some. It wasn't exactly smooth and polished, but at least I got around. It must have looked a little better than it felt;

John later told me that when I finished, Joe sniffed, and remarked that it "wasn't too bad, for an American."

I was sad to leave Ireland, where I had spent most of my time with horses, thus continuing my equestrian education. I now faced new challenges. When I left Dublin, I was headed for the University of Colorado, once again sentenced to academic incarceration. ■

5

Colorado: My Horizons Widen

*Wherever we go in the mountains,
we find more than we seek.*

John Muir
Naturalist and author

fter his graduation from Harvard, Ralph Waldo Emerson remarked that even though you knew the university was hostile to genius, you sent your children there and hoped for the best.

If Emerson has it right about hostility to genius, that would explain the warm welcome that the University of Colorado extended to me in the fall of 1962. There was no genius involved in this transaction. Because the university (CU to its friends) had recently been short of out-of-state students, they snatched my application, stamped it "accepted" without a careful examination of its contents, and arranged for my incarceration in the School of Business. I forgive them, as they were working under economic pressure. At the same time, I was working under pressures of my own.

First, I was about to turn 18, and there was this horrible prospect looming in my future called THE DRAFT. More about that in a minute. Second, but just as important, my family's rule—get good grades and get a chance to ride—had been adjusted to suit my new circumstances. "Stay in school, and you will be able to ride" became "stay in school, get good grades for the first semester, and we will discuss a car and horses." The car was a necessity, because the closest training facility was about a 45-minute drive south of Denver. In fact, that facility was one of the major reasons I had applied to CU. The other major reason was a certain blonde young lady who lived in Colorado Springs. I needed wheels to ride, and to be able to see my future bride—a twofer of massive proportions.

CU back then had a lovely campus with reddish sandstone buildings set against the foothills of the Rocky Mountains and boasted more than 300 days of sunshine yearly. Its vast lawns and fields were irrigated by water from the foothills, supplied to the campus via irrigation ditches laid throughout the area. The student body numbered about 16,000, so once again I was plunged into a much larger community than I was used to. Fortunately, I had signed up for fraternity Rush Week and wound up pledging to join Sigma Nu.

CU was known as a party school and deserved its reputation. According to state law, the legal drinking age for hard alcohol was 21, but at age 18 one could purchase "3.2 beer" with only 3.2 percent alcohol. The theory was that because of the relatively low alcohol content, one could not consume enough at a sitting to induce a state of inebriation. This is just another example of how wrong politicians can be.

When you combine an active social scene with the recreational activities available, you can see why CU expected to lose about a third of each incoming freshman class. It's hard to go to class when the local ski areas have just gotten 6 inches of fresh powder. But for the most part I kept my nose to the grindstone during my first semester. I'd like to say that I was mindful of the requirement that I keep my grades up, but the truth is closer to the fact that I did not have a car, so my recreational opportunities were limited.

I did play hooky occasionally. One of my fraternity brothers had a car. We shared a Tuesday class that we both loathed, and a desire to take advantage of local skiing. Thus it was that for a while, Townes Van Zandt (yes, *that* Townes Van Zandt) would appear at seven in the morning on Tuesdays in a souped-up Pontiac V-8 with his skis poking out the back window and a half-gallon of Gallo Hearty Burgundy on the seat. I would barely have one foot inside the car before he punched the accelerator and away we sped, as if we were already late for an appointment. After several of these expeditions, however, I realized that Townes would already have been up all night, playing his guitar and writing the songs that would later make him famous, and I eased myself out of the habits of cutting class and living a dissolute life.

If you want to hear a songwriting genius, look Townes up. He later wrote hits like "Pancho and Lefty," "Marie," and my personal favorite, "Quicksilver Dreams of Maria." For his humorous take on life at CU, try "Fraternity Blues." Townes was born with a broken heart. He was destined to burn out and lived his life at a frantic pace, a pace that eventually caught up with him. I was sad to read his obituary, but I was not surprised.

I mention our brief friendship not because it represented my college experience but because it was unusual for me. I was finding my way into a new life, one without uniforms and regulations. The looming threat of no grades, no horses kept me focused; besides, if I didn't stay enrolled in school, I would become eligible for the draft. Although I had grown up in a military family, the days of Army horse show teams was long gone, and the military would no longer provide me the opportunity I longed for. I remained focused on horses and was not paying attention to the nightly news as it started to refer to faraway places in Southeast Asia. This would later pose a moral dilemma for me; I was patriotic but didn't feel that I could add much to the course of events in Vietnam. I had far more to offer to the horse world. I wrestled with this quandary for the next several years.

In the meantime, I found that if I went to most of my classes, read the assigned material, and took the tests, I could get surprisingly good grades. I was on the Dean's list my first semester, and resuming my riding career was looking more and more likely. (I was too dumb to realize that Culver had prepared me so well that my first year of college was a repetition of my classes at Culver, a fool's paradise that could not last.)

A Key to Every Door

——As promised, a car arrived at my doorstep, and suddenly in the spring semester a whole new world opened up for me. I could both attend college and ride—what could go wrong? I wandered into the next chapter of my life, ignorant of the ominous clouds gathering on my horizon. My academic education took a back seat to horses as off I went to ride with a man named Bill Bilwin.

One of the few eventing trainers in the United States at that time, Zygmunt (Bill) Bilwin ran a training facility on the outskirts of Denver. He is gone now, like so many of my mentors, but his effect on my riding was palpable. He had been an officer in the Polish cavalry, which suffered terrible casualties when World War II broke out in the fall of 1939. There is a legend that early in the war, the Polish cavalry, armed only with their lances, charged German tanks. There is no historical record of this happening, although Bill would have been the type to grin, shrug, take one more pull on his flask, pat his horse on the neck, and obey suicidal orders.

As a trainer, Bill was a product of his country's cavalry school. This is meaningful, because there were very different "schools" of military equestrian thought between the World Wars. For example, the Polish cavalry school was heavily influenced by the Italian cavalry schools at Tor di Quinto and Pinerolo in Italy. The Royal Hungarian cavalry school, on the other hand, was (as I would find out later in my career) greatly influenced by the German school at Hanover. Bill's riding and teaching was reflective of his experiences in the Polish cavalry, which made his teaching very similar to that of the founder of the forward seat, Federico Caprilli.

Bill arrived in the United States in the early 1950s and initially made his living as a racehorse trainer. (If rumor is to be believed, he generously supplemented his income by a keen appreciation of the odds of drawing to an inside straight in a poker game.) However, once the U.S. horse world learned he had been named to the 1940 Polish Olympic eventing team (before the onset of World War II caused the cancellation of those Olympics), he found his calling and managed large hunter, jumper, and eventer training facilities in the Denver area until his death.

Bill taught me to listen to the balance of my horse, and to improve that balance using gymnastics. I was so intrigued by the effectiveness of gymnastics as a training tool that years later I wrote a book about them.

I did not realize it at the time, but all my instruction—beginning with my father, from my readings of Chamberlin, continuing with Culver's Black Horse Troop, and on through Bill Bilwin's teaching—was based on the same system of riding and training. The longer I stayed with this system, the more comfortable I became with it, and the less I realized that there were other systems. This was storing up trouble for the future, but I was content at the time.

My schedule at CU assumed a consistent pattern beginning with the spring semester of my freshman year. I applied for "work scheduling" when I registered for classes; this meant all my classes were held in the morning and I was finished by noon. I skipped lunch, drove 45 minutes to Bill's facility, rode several horses, and was back at the fraternity house in time for dinner. I made a half-hearted attempt at my homework after dinner, but soon was in bed to sleep the sleep of the ignorant. Aside from saving time, I skipped lunch because I had already started to struggle with my weight. Event horses of that era were required to carry a minimum weight of 165 pounds, including saddle and bridle, which then weighed about 20 pounds, and riders tried hard to "make the weight" so that their horse was carrying no more than 165 pounds. Maintaining at 145 pounds was difficult for me. (Do the math: I was on some sort of diet for the next 20 years.)

The next time you drive south out of Denver on I-25 and cross over Arapaho Road, look to the east. All you will see now is pavement and sterile high-rise office buildings, but in the early 1960s this was semi-arid, high altitude prairie as far to the east as you could see. All this space meant one thing to Bill Bilwin: there was ample room to run a three-day event.

One of the aspects of my career in the horse world that I'm proud of is the wide array of things I have done. In no particular order, I've been a rider, trainer, judge, organizer, and course designer. I stuffed my resumé while in Colorado, adding "course builder" to that list. Bill would sketch a cross-country obstacle during the week, and I helped build it over the weekend. This pattern continued for the next two years and was invaluable in introducing me to the intricacies of construction and the vast number of tasks that took place behind the scenes of a competition. As a result, I did not begrudge the labor involved in organizing an event of this nature, or the long-term, painstaking conditioning my horse needed to participate in a full-scale Classic.

All of this was educational, but it didn't help me when I got the results of my spring final exams. In a word, *gulp*. I had sunk from Dean's List to academic probation in one semester, and I was in trouble. The draft lurked in the lives of all single men between 18 and 25 at that time; if your classification was 1-A, you were next. If you were classified 2-S (matriculating student) you were safe—as long as you stayed in school with a C, or 2.0, average. (A 4.0 average was straight As.) I had managed to plunge from a 3.25 in my first semester to a 1.9 in my second semester—thus, probation. My options were clear: I could stay in school, somehow pull my grades up, and ride, or I could join the Army, thereby putting my serious riding ambitions and dreams on hold and, quite likely, my life at risk. My morale had hit rock bottom when I left school for the summer.

My family wasn't too rough on me, considering the hole I had dug for myself. They couldn't have been any harder on me than I was on myself. I rode in Colorado all that summer, and successfully completed the Classic on the course I'd helped to build, placing second on a horse of my mother's named Goretor. He was a leggy 16.3-hand Irish/Thoroughbred chestnut of limited athleticism and no initiative, but it didn't matter. I have done a lot of things on horseback, but nothing has ever compared to the sensation I experienced whenever I galloped across the finish line of a cross-country course. I have never gotten such a feeling of partnership with a horse as when eventing. It seemed to me that the work involved in getting a horse fit enough to complete a Classic was worth it for the psychological and emotional payoff. The wide range of skills required from the Classic horse and rider intrigued me, and I was hooked. Still am, for that matter.

My riding improved over the summer of 1963, but I knew that wasn't the only area in which I had to do better. I returned to CU with a new attitude, and I was now going to get help maintaining it. Gail joined me at school, and things were immediately different. She had a much more disciplined approach to homework than I, and time spent in the library with her showed up in my grades. They were not wonderful, but they were good enough to keep me in school and out of the draft. She was able to arrange work scheduling for herself after the fall semester, and together we resumed my practice of driving to Denver every afternoon to ride.

Bringing Up Babies

⸺My mother had paused her breeding program following the death of my father but started it up again once I went away to Culver. Soon she had young stock ready to be handled and started under saddle, and I worked with the two- and three-year-olds while at home for the Thanksgiving and Christmas holidays, and during spring breaks. Gail took part in these sessions after she joined me at CU (I think I mentioned earlier that she started to take a more serious interest in me once she found out my family had a horse farm).

Part of my mother's renewed interest was due to our new farm manager, who was supposed to be able to work with draft horses and was "a good man with young stock." Dan Hannah weighed about 300 pounds, stood 6 foot 3 inches in his bib overalls, and had a cigarette forever stuck between his fingers and a twinkle in his eye. When I met Dan, I also met Barney and Babe, a matched pair of chestnut Belgians who had come with him.

I was soon impressed by his knowledge on my first visit home. Long before "natural horsemanship" was branded and marketed, Dan was applying those techniques to our young stock. He never hurried and never raised his voice; young horses seemed to trust him and relax in his presence. By the time Gail and I showed up to help, he had the youngsters voice-trained to walk, trot, and canter in both directions on a longe line. Then we were ready to back them for the first time. We placed a straw bale in the middle of the horse's stall and Dan held them as we stood on the bale, leaned over and put our weight on the saddle, easing back at the first sign of tension. Before long we had a leg on each side while Dan led them around the stall for a couple of turns.

Occasionally, one of the babies would think about bucking, and it was a comfort to have Dan holding the halter. His strength and stability soon quieted even the most nervous ones. When we had them settled in the stall, we repeated the mounting procedure in a small paddock, again backing off when they showed signs of tension. Before long we could walk, trot, and canter in both directions, using voice commands to produce the desired gait while we introduced the leg aids. All of this was accomplished with a minimum of drama. I don't mean to say that we never wound up in a pile after getting bucked off, but it was a rare occurrence, and one that we accepted as part of the process. It's easy to be brave, when you are young.

Breaking the Breaking Cart

——As the summer of 1964 approached, Mom announced that she would have a new project for us when we arrived. You guessed it; she had been to the local livestock auction. We came home to the news that she had purchased at auction a 13.2-hand pony mare that was ostensibly safe to ride and drive.

You can see where this is going. The mare stepped off the stock trailer looking somewhat the worse for wear, but obviously taking a keen interest in her new surroundings. Did I say, "stepped off" the trailer? "Launched like a rocket" would be more like it. The gentleman delivering her seemed to anticipate this. He snubbed her up pretty quickly and made some smiling comment about how glad she was to get here. Turning down our offer of a cup of coffee and some homemade pie, he sped out the driveway. This seemed a bit odd at the time; later on, we understood.

The auction program had dubbed the mare "Miss Fortune," and we decided to keep her name, not knowing it was spelled as one word, not two. I was about to say we led her back to a stall, but it was more that she bolted in that direction, and I just aimed her at the first open door. "Aw," I thought, "she's just a little skittish." Ignoring these portents of disaster, Dan and I immediately decided to hitch her up and take her for a drive.

My older brothers and sister were the last children I know of who actually drove a pony cart to school. Pickup trucks had been invented by the time I came along. So, despite my varied farm upbringing, I had never actually driven a horse, much less a new pony. "How hard can this be?" I said to myself.

Here's how hard it can be. Although we had a small corral with 4-foot board fence all around, we naturally just parked the breaking cart out in the middle of a 50-acre pasture and proceeded to tack up Miss Fortune. She kicked at the harness traces a few times and bucked a little, but she seemed to accept things fairly well; we put the bucking and kicking down to the natural high spirits of youth.

Mom drove up as we led the pony out. She parked her car, and got ready to watch us put her new driving pony through her paces. We tried to back Miss Fortune into the extra-long shafts of the breaking cart, but we couldn't seem to get her to do it. "Funny," I thought, "she acts like she has never backed up before. Oh, well, we'll bring the cart to her." Talk about putting the cart before the horse.

Anyway, that's what we did: held her and walked the cart up so that we could hook up all the straps and other stuff. She flinched when the shafts touched her sides but otherwise stood like a rock. Dan was not going to fit on the cart; there was no doubt who was going to have the honor of driving the newest member of our four-legged family. He handed the reins to me and I climbed up into the flat seat of the cart, stuck my feet into the metal stirrups on each side, clucked to Miss Fortune, and slapped her on the rump with the reins as if I knew what I was doing.

Nothing. I clucked louder and slapped harder. Still nothing. I squalled at her pretty strong and cracked the reins along her flanks. *Zip!* She kicked out quicker than a rattlesnake and twice as deadly. "That was close," I thought. "Good thing this breaking cart has long shafts and she is up at the front of them, else she would have kicked my lights out." Still not fully aware of the situation, I yelled at her again, and flapped the reins even harder. *Zip! Ping-ping!* "I understand the *zip* part," I thought. "That was her hind feet slicing through the air in front of me. But what was that *ping-ping* noise?"

Later I figured out that *ping-ping* was the sound of both metal studs breaking—you know, the ones that keep the horse firmly attached to the shafts, which keep the horse a safe distance from the driver? So I slapped the reins another couple of times; every time I did, she let fly with both hind feet, and now every time she kicked she wound up a few inches closer to me. The reason I figured this out was that her feet started to pass either side of my ears. "Time to go," I thought, and bailed out of that cart backward. And just in time, too.

Her very next kick made contact with the front of the seat. This gave her a split-second pause, and then she redoubled her efforts. That mare stood in one place and proceeded to kick the breaking cart into splintereens. By the time I rolled away, stood up, and dusted myself off, there was not enough left of that cart to make a good toothpick, and the harness was in a million pieces. I looked over at Mom, and she was laughing so hard she had opened the car door so that she could get her head down on her knees.

Dan was having a pretty good chuckle, too. When he settled down he said something about."Next time, we will start her in the corral." "I'm not too sure about that 'next time' stuff," I replied. Miss Fortune went on to be a suitable ride for my nieces and nephews, but we never talked about hitching her to a cart again.

New Horses, New Horizons

——As usual, my older brothers had absconded with all the good horses. Goretor (my first Classic ride) had become unsound, and I didn't have anything to ride that summer, so Mom bought from Bill Bilwin a 15.3-hand Appaloosa named Atos. He had been bought cheaply from the

Nez Perce reservation in Idaho, because he bucked off all the young braves who wanted a challenge. As he subsequently passed through several hands, he forgot how to buck but learned how to jump. He was still cheap when Mom bought him; I guess there wasn't much demand for a small Quarter Horse-type with a jug head, a pig eye, and a fiercely independent streak.

Bill Bilwin hosted another Classic three-day event that summer of 1964, and I needed something to ride, so...Atos. I quickly learned that telling Atos how to approach a jump was a prescription for disaster. I had to point him, make sure he had enough speed to get to the other side, and let him do the rest. This was disconcerting, but Atos had cat-like agility and reflexes, and, when left to his own devices, was brave as a lion. He seemed to know what he was doing, and I wasn't too proud to be a passenger; by the time the event rolled around we had a workable partnership.

When the dust from the Classic settled, I had won the event, and found I was starting to be recognized as a competitor with a future. My 1963 Classic placing had been good; it was even better this year, and I had high hopes for the 1965 talent search. In 1961, I had entered the talent search and had been told to get better and come back in four years—so I was back again, this time with some recent success on my record. In the meantime, my grades were good enough to keep my riding plans on track, and my draft board seemed happy to maintain my 2-S classification.

The board did not require you to graduate in a certain number of years; if you stayed in school that was good enough. I had been signing up for the minimum number of hours to keep my draft status, using "work scheduling" to free my afternoons for riding, but I was starting to run into difficulties. The School of Business had certain required classes, and I had been taking them whenever they were available at times that enabled me to ride every afternoon. However, as I worked my way through the curriculum, I found some required classes were not offered in the mornings. I solved this by taking courses outside the Business curriculum that counted toward my draft status and interested me. Without thinking it through, I discovered the secret to improving my grades and maintaining my 2-S status: just take classes in things that I liked. What a concept.

Given my equestrian interests, it is fair for you to ask, "Jimbo, if you weren't interested in business, then why Business School?" The answer is that at that time Olympic participation was only available to amateurs, and riders typically competed in one, sometimes two Olympics before going on to the real world. I confess I did not have an "after the Olympics" plan but had a vague sense that someday in the far distant future, say when I was 25 or so, I would have to get a job. That meant going into some form of business, so there I was at the CU Business School. As it turned out, during my last couple of years at CU I took enough extra hours in liberal arts to (eventually) graduate with both a BS from the Business School and "minors" in personnel management, history, and Shakespearean literature.

My grade average had stabilized and my riding career was looking up. A family friend, Jane Luce, owned a mare (Play the Field) who had been the reserve horse for the 1964 Olympic eventing team. Jane was willing to loan her to me for a while, as a second ride during my preparations for the 1965 talent search. Naturally, I was excited at the prospect, even though the mare had the reputation of being physically fragile and a difficult ride. She was a dark bay, 16.1-hand Thoroughbred with no chrome, lovely large, expressive ears, and luminous eyes. I quickly found that she was ultrasensitive, had a fiery temperament, and resented any attempt to interfere with her efforts to get to the other side of an obstacle that had the effrontery to get in her way. My experiences with Atos had taught me how to compromise, and I applied the same attitude to my new ride, with surprising results. In a few months she was winning low ribbons in working hunter classes, cantering around quite happily on a soft rein. This was fine with me, as it meant I could compete her in more than one division at a show.

Part of the allure of the talent search was that I would have a chance to compete in the U.S. Intermediate Championships immediately after the training sessions. This was an exciting prospect, but it meant that my horses had to be at a higher level of fitness than they had achieved so far. Developing this fitness had its challenges, both due to the high altitude of my training facility and a tendon injury that Play the Field had suffered several years before. Bill Bilwin dealt with her fragility in a clever way; it took more time and effort, but it was worth it. To this day, I apply many of the basic concepts to my fitness programs.

Simply put, I walked my horses into shape. An extensive network of dirt farm roads, including one long gradual uphill slope, surrounded the facility. Several days a week, I walked them for an hour on the roads, then gradually added the hill, first walking, then trotting, finally cantering up the hill an increasing number of times. There was no speed work involved, because the event wasn't until early August, and this conditioning took place in the spring and early summer.

The summer of 1965 was a turning point in my career. The Talent Squad sessions went well for me and a couple of weeks later a letter from the USET arrived, telling me that I had been selected for further training at the USET headquarters in Gladstone, New Jersey. By the time my two horses shipped to Gladstone, I felt that we were ready for new challenges.

As I turned my car toward New Jersey, the Rockies gradually lessened in my rearview mirror, and visions of "riding on the Team" filled my thoughts. I was on my way. ■

6

__New Jersey—
the First Time

I learn by going where I have to go.

Theodore Roethke
The Waking

T rue, I was in a hurry to get to New Jersey by mid-summer of 1965; however, I had other things on my mind the morning I left Colorado. First, I had an important detail to take care of at the Denver Customs House: I had ordered a brand-new Hermès saddle—a Bill Steinkraus model—the previous spring, and it arrived just in time to make the trip with me. It cost $250, a lot of money at the time, but I figured that if it would enable me to ride like Bill Steinkraus, it was worth it.

That's not the way things work, as I know now, but I still have the saddle. I got a valuable lesson, too—but like a lot of the lessons I learned, the process resembled a birddog lifting his leg on a fire hydrant: it took a while to sink in. There had been no shortcuts to New Jersey, and there were no shortcuts to learning how to ride. I couldn't buy success with a saddle; I was going to have to go to New Jersey and learn.

My next stop was Rimrock Farm. I had told Mom I needed to talk with her on my way east. We sat down in the library when I got there, and I told her I wanted to ask Gail to marry me. She smiled and said, "It's about time." I agreed, because we had been together for eight years. I had already asked Gail if she would say "yes" if I asked her...and she said "yes."

The process began to slip out of my control immediately, as Mom started talking about engagement rings, wedding dates, and so on. I realized that the situation was in good hands, mentioned I had a long drive ahead of me, and was gone like a shot.

Although modern horse people know that Gladstone is the headquarters of the USET (the "Team"), it is hard to appreciate now the grip the place had on the horse world's imagination in the mid-1960s. The Team had established a permanent training center there after the 1960 Rome Olympics. Bert de Némethy trained the show-jumping team, and Stefan von Visy was the eventing coach. With its first permanent base in a decade, the Team immediately started producing winners: both the show jumping and eventing teams won medals at the 1963 Pan American Games in Brazil, and eventers medaled again at the 1964 Olympics in Tokyo. In a short time, Gladstone had become the Mecca of the U.S. horse world. To be selected to ride there, even on a probationary basis, was (in some equestrians' minds, anyway) to have been anointed.

I had been to Gladstone once before, to watch the 1964 Olympic selection trials. Now, a year later, my heart jumped in my chest when I turned up that drive, saw the huge office and stables, and looked through the front and back tall archways in the rotunda and saw the main arena behind the building. Suddenly I realized I was not there as a spectator, but as a rider.

Built by the Brady family in the early 1900s to house their driving horses and carriages, Gladstone was an imposing three-story building with stabling on the middle and basement floors, and apartments and hay storage on the top level. Administrative offices on the east end spoke of the growing organizational efforts of the Team. All the Team trips were planned in these offices; occasional meetings of the Board of Directors were held, monthly meetings of the Executive Committee were scheduled, and a growing fundraising effort was coordinated from Gladstone.

As a sign of the continuing reach of the Old Army into national horse sport, the executive director and treasurer of the Team was General F.F. ("Fuddy") Wing, a close family friend. I was a long way from home, and it was good to see a face I recognized. There were quite a few new faces at Gladstone as well, which was the point of the next couple of weeks. Out of the 175 riders who participated in Bert's early-summer, 1965, talent-search clinics around the country, 24 young men and women selected for the talent squad were invited to Gladstone from July nineteenth to July thirty-first for more advanced training. No scores were kept, but it was clear to all of us that only a few from each discipline would then be named to the "rider in residence" program, so we were serious about our efforts. In addition, the U.S. National Intermediate Eventing Championships were planned for Gladstone and would serve as a graduation exercise for the eventing riders.

When I say Bert and Stefan were in charge, I mean it. They had established themselves as successful Olympic coaches, and their reputations ensured our rapt attention. Both were graduates of the Royal Hungarian Riding School, former Olympic riders, and career military officers before World War II. Our surroundings reflected their military backgrounds:

Gladstone in the 1960s was run like a military operation. A work list was posted at four o'clock every afternoon, stating the times of the next day's training sessions, and I guarantee we were there at the appointed hour, wearing clean breeches and highly shined boots. Those few unfortunates who once came late to a session made sure never to do it again; Bert was a stern disciplinarian, and Stefan's temper was like a volcano, bubbling just beneath the surface. The aisle floors were scrubbed every day, the brass fittings on the stalls were polished once a week, and cobwebs were an endangered species. The show jumpers and eventers had their own stable managers, George Simmons and René Williams, and there were grooms for the horses.

This last was a revelation to me, as I had always done my own work around the barn. However, another family friend, Billy Haggard, lived near Gladstone and heard that I had been named to the squad. He called my mother and convinced her that hiring a groom would make my efforts more productive. Atos and Play the Field had arrived a day ahead of me, and Alex Edmonds was there to greet them. By the time I showed up, my tack stall was organized, my tack was clean and hanging up in order, and both horses were sparkling while standing knee-deep in the whitest straw I had ever seen. I suddenly realized that all I had to do was ride; everything else was taken care of.

I was impressed by all this, and quickly noted that Alex was a treasure. A Black man of undisclosed age, short and thickening at the waist, he was a fountain of knowledge about horses. He had been raised in Middleburg, Virginia, and gradually made his way north working as an exercise rider and groom for foxhunting families, eventually winding up in New Jersey. He had never been able to find a permanent situation, due to an unfortunate tendency to "fall off the wagon" every six months or so. His age, his lovely wife, Corrie, and his part-time employment as a lay reader at his local church had almost effected a cure. I say "almost," because during the several years that Alex managed my horses, he succumbed a couple of times. But he would soon reappear, asking forgiveness and promising never to do it again. He was invaluable to me, and we worked it out.

Not in Colorado Any More

——At Gladstone, everything that could be done was done, so now it was up to me to go to work. And this training session *was* work, done in the blazing sun and thick humidity of a New Jersey summer. After my stay in Colorado, where fog in the summer meant a chill was in the air, I peered out the motel window that first New Jersey morning, saw a thick fog, and naturally assumed it was chilly. I put on a sweater and stepped outside, where I was immediately enveloped in a noisome steam bath—because that's what summer fog means in New Jersey. I hastily took my sweater off and left it in the room. I wasn't in Colorado anymore.

The heat added to our discomfort during the training sessions. We finished drenched in sweat, with raw sores on various parts of our anatomy. The emphasis throughout was on the fundamentals of our position, and a fair amount of pressure was put on us to improve. Somehow, this pressure always wound up in our seat bones, and I soon had a large knee bandage on each seat bone—and a life-long preference for boxers, not briefs.

In 1964, the main arena at Gladstone was a sand oval around a grass island, but this had become a modern training arena by the following year, and after we were through riding for the day we spent afternoons setting or taking down show-jumping courses and picking rocks out of the footing in the hot sun. This occasioned a fair amount of grumbling, as the rocks in the arena were like the mythological Hydra's heads which, if you cut one off, it grew back as two. (Space-age footing and arena design were 30 years away.) After we cleared the arena it was chain-harrowed for the next day's sessions, turning up a whole new bunch of rocks. If those rocks had been a cash crop, the team's fund-raising problems would have been solved for years.

Looking back, there was probably method in Bert and Stefan's madness. It made perfect sense that we should work on the footing, as it would then be safer for our horses. In addition, they recognized the dangerous possibilities of gathering 25 young men and women and leaving them with too much time on their hands. By the time they got done with us every day, most of us had little interest in going out and raising hell.

This wasn't universal, of course, seeing as how we *were* a young group. A couple of young men (the names have been changed to protect the guilty) were from the Southwest and wore their 20-gallon Stetsons as a badge of pride. They quickly found that if they walked into the Gladstone American Legion bar, they would get all the excitement they could handle. To a New Jersey redneck, a cowboy hat was like a red flag to a bull.

After a couple of drinks, the dialogue would usually go something like this...

Redneck: "Where's your horse, cowboy?"

Cowboy: "I'm looking at his hind end right now."

...and they'd be off to the races. The local deputy got tired of responding to public disturbance calls and told them they could keep coming to the bar, but they had to leave those blankety-blank hats in the car.

The strangely monastic attitude at Gladstone produced a serious atmosphere, punctuated by brief explosions of youthful energy. Bert was single at the time and lived in an apartment on the west side of the third floor, serving as a sort of Mother Superior to the novitiates living there. The male riders' rooms were on the east side and were off-limits to females. What can I tell you? The sexual revolution had not arrived. Both my brother Warren and Hugh Wiley told me that when the show-jumping team was on tour in Europe in 1956 and '57, Bert enforced a strict curfew on the young male and single riders. At every show, they went up to bed after dinner, only to see a very dapper Bert in black tie, stepping into the limousine of a local countess or duchess, obviously headed out for the evening. Do as I say, not as I do.

Anyway, boys will be boys, and at Gladstone that summer one of them talked a young lady into coming up to his room, based on the premise that it was Sunday, Bert was away, and everything was quiet. Things were proceeding nicely until two other riders decided to creep down the hall and peek over the transom. Naturally, they were not as quiet as they needed to be, and the lady in question inquired, "What's that noise?" Her partner stepped out into the hall, but by that time his "friends" had receded into their room. "Oh, nothing, dear...where were we?"

His friends, intensely curious by now, decided to take turns holding each other upside down by the ankles from the upper floor, while each snuck a look into the window. This was working until one of them had a giggle-fit—and dropped the other one down two stories into the giant boxwoods. The bushes broke his fall, but the noise broke up the proceedings, and there were some harsh words exchanged between teammates.

Those discussions were not nearly as heated as when a rookie transgressed the one inviolate rule at Gladstone: you never, but *never*, ride or drive through the main rotunda. Of course, "never" means "why not?" to some young fellows, so one enterprising new arrival spent Sunday afternoon washing his sports car in the main rotunda and went off to have a beer without cleaning up after himself, leaving the mud and wet towels as evidence of his disdain for rules and regulations. When we heard about this, the general feeling was, "He seemed like such a nice guy, but he is history."

Sure enough, he was quickly told that he wasn't Team material. To celebrate his walking papers, he had several more drinks than necessary that night, came home, started at the end of the driveway, shot through into the outdoor arena at about 60 miles per hour, hit the hand-brake in the middle, and left a satisfying series of "doughnuts" in the sand. After several repetitions of this he parked beneath his upstairs window, went up and threw his duffle bag and dirty laundry out the window into his open car, and hit the road. The last time I heard of him he was a big shot with NASCAR.

A Different System Means a Struggle

——I wasn't any part of these escapades, because things were not going well for me. For the first time in my life, I was being taught a different system of riding than I was used to, and I was struggling. I mentioned earlier that I had always ridden with instructors who based their teaching on the U.S. Cavalry system, as developed by General Harry Chamberlin. Dressage was taught under his system, but the exercises were aimed at improving the rider's control of the horse, not as specific exercises and movements produced at an exact spot and designed to produce a numerical score. According to Stefan, the rider should control every movement of the horse, especially when approaching a jump. For the first time in my life, I was introduced to the concept of "timing," which I later defined as the rider's ability to predict and influence the remaining increments of stride before an obstacle.

In short, I had never known that it was possible to get to a jump "wrong," so usually produced acceptable efforts from my horses, who were willing partners in our attempts to get to the other side. Not only was I now required to regulate my horse's approach and arrive at a pre-determined spot in front of each jump, but also I was a terrible rider and a stupid boy when I failed to do this. Stefan had a short fuse, but there were twelve of us on the eventing talent squad (and another twelve on the show-jumping squad), so there were plenty of other stupid boys and girls around to share his critical comments. I didn't complain; I had expected it to be tough. My military background had accustomed me to discipline and strict behavioral parameters. However, I had expected to be able to improve, and that wasn't happening.

All this was from my perspective; from the Team's perspective, I must have been among the best of an unskilled lot. At the end of the two-week clinic, the show jumping and eventing squads each named six riders who would remain at Gladstone for further training, and I made the list.

30 YEARS' PRACTICE WILL DO IT

When I first came to Gladstone in 1965, Richard Wätjen was coaching the dressage team, and I audited his lessons whenever possible. Wätjen, German by birth, was classically trained at the Spanish Riding School in Vienna after WWI and had become a coach after WWII. Tall and portly, he was a legend in the dressage world, and must have been a tough old buzzard as well. In the winter of 1966–67, Nautical Hall, the indoor riding arena at Gladstone, was one of the coldest places on Earth, but no matter how cold it was, Wätjen taught in slacks and street shoes, wearing a dark green Loden greatcoat. He was not an inspiring instructor, and his comments were brief and pungent. "More," was one of his favorites, along with "Again," and "No." I never knew if teaching in a second language was a problem for him, or if it was just his style, and I was too intimidated to ask.

He was dedicated to obtaining a correct response from his horses by establishing an inside leg to outside rein connection. One day a student remarked that he wanted to start work in half-pass. "No," said Wätjen, in his heavy German accent. "Vee vill put him in shoulder-in for two years, und zen vee vill put him in half-pass in two days." His point was that once the basic response was correctly established, the horse would put his forces completely at our disposal. In terms of my overall development as a horseman, I might have gotten as much from my auditing as from riding at the time.

Once Wätjen had finished his work with the Team horses, he taught occasional outside lessons for dressage riders. A woman showed up for one lesson with a very fancy, recently imported horse reputed to have set her back a princely sum. (Given the fur coat and diamonds she was sporting, I don't think she noticed the cost a bit.) It was obvious after she careened around the ring for a few minutes that she couldn't get this creature even close to being on the bit.

Then magic happened. Telling this unfortunate lady to ride in and "get down," Wätjen turned toward the corner of the arena where Rick Eckhart and I were cowering. Pointing at us, he said, "Boys. Come here."

Next thing we knew, we were holding the horse while, in street shoes and gabardine slacks, Wätjen laboriously stepped aboard. He would have been in his late seventies by this time, and his beer belly indicated he wasn't much for exercise. I knew he had been a fabulous rider in his day—a long time ago. He walked off gathering his reins, then moved into working trot. By now the horse was starting to settle into the contact and produced a few transitions from working trot to collected trot, followed by extended trot across each diagonal. This happened with no discernable aids, as Wätjen sat bolt upright in the saddle. Some canter work followed, including several flying changes remarkable for their straightness and fluidity.

All this only took a few minutes, with no preparation or warm-up. In the meantime, the dressage rider was standing with a stupefied look on her face, and I was pretty impressed as well. Wätjen walked back to the center and gestured that we should hold the horse while he carefully stepped down, gave him a pat, and said, "Nice horse." The owner began to babble about how grateful she was, and how impressed. "How ever did you do that?" she inquired.

Gesturing with his hand toward her shoulder, Wätjen said, "Vell, you must sit mit a straight line from shoulder, to hip, to heel." She replied eagerly, "Yes, yes, I am doing that." Wätjen continued, "... und zen you are riding mit a straight line from elbow to horse's mouth."

The lady pounced on this statement with glee, "Yes, yes. I have been doing this." "Goot!" said Wätjen. "Now you must practice for 30 years." I started to crack up at what I thought was a masterful put-down, but I happened to take a look at Wätjen's face. He wasn't putting her down, or kidding. He was serious. ∎

The training became more useful as the Intermediate Championships approached. We had a couple of cross-country schools, and we now galloped on a regular basis. Stefan was as organized in his conditioning work as in everything else, and I quickly realized what an advantage I had in coming from a high-altitude location. Both of my horses were obviously fitter than the rest and handled the work easily. My long, slow, progressive conditioning was paying off. Play the Field looked especially good—her old tendon injury did not seem to be an issue—and Atos sniffed disdainfully at his workload.

When the event was over I had placed in the top five, but I suffered one of my most embarrassing moments to do it. The Championships used the Classic format, including road and tracks, steeplechase, and so on. In those days, riders got down after steeplechase and ran alongside their horses on Phase C in order to take the weight off the horse's back. Atos and I were jogging happily along a gravel road behind the Gladstone estate after steeplechase, heading for the ten-minute vet box, when a car full of young ladies including Lana du Pont, Carol Hoffman, and Donnan Sharp pulled up alongside and started to tell me how good we had looked on the steeplechase. Carol was already a successful show jumper, Lana was an Olympic veteran, and Donnan soon would be. I was consorting with equestrian royalty, and good-looking ones to boot, plus I was fit enough to jog and talk at the same time. But just at the moment I started to think that maybe I was pretty cool, I caught one spur in my other spur strap, tripped, and fell flat on my face in the gravel. Atos never suffered fools gladly and bolted up the road, heading for the barn.

I knew if he ever got loose from me, I wouldn't catch him until next week, so I held onto the reins like grim death. He pulled me up the gravel road for a while, but finally got tired of my weight on the bridle and stopped. I got to my feet with bloody knees and torn breeches, looking as if I had been pulled backward through a hedge, while the girls in the car pulled past me. I could hear them shrieking with laughter as they

DETAILS MATTERED

I mentioned earlier that I was on the 1965 Talent Squad; when we arrived that summer Stefan called us together and gave us a brief talk about what an event was, and how important it was for us to understand the inner workings of the competition, the rules, the scoring, and so on. He then handed each of us an enormous stack of paper, which turned out to be Michael Page's raw scores from the Tokyo Olympics. This was the start of our education about eventing; we had to understand how riders were awarded the scores they got.

We started with the raw dressage marks from each of the three judges, applied the "coefficient of difficulty" to went around the bend. I can laugh now, but at the time I was in a suitably grumpy mood for cross-country.

I wasn't in a hurry to share that story, and obviously Stefan did not hear about it, as I survived the next cut and remained in residence at Gladstone, preparing for the U.S. National Championships in early September. This event would be held in upstate New York, outside of Geneseo, and would provide my most serious test to date. Although I was secretly in turmoil at my riding not having improved as I thought it should, I must have successfully concealed it; I was given a third horse to ride. This was Brado, a young horse owned by the team and currently competing at the Preliminary level.

Since its inception, the Team had made a practice of owning horses, and picking riders to suit those horses. In an era where the cost of purchasing

produce the average score of the three judges (never mind, you don't want to know—event scoring in the sixties was insanely complicated), computed the start and finish times on each phase of the speed and endurance test (yes, including Phase E) and the time taken plus time and jump faults from the final show jumping. Stefan had us score the event, starting with the dressage, computing the final dressage scores of each judge, and so on. Most of us messed up the math involved in computing the dressage score and had to do it again.

Once we all had the correct final score for Michael, who had placed fourth, Stefan made us recompute the entire results, this time giving Michael one mark better from one dressage judge for Michael's position, while keeping all the other results the same. Stefan's point? If Michael had gotten that additional mark from one judge, he would have won the bronze individual medal by a fraction, instead of losing by a fraction. That's how competitive life is at the Olympic level. Winning and losing is a matter of fractions. Details matter, was Stefan's point. Details matter. ∎

and maintaining high-level competition horses was low, this practice made sense. It ensured that the Team would always have horses who could compete internationally. However, it had negative effects as well. What the Team could loan to a rider, the Team could take away again. This gave the Team a huge role in determining the direction of a rider's career and engendered a feeling that riders were merely interchangeable cogs in a giant machine. None of this occurred to me at the time. I was thrilled at the prospect of another horse to ride, and those negative ramifications waited for me a little farther down my career path.

The National Championship: Mixed Results

——Arriving at Geneseo for the National Championships, for the first time I experienced the problems that upper-level eventers encounter when their horses get truly and completely fit. Atos especially reacted to never having been this fit before in his life and gave me an uncomfortable few moments in the dressage ring. If there were bonus marks for airs above the ground, I would have come out way ahead. He bucked and reared through most of the test, and I was complimented on my ability to stay on. It didn't help my score, but it made me feel a little better going into the speed and endurance day.

Having two rides (Atos and Play the Field), I was first on course and so first to discover that the cows had not yet been removed from the stee-plechase field. Atos wove his way through them with the relaxed air of the cow pony he used to be, and things were going well until we stepped in a cow pie a couple of strides before a brush fence. However, Atos was like a cat with his footwork and we scrambled over it safely. The rest of the event went well for me, until the very last fence on the cross-country course, which was an open ditch. Being tired at the end of fifteen miles, Atos stumbled badly, pitching me over his neck. I landed equally on my head and my shoulder, but got to my feet, remounted, and finished. My mother and General Frank Henry met me at the finish line and decided after a brief examination that I was concussed and should not ride Play the Field. This was a bitter disappointment, as I thought I had a good chance to win it on her. She was only on loan for the summer; her owner intended to use her for a broodmare. I never saw her again, but often think of her, and of what might have been.

Although somewhat the worse for wear, I was able to show jump on Sunday, and thus had the honor of finishing second in the National Championships to Charlie Plumb, Mike Plumb's father. Mr. Plumb was the only person to have won the Maryland Hunt Cup in 1929 and the U.S. National Eventing Championship 36 years later, by then in his mid-fifties. As I flew back to Colorado to finish my last year of college, I considered that my second-place finish in the Nationals would sound pretty good on a young rider's resumé, but there was more to consider. Over the next six months I had to figure out how to stay in school, not get drafted, and improve my riding. Considering that I also had a wedding to plan for, I had a lot on my mind.

My future in-laws met us at the Denver airport. By prearrangement, Gail and her mother took Gail's car back to Boulder, while Jon, her dad, drove me back. I later thought that drive might have been the most dangerous part of my summer. I screwed my courage up while we were en route, and asked Jon for his daughter's hand in marriage. Gail says she could tell the exact moment when I popped the question, because Jon headed for the ditch, over-corrected, and swerved several more times before getting the car back on the highway. Jon was never the safest of drivers, and the conversation compounded his difficulty. Once safely back in control, he agreed that the wedding plans could continue. Thus, I completed yet another rite of passage along my way.

Years later, I twice had the pleasure of sitting on the other side of what I now realize is a carefully choreographed production. Both my future sons-in-law successfully passed the test. After one of them got the desired response that he could indeed ask for my daughter's hand in marriage, he leaned back in his chair with a blank stare on his face, stunned at the enormity of the step he had just taken. After a moment, he looked at me and asked, "So what happens now?" I laughed and told him to relax, because the ladies in both families would control the rest. I wish someone had told *me* that when I was driving into Boulder that afternoon in 1965. Regardless, I was headed back to a comfortable situation, one I was looking forward to. ∎

__Meanwhile, Back in Colorado...

I can't go back to yesterday, she said, *because I was a different person then.*

Lewis Carroll
Alice in Wonderland

From the outside, things were looking good for me. My grades continued to improve because I was taking courses that interested me. I had a gorgeous fiancée, and I had a spot on the USET Eventing training squad waiting for me at Gladstone. But things were different on the inside. Put crudely, I was changing my riding from an Italian system to a German system, and it still wasn't working. In addition, I did not have a coach who could guide me through the process. As I mentioned earlier, all my instruction to this point had been firmly of the Italian system, with the adjustments that my father's coach, Harry Chamberlin, had explained in his books. They were not useful in my search to transition to a new attitude toward riding and training.

Stefan von Visy was a better organizer than he was an instructor. An Olympic rider himself, he could not understand why someone else could not immediately do something in the saddle as he instructed. To top it off, I could feel that my horses were not happy. A year earlier, I had been getting ribbons in hunter classes on horses other people had found difficult. Now, however, my horses were increasingly difficult to ride, and my daily practices were not fun. I persevered, looking for more accuracy in my jumping and more compression in my dressage, but finding neither.

I did not realize it, but neither of those two systems, Italian or German, was the complete answer to the requirements of eventing in the 1960s. One of the many reasons I later became a coach is that I could explain to riders how to combine elements of each system, and produce comfortable and effective results. But that was far in my future; for now, I just kept working.

It was not all doom and gloom. I was a senior, and the draft was a distant threat. Because I had taken the minimum number of hours necessary to keep my draft deferment, I would not graduate with my classmates. This was fine with me; if I wanted to keep riding, I needed to stay in school. I discussed this with my mother that fall and mentioned I had to transfer to a college close to Gladstone.

Mom's eyes lit up and once again my family's network sprang into action. My mother had been a founding member of the U.S. Combined Training Association (it would later become the U.S. Eventing Association) at its first meeting during the 1959 Chicago Pan American Games. While there, she had formed a friendship with another founding member and the USCTA's first president, Philip Hofmann. The Hofmann and Wofford families were equally horse crazy. Phil's daughters,

Carol Hofmann Thompson and Judy Hofmann Richter, were fabulous riders who would go on to lifelong careers at the top of their discipline. The point was that Phil was somehow involved with Rutgers, which had a good business school and an active night school program. I was to leave it to her, and she would see what the situation was there.

A week or so later I received a letter from Rutgers, welcoming me to the School of Business Night School Program as a "non-matriculating student" (taking classes for credit, but transferring those credits to another institution). I was to present this letter upon registration at the start of the 1966 fall session. I had enough sense to keep the letter, but I didn't bother to think about the favors that were being done for me, based not on merit but entirely on my family connections. From my point of view, at least I was safe from the draft for a while.

As seen from New Jersey, returning to Colorado was an attractive prospect. However, I soon realized that I was looking forward to a lot of changes in my life, and they all involved the east coast. I put in the rest of my time at CU and took my spring finals successfully. Of course, "successfully" meant different things to different people. I knew to a decimal point what grade I needed in each subject in order to maintain an average that would keep me in school and out of the draft. I could afford one D for my final semester, but an F would sink me.

I had avoided anything to do with numbers since wrestling algebra to a draw eight years before, but Accounting 201 and 202 were core Business School curriculum and I had to complete them. Accounting 201 was easy for me because one of my fraternity brothers had suffered through the same course from the same professor a semester before me and told me what to expect in the way of tests. My professor for 202, however, was a transfer from another university and thus an unknown quantity.

In those days, after the exam your grade was posted on a list on the professor's door. I approached the office of the 202 professor with some trepidation, and saw to my immense relief a D next to my name—but also an asterisk, and a terse note from my professor: "See me."

I knocked, entered, and was told—with some asperity—that throughout 30 years of teaching accounting my professor had always graded on a curve. My class's curve had forced him to give me a passing grade, but he wanted me to know that in the future, I would not have escaped his clutches; he would never grade on a curve again. I thanked him politely, skipped down the hallway and out to my car. I needed to put CU in my rearview mirror—I had a wedding to go to.

Looking back at June of 1966, I could have predicted what was going to happen. Final exams at various colleges and universities had just finished, and our bridesmaids and groomsmen arrived from around the country, all of them stressed out and sleep deprived. Most of the groomsmen were fraternity brothers, which seemed like a good idea at the time. In addition, people took one look at the invitation for a party at the Garden of the Gods Club following our wedding and said, "Colorado Springs in early June—hell, yeah!"

By this time, Gail was looking a little deer in the headlights, and sought out my sister, Dodie, with a burning question. The Wofford clan that had shown up in force included a sizeable number of eccentrics and oddballs that Gail was meeting for the first time. She asked Dodie, "Is there a lot of insanity in the Wofford family?" Dodie agreed that a lot of cuckoos had come out of the Wofford cuckoo-clock, but Gail wasn't to worry for a moment. Besides, she had more immediate problems; the parties were developing a dangerous momentum.

Most of the wedding party was either 21 or had a good fake ID, so glorious uncertainty awaited us all. My brother-in-law, Paul Seymour, foolishly offered to pay for my bachelor's party. Held near the Broadmoor Hotel at a pub called the Golden Bee, the celebrations quickly became bacchanalian, and the glass breakage exceeded the bar bill. Leaving the party, one of the participants, the son of the governor of Colorado at the time, was pulled over for speeding. He uttered those fateful words to the arresting officer: "Don't you know who I am?" We got him bailed out just in time to attend.

Decorum prevailed during the ceremony, but things got pretty wild at the reception, and my fraternity brothers decided they would cool things off by throwing each other in the pool. Gail—now Mrs. Wofford—and her bridesmaids fled the scene, and wiser heads prevailed. I shrugged and figured, what the heck, I had to change clothes anyway, so in I went. Gail and I were headed for a honeymoon in Europe, then to Gladstone, starting our new life together. ∎

8

New Jersey Redux

There are no shortcuts to any place worth going.

Beverly Sills
American soprano

The thing about being young is that you are brave without knowing it. You decide what you want to do, and away you go; there's no messing around, no serious analysis, no "what if." You just do it. So Gail and I got married, left Colorado, took a ten-day honeymoon in Europe, and landed in New Jersey. We had no place to live, no household goods, no furniture, two cars, two horses, no friends, and no worries.

We got to New Jersey at a time when the U.S. equestrian world's hopes were rising, and those hopes were focused on Gladstone. The Team's results had improved beginning in the late 1950s with Bert de Némethy as the show-jumping coach, and after 1961, Stefan von Visy's event team added to these results. If you wanted to see equestrian excellence in action, Gladstone was the place. When I arrived, the pressure-cooker atmosphere was already hot enough to match the steamy New Jersey weather. The FEI had announced that World Championships would be held in both show jumping (Buenos Aires, Argentina) and eventing (Burghley, England) in 1966. I knew it would be hard to make the eventing team riding a 15.3-hand Appaloosa, but stranger things had happened; I was prepared to give it my best shot.

Because of the importance of the eventing team's performance, two-time Olympic veteran Mike Plumb had moved back to Gladstone, along with his lovely wife Donnan and their infant son Charley. Donnan was still chuckling over my faceplant of the year before. Another veteran, Kevin Freeman, had taken a sabbatical from his job in Portland, Oregon, and moved to Gladstone for the summer. I joined Mason Phelps and Brad Smith, who had both been on the talent squad the year before, along with Rick Eckhart, who had been named to the training squad during the winter of 1965. We would ride at Gladstone all summer, and ship to England in time for the World Championships at Burghley.

Stefan had a party to welcome all the riders at the start of the session. By that time, the only rider I didn't know was Kevin Freeman. The next thing I knew, Kevin and I were standing in the corner, knocking back the cocktails, talking a mile a minute and immediately becoming fast friends for life. Kevin and I had such a good time during that party that we didn't talk with anyone else.

While I was getting into the groove at Gladstone, Gail was quietly making a life for us in New Jersey. It was she who found an apartment just off the traffic circle in Somerville, centrally located between Gladstone,

Rutgers (where I would be attending classes), and her horse's stabling near Princeton. She opened checking accounts, arranged lessons for herself with Major Dezsö Szilágyi (a local dressage expert), and put out preliminary feelers about foxhunting with the local hunt, the Essex Fox Hounds. Groceries appeared in the refrigerator, invitations to parties arrived and were answered, and we settled into a quiet routine. I was operating with my usual tunnel vision, so all of this happened offstage; things just miraculously showed up on time. However, one thing that appeared on our doorstep took Gail by surprise.

Gail had heard of Kevin Freeman by now but had not really met him. She answered the doorbell one day to see a guy in filthy blue jeans and a ragged tee-shirt, covered in motorcycle oil, grease, dirt, dead bugs, and general road grime, with Barney Oldfield goggles pushed up on his head. He said, "Hi, I'm Kevin...got any beer?" As luck would have it, we had a couple of cold ones in the fridge. Kevin was the best friend we made that summer and remains so.

Putting a Team Together

——The 1966 U.S. eventing team barely existed at this point. We had assembled every conceivably qualified horse in the country when the training session started, and it wasn't an impressive list. The Team owned several horses, including M'Lord Connolly and Gallopade, both Olympic veterans. Although M'Lord had been given to Mike as a wedding present after the 1964 Olympics in Tokyo, Mike was never on the same page as his horse and donated him to the Team; he was assigned to Kevin to ride, with Royal Imp as his second ride. Mike was to ride Foster and Chakola. Rick had been riding Gallopade successfully over the winter, so that combination had a good chance of competing at Burghley if Gallopade stayed sound. The horse was a bit of a tank, but he was honest and had successfully completed the 1964 Olympics with Kevin.

At that time, FEI World Championship rules stipulated that each country entered a team of four riders, plus two individuals; the host nation entered the same, plus an additional six individuals. The selectors' plan for our team was that Mike and Kevin would make up half of the team on their best horses, and also ride two of the younger horses as individuals. This left only two places available, to be divided among four other riders, all with no international experience. To further complicate matters, none of us owned horses that were good enough. Atos had developed a deep bone bruise in his foot and was out for the season, so—like the rest of the rookies—I now depended on the Team to provide a horse. Although this made for an interesting group dynamic, I don't remember any jealousies or competitive problems. As rookies, none of us had any kind of record to be jealous about.

Because Rick and Gallopade looked like a dependable combination, there was actually only one slot left. Stefan was desperately seeking one more partnership to make up his team. We weren't making it easy on him—nor was he making it easy on us.

We read the next day's work list with trepidation every afternoon. Bean Platter was the only USET horse left who had the quality necessary for a Classic event (totaling over 20 miles of roads and tracks, steeplechase, and cross-country) and Stefan gave us all a fair chance at riding him. The problem was that none of us did a good enough job to incline Stefan to leave us on the horse for more than one or two days. The pattern was that one of us was assigned to ride Beans, would not do a very good job of it, and Stefan then assigned him to the next rider.

This rotation continued throughout the summer with no improvement in results. Finally, Stefan decided that Brad Smith would get the final team slot, Mason would stay behind (on the basis that seventeen was a bit young to ride in the World Championships), and I would be the non-riding reserve.

Over the next two decades I tried out for twelve teams, made seven of them, and filled every kind of role imaginable for the selectors: just plain not good enough, non-riding reserve, good enough to make the team but nothing miraculous expected, fair-haired boy wonder, and team captain—I've been all of the above. From personal experience, I can tell you that being named non-riding reserve is like kissing your sister.

I quickly figured out there were a couple of rules for making a team. First, you needed a horse that was good enough, and that *you controlled*, either because you owned it, or you rode for an owner who believed in you. Next, and equally important, you never gave the selectors a reason to leave you off the team. For instance, it is amazing how winning all the selection trials takes the politics out of team selection.

Our results at Burghley were a big disappointment for the United States. We did not finish a team. Kevin, in eighth place with M'Lord Connolly, was our best-placed rider. Following the team's return to the United States, I was named to the fall training squad. As a consolation prize, my mother had taken Gail and me to Burghley. I came home with a deeper appreciation for what it took to succeed at the international level and more determined than ever to become a good rider.

Then, suddenly, the fall semester was looming. It was time to refocus on school, and a whole new world outside the narrow confines of Gladstone. Now, where had I put that letter from Philip Hofmann?

I (Just Barely) Enroll at Rutgers

——After finally retrieving my acceptance letter, I showed up at the Rutgers registrar's office about fifteen minutes before closing on the last day of registration. The clerk behind the counter, looking at the clock, said he wasn't sure he could help me. Suddenly realizing I should have been more proactive about my educational career, I whipped the letter out and presented it. The clerk glanced at it, said, "I'll be right back," and went into the next room.

The next thing I knew, the Dean of Admissions was shaking my hand, telling me how glad and relieved he was to see me, how worried he was that I had not shown up until now, and asking about my health and the health of my close personal friend, the Chairman of the Board of Regents at Rutgers, Philip Hofmann. This was news to me (as I had not really studied the letter), but I managed to tap dance around the questions and register for classes beginning the following week.

The letter, when I finally read it carefully, was a doozie. I got special scheduling privileges, a private number to call if I needed any assistance, and the assurance of the undying personal dedication of the Dean of Admissions to the well-being of my college career. I kept the letter for a while, but it was lost forever during one of the ten times we moved in the first ten years Gail and I were married. I still shake my head at my younger self when thinking of this. Thank you, Mom; thank you, Phil.

The Rutgers School of Business was very well regarded at that time, and Rutgers applied all the credit hours I earned there toward my CU graduation. (This would cause me trouble later on, but I wasn't focused enough on school to be able to foresee it.) Meanwhile, I continued riding at Gladstone, still with a gnawing sense that I was not only failing to improve but was *unable* to improve. I could not get my horses on the bit in the way that I was being taught and their jumping was erratic at best. Despite all this, I vowed to continue.

It was not as if I didn't have enough other activities to occupy my time. I had barely settled into my fall 1966 schedule and was sitting down to lunch one day when the phone rang. Out of the blue, I was offered a catch-ride in the U.S. Eventing Championships the following weekend. (We had a much more relaxed attitude about qualifications and entries than in modern times.)

I had been on a strict diet for the previous couple of years, due to the weight rules I explained earlier. I had given in to temptation while at Burghley and had vowed to get serious about my diet once school started. But the phone rang as I was finishing the first of two lovely ham sandwiches. I accepted the ride, hung up the phone, and sadly put the second sandwich away. I was back on my diet, because I had a ride in the Nationals on Duck Soup.

Gail is still laughing at me about this.

Duck Soup's owner, Gibson ("Gibbie") Semmes, told me a nice young lady would ship the horse up to Geneseo Valley—the same site as the previous year's Nationals. Patricia Guest (we know her as Trish Gilbert these days) arrived in a flurry of organization and couldn't have been nicer about the whole thing. Gail and I admired her ability to control a two-year-old daughter and her horse, all without a groom or a nanny. Fortunately for the eventing world, that organizational skill has continued for the duration of her involvement in our sport, culminating in her organizing the new Five Star event at Fair Hill, Maryland.

Gibbie said Trish would bring up Duckie's bridle, if I could bring my saddles. Oh, and by the way, he would send up the long polo whip that he carried on cross-country, because Duckie needed some aggressive encouragement in order to jump. This should have told me that I wasn't bound for glory during my second attempt at the Nationals, but I was an eternal optimist and figured I would work it out. I was wrong, but I got halfway around the cross-country before Duckie decided he had gone far enough. His owner later told me that I had gotten him much farther than he had expected; he just wanted me to have a ride at that level. I wasn't too discouraged.

Education Continues, on Two Fronts

——Night school was a perfect fit for me. I got good grades if I came to class, read the material, and passed the tests. The professors knew their students were working other jobs during the day, so there was never any outside written homework. I didn't have a job as such, but I was busy enough. I rode two sets at Gladstone in the morning, stopped off at a local barn and galloped a couple of racehorses, went home, took a short nap, read the material for my evening classes, and drove to Rutgers. I was usually home by eleven. Reading for my classes was a necessity but in my spare time I devoured every book I could find on horses. I was consumed with learning about them.

While there was not much spare time in my schedule, I was living the life I had dreamed about. I was riding at Gladstone, staying in school, and foxhunting at every opportunity. The Team's training center was only five years old but the local horse community had embraced the riders and involved them in other local horse activities. There were not many events during that time, so we participated in whatever was available. We went to horse shows, foxhunted, and (during the racing season) rode in timber races. In addition, riders were swept into the area's busy social scene.

Gail had approached Jill Slater, the local Master of the Essex Fox Hounds, and asked if we could foxhunt. Jill immediately adopted us, and literally changed our lives. She welcomed us to the foxhunting scene, and loaned me horses to exercise and hunt. She invited us to her fancy dinner parties, black tie and all, and generally became our supervisor, big sister, and tour guide. For a couple of young kids from the Midwest, we were in tall cotton. To top it all off, we had picked out a black Labrador retriever puppy and named her Petunia. This was the start of my lifelong love for Labs, and I would rarely be without at least one by my side for the rest of my life. Life was good.

If something is too good to last, it usually doesn't—but in my case, it got even better first. Atos had recovered from his bone bruise and I was riding him again, plus getting on anything that Stefan assigned to me. The breeding program at Rimrock Farm was shifting into high gear again, and with the prospect of more young horses soon to arrive, Gail and I moved from our apartment in Somerville to a farm just outside of Pluckemin, where we would have stalls for the string we were developing. The Team was very strict about outside horses at Gladstone, and required every horse stabled there to have an immediate future as a Team horse; four- and five-year-olds need not apply. But the local market for nice young Thoroughbreds who had never raced and had been started over fences enabled Gail and me to quietly develop a nice side hustle in selling young horses. It got them off my mother's stable expenses, paid for our activities, and was legal as far as the IOC was concerned; I could maintain my amateur status, yet help pay for my riding.

Riding enough horses was not my problem. My problem was getting *good* horses to ride. I was so horse crazy that I confused riding any horse with riding a horse good enough to be successful at the upper levels. If my competition record had been that of a football game, it would have read punt-punt-fumble-punt. The 1967 Pan American Games in Winnipeg, Canada, were my next goal; this meant that the United States had to train and select a team, and once again the training intensity picked up around Gladstone.

By now Kevin had gone home to help run his family firm in Portland, Oregon. Mike Plumb, Rick Eckhart, Mason Phelps, and I were in residence, and we were joined by another Olympic veteran, Michael Page. This was personally exciting for me as Michael was one of my heroes; I had followed his career since he rode Grasshopper at the 1959 Pan Ams in Chicago, at the Rome Olympics in 1960, and again at Tokyo in 1964, where he had placed fourth. Like that of Mike Plumb and Kevin Freeman, his riding showed a quiet competence that I envied and tried to copy. Michael had taken over the ride on Foster from Mike Plumb and planned to ride at Badminton that spring as preparation for the Winnipeg Pan Ams. The rest of us were going to train at Gladstone until the Games.

It is not so much that I remember specific details about riding with Mike, Michael, and Kevin; rather, I remember their general attitude. This was a group of guys who were used to winning. They had gold and silver medals to prove it. Although we had come home from the World Championships disappointed, our results were a wake-up call, not a destructive blow. My training partners' affect was a strange mixture of, "It's never good enough," and "I'm going to win when I get there." Between Stefan's attitude toward details, and the veterans' quiet determination and confidence, I found myself subconsciously feeling the same way. I knew if I could make the team, I could rise to the challenge.

My lack of a good horse was holding me back, but that was about to change.

Then Came Kilkenny...AND THE DRAFT

—— The first couple of months of 1967 passed quietly. Gail and I had been back to Kansas over the recent holidays and picked out the young horses that would come east for further training. I had passed my fall courses at Rutgers; I was galloping racehorses, had the prospect of being able to ride in some point-to-points, and was happily living my dream, with Pan American visions—no matter how far-fetched—dancing in my head. I can see now that an Appaloosa with a jack-hammer trot, no dressage manners to speak of, and an utter disregard for any instruction from his rider about how to jump anything—that horse was not going to be at the head of the queue when it came to choosing a team.

Then the phone rang. "I have bought Kilkenny for you to ride, and he will arrive at JFK Airport tomorrow," my mother informed me.

I babbled something, thanked her, hung up the phone, and sat there in the kitchen considering how my life had changed in a flash. I now had a horse to ride that was good enough.

"Good enough"—that's a laugh. Kilkenny ("Henry" to his friends) had been on the 1964 Irish Olympic eventing team as a six-year-old, and on the gold medal Irish World Championship team in 1966 with Tommy Brennan riding him. (Tommy actually was a show jumper who had started eventing out of curiosity. Henry did not event in 1965, so to keep him in work that year Tommy took him show jumping in Europe for additional experience.) I had seen Henry go at Burghley and loved him immediately, but the thought of riding him never crossed my mind.

My brother Warren, a show jumper, was living in England at the time. He was in Ireland looking for jumpers when Tommy mentioned to him that, considering his mileage and experience, Henry might make a good schoolmaster for someone. Warren wisely said he wasn't interested but if he thought of anyone, he would get back to Tommy. (This wasn't Warren's first experience with Irish horse dealers, who are all born with a streak of larceny in their hearts and a subtle conception of the truth.)

As it happened, however, Warren and Mom had a more realistic evaluation than I of my chances of riding for the Team, given their also more realistic evaluation of Atos's limitations. Several Irish Team members had expressed an interest in buying Henry, and one rider went so far as to have him vetted, but the veterinarian (bless his heart) said that Henry had too much mileage (even though he was only eight at the time), and he wouldn't recommend buying him. Then some dumb Americans came along and paid the princely sum of $7,500 for him. I suppose Mom thought that if Henry would hold up for another year or so, he would be a wise investment in my future while she waited for her homebreds to mature. After all, Henry had already been around Badminton, plus the Olympics and the World Championships. We couldn't expect him to do much more.

Of course, all this had happened without my knowledge and now I was trying to deal with the possibility that I indeed had a future as a Team rider. My future looked bright indeed—until I opened a letter that said, "Greetings from your fellow citizens..."

What Would General Wofford Have Done?

——That's right, I was headed for the Army. Without my realizing it, my additional hours of classes at Rutgers had generated enough credits at CU for me to graduate. This automatically changed my draft classification, and the long arm of the draft board had reached out to tap me on the shoulder.

When I shared the news with Gail and Mom, the Wofford family network once again came to the rescue. "Oh, what a coincidence," Mom said. "That nice Ralph Mendenhall, who was one of your father's favorite young officers, stopped by the other day to say hello. He is now a colonel at the Pentagon. He asked about you, left his business card, and said you should call him if he could be of any assistance. Here's his number; you should give him a call and explain your problem."

As soon as we hung up, I called the number Mom had given me and asked for Colonel Mendenhall. A very official-sounding voice at the other end of the phone line answered, "Office of the U.S. Army Sports Program, Sergeant Something speaking." I had never met Colonel Mendenhall, never heard of him, and didn't know there was even such a thing as the U.S. Army Sports Program—but such was the power of the Old Army network that as soon as I was put through to him I immediately felt that I had a friend at the other end of the line.

Colonel Mendenhall explained that I was going to get drafted; there was nothing he could do about that. I was going to spend the next few years of my life in uniform like most young, eligible males of that era. But he had a deal for me. Young men at that time were obligated to serve for a total of six years. If I waited to get drafted, I would have to serve two years of active duty, two years of occasional duty, and two years in the inactive reserve. His deal was this: I could sign up for three years' active duty, followed by three years' inactive. If I volunteered, I could choose my MOS (military occupational specialty) and that would guarantee I would not be shipped to Vietnam. In the meantime, once I finished basic training, Colonel Mendenhall would have me placed on TDY (temporary detached duty) at Gladstone. I would be in the Army—but as long as I maintained my Olympic eligibility, I would not have any duties other than training for the Olympics. If I made the Olympic team I, of course, would be assigned to participate in the Games. When I came home, Colonel Mendenhall would assign me to the U. S. Army Pentathlon Training Center (USMPTC) at Fort Sam Houston, Texas, where I could serve out my remaining time in the army as the assistant riding coach to the Pentathlon team. "How does that sound?" he asked me. I said his deal sounded like the answer to my prayers, and where did I sign?

I still had some questions. First, this whole plan was based on my ability to ride a horse I had not yet ridden. If I didn't form a partnership with Henry, the rest of the deal would fall apart. Also, I was married now. How was the plan going to work for Gail with me gone, leaving her to manage the farm where we planned to move the new young horses, the additional groom for those horses, plus Alex Edmonds to run it for her?

My inner turmoil was nothing when compared to the turmoil in American society. This was especially true regarding the war in Vietnam. I had grown up in a military, deeply patriotic family. I didn't know much about my forefathers in Scotland and England, but Woffords fought in the Revolutionary War. During the Civil War, General William T. Wofford's Confederate brigade charged through the Peach Orchard at Gettysburg on Pickett's right flank. One of his commanding officers later referred to him as "one of the most daring of men." I spent a lot of time thinking about him, about how such a courageous man could be so wrong in his choice of a cause to fight for.

Although wounded three times, General Wofford survived the Civil War, returned home to northwestern Georgia, was elected to the Georgia assembly, and for the rest of his life was a leading proponent of civil rights during Reconstruction. I had thought about relations between races ever since my early experiences with Bessie Smith and Doris Payne at Rimrock Farm. While I sat in the apartment kitchen in Somerville, New Jersey, after talking with Colonel Mendenhall, there were deadly race riots occurring a few miles away. Those riots were a reminder of the toxic after-effects of slavery. W.T. Wofford's career after the Civil War showed a dramatic change in his belief system; I wish I could have talked with him about it.

I wished even more fervently that I could discuss my life plans and decisions with my father. He was never far from my thoughts. I wondered, if he could offer advice, what he would think I should do—and most importantly, if he approved of me. He had volunteered for West Point and the Army during World War I, knowing that if the war continued he would be sent abroad to fight. What would he think of me as I strove to avoid a similar situation one generation later? I thought about this continuously, but deep down I was sure of my answer.

I could not explain the instinctive, irresistible power that drew me to horses, but I was going to follow that path. If it led to a schism with my family I would be sorry, but I was committed. No matter what, I was going to pursue a life that revolved around horses. I signed on the dotted line, promising to give the U.S. government three years of my life.

One Horse's Power

——When Henry stepped off the van at the USET not long after this, I was about to experience the power of a horse to change a life. And talk about power—throwing your leg across Henry was like strapping on a rocket.

I had liked Henry when I saw him at the World Championships, but I fell in love with him when he stepped off the van and looked around the Gladstone stable yard. If ever you wanted to see "the look of eagles," you had only to look at Henry and you would know it for life. I later remarked that Henry had a trot with all four feet off the ground, and a gallop it took a young man to enjoy. I was never sure I would be able to control his power, much less direct it at an obstacle. Throughout his career, Henry never saw an obstacle he did not want to extend his stride toward.

I was lucky enough to compete with him for six years, and it was *his* superlative talent that first made people think I could ride. Henry and I knew better, but Henry was Irish, and my lack of skill never bothered him in the slightest. His motto at that time was probably, "Kid, sit still and shut up."

Foaled in 1958, Henry was a 17-hand brown gelding by Water Serpent, out of an unknown mare. He eventually competed in three Olympic Games, all of them using the Classic format. In addition, he went to two World Championships, one Pan American Games, one Canadian Championships, three Badmintons, and two National Championships, again all Classic events.

He first went to the Olympics with the Irish team in 1964, when he finished sixth. In 1965 he jumped 6 feet, 7 inches to win the Puissance class at the Rotterdam CSI. (You can see why I never worried about having enough scope to jump anything in our path.) Henry was part of two gold-medal and two silver-medal teams. He won an individual bronze medal at the 1970 World Championships and won the National Championship at Ledyard in 1967. In all, (using modern nomenclature) he completed six CCIO Five Stars and nine CCI Four Stars, all Classic formats. I'm getting ahead of my story, but in 2000 the Irish Horse Board would name Henry the Irish Sport Horse of the Century.

About all I can say for myself was that I had nerve enough to let him be himself. Henry was a young man's ride, and I am quite sure he would not be successful in a modern short format. He disliked dressage and only put up with it because of his affection for me. An Irish friend, Jock Ferrie, came up to me laughing after my dressage test at the 1970 World Championships at Punchestown. I had cantered down the center line and stopped at "X"—I say "stopped" because it was a cessation of forward motion, but it wasn't any kind of halt that dressage judges would recognize. Henry planted all four feet at different angles, came well above the bit, and stared longingly toward the Wicklow Mountains visible in the far distance. "Never mind, Jimmy," said Jock. "Sure now, wasn't he looking at the Wicklow Mountains, and deciding whether to stride them, or jump them as one." That was Henry.

He hunted with the Piedmont Fox Hounds after his retirement in 1972 and is buried in my east paddock, where the light of the morning sun first touches the farm. Throughout his life, he was only afraid of two things: bagpipes and not doing his best. I miss him still.

But all this was in the future; for now it was 1967, there was a big competition in my sights, and I had to learn how to do my best with this horse. After more than a year riding under Stefan's tutelage, I knew his system pretty well. One thing I had noticed was that Stefan expected all his horses to match his work ethic—which meant Team horses had a high rate of injuries. I was determined to keep Henry sound, so I did not join in the Team training at first; instead, I hacked him out in the countryside around Gladstone. Although I was committed to slowly, progressively improving his fitness, I do admit to immediately taking a couple of long trots up Larger Cross Road, and a couple of canters up hills in the back of the Brady estate. I realized I was on a different creature than I had ever been on before, and I was excited at the prospect of competing with him. Wouldn't you have wanted to play with your new toy while nobody was watching?

I joined the daily Team training sessions after a few weeks, and after another few weeks it was time for our first cross-country school. Word of Henry had gotten out in the community. There were a lot of spectators watching the squad practice and to my horror, I was not having a good session—at all. If I wasn't "chipping in" at a jump, I was leaving a stride too soon—and was hearing that old refrain from Stefan about stupid boy.

Fortunately, one of the spectators was an old family friend whom I've mentioned before, General John "Tupper" Cole. Tupper, a famous horseman, was reserve rider in 1932 when my father rode in the Los Angeles Olympics. He called me aside during a break and delivered a blistering lecture, as only an officer from the Old Army could. I won't bore you with the details; it boiled down to, "Boy, get your head out of your backside. Your horse knows his job. Get out of his way and let him do it."

I nodded grimly, got back on, gathered my reins, struck off in a canter toward a simple brush and rail, and put my hands down to see how Henry would react to it—rather than my *telling* him how to react to it. Something clicked. We jumped it well, and the subsequent obstacles went even better. For the first time in more than a year I was meeting the jumps on normal distances, landing comfortably, and feeling as if I knew what I was doing. I'd like to think Stefan was secretly pleased, but he never mentioned it.

My confidence grew each day I rode Henry, and I went from the blackest of depressions to feeling that I had a good chance of making the Pan American team. Olympic veterans like Mike Plumb and Michael Page set a standard of intensity every day they stepped into the ring, and I did my best to copy them. Training with them was a great treat, but I had other disciplines to watch as well. If you got to jump-crew for Bert De Némethy while Bill Steinkraus and Frank Chapot were schooling their Team horses, you would be a real dumb bunny if you didn't learn something every time they cantered down to a fence.

The most dedicated practitioner of the "Gladstone attitude" (nothing was ever good enough, and we were going to win anyway) I ever saw was Mike Plumb. Nothing was ever good enough for Mike, and he trained with a frightening intensity, always working to get better. When your team captain brings that attitude to work every day, the rest of the team quickly picks it up. I wasn't remotely in Mike's class, but I could copy his work ethic, and after a while it became a lifelong habit.

Between my growing confidence in Henry and the lengthening hours of daylight, I felt ready for the spring season of competition, which would culminate in an early June three-day event at the Myopia Hunt Club in Ipswich, Massachusetts.

Eventing Then and Now: Two Different Sports

——Before telling you about the spring of 1967, and the Pan American Games in Winnipeg later that summer, I need to set the stage. Eventing half a century ago was a different sport from what we are accustomed to in the early twenty-first century. When my mother gave me a USCTA life membership in 1959, the Association was comprised of approximately 100 members. By the time I was training at Gladstone in 1966, it had grown to 250 or more. (Remember, these numbers are national totals.) There were fewer than 10 events scheduled for 1966, two of them Classics. The final Pan Am selection trial at Myopia was one; the other was the Pebble Beach Three-Day Event on the West Coast.

Eventers were tolerated by the USET, which was run by people predominantly interested in show jumping. Dressage hardly existed, and my mother referred to eventing and dressage as "the poor stepchildren" of the Team. My father's successor as USET president, Whitney Stone, was a big supporter of show jumping, but he also had the foresight to provide funding for an eventing coach and some administrative staff and made the facilities at Gladstone available to eventers. Things began looking up by 1962 when, in addition to a permanent training base, the discipline had a grass-roots organization behind its efforts.

The Founding Fathers of eventing included Philip Hofmann, Alexander Mackay-Smith, and Stuart Treviranus—also Jack Burton and Jack Fritz, who jointly wrote the first rulebook, trained judges and officials, organized events, and generally provided the administrative structure needed for the sport to grow. At one point Jack Burton was called "the Johnny Appleseed of eventing" because a local competition started and flourished everywhere he went.

The closeness of the people behind the scenes was duplicated among the competitors. Event riders all knew each other, knew each other's horses, and could recite the competitive records of all their fellow participants. Those of us competing at the national level were rivals, but with no hint of "win-or-die" mentality. We were all simply intrigued by the cross-training nature of the sport and intoxicated by the prospect of riding long distances at speed over fixed obstacles. In our minds, one successful cross-country ride could make a year's worth of effort worthwhile. This was the mindset of the Team as we began our spring season of preparation aimed at two horse trials in Virginia, followed by the Myopia Three-Day Event. The Pan American team's short list would be announced at Myopia, and we would resume training at Gladstone after a short break.

A Do-It-Yourself Sport

—— But first things first. As Rick Eckhart and I stepped out of my car in Warrenton, Virginia, to walk the cross-country course at our first spring horse trials, we were greeted by organizer Stuart Treviranus. He exclaimed how glad he was to see us and handed us a stack of both red and white paper plates, a hammer, a coffee can full of nails, and several black broad-tipped pens, asking, "Rick, would you and Jim flag and number the course while you walk it?"

Slightly startled, we acquiesced, but gently inquired about a course map. "Oh, Rick, you rode here last year—it is the same course." We gathered our plunder and set out, happily flagging and numbering the course as we went. So the event was disorganized! We didn't care. We were about to go cross-country.

The Team's efforts were usually better organized than the events we attended. All we had to do was ride, while the administrative staff at Gladstone arranged motels and stabling. General F.F. "Fuddy" Wing was the Executive Director, and trips that he and his staff organized usually ran like clockwork. Another of my U.S. Army Dutch Uncles, Fuddy was a lifelong cavalryman and a member of the 1948 Olympic show-jumping team. Given his experience, it is no surprise that he was accustomed to organizing large groups of horses and people.

However, when things went off the rails, they went off badly. Our second horse trials (we used the terms "events" and "horse trials" interchangeably) that spring, the Blue Ridge Horse Trials (also in Virginia), was on the western slope of the Blue Ridge Mountains, and a huge scuffle had broken out behind the scenes by the time we riders arrived at the site.

The Team paid for our grooms during our training periods and made all the arrangements for them—transport, lodging, and so on. At that time, there was a huge social barrier between grooms and riders, as "one didn't mingle with the help, don'cha know." These barriers were even more immutable in the case of my groom, Alex, who was Black.

The story went like this. The closest motel to the horses' stabling was the Mountain View Motel. (It still stands on U.S. Route 50, near the Shenandoah River.) Several young ladies were grooming for the USET that year. They walked into their accommodations, took one look around, and promptly went on strike. They said the motel was a roach-trap, they were not staying there, and that was that. Hearing this, Stefan, who was in charge of our trip, did what any self-respecting retired army officer would have done: he delegated it to our barn manager. René Williams assessed the situation and reported back that the grooms were united and adamant. No clean sheets and hot water, no grooms. Fortunately, there was sufficient space at the Holiday Inn and peace descended on the Blue Ridge.

All this was reported to me later. Looking back, I recognize trends and issues that would emerge from the 1960s and cause turmoil throughout society. Fissures caused by attitudes toward race and gender, the same ones we are dealing with today, had begun to manifest.

I was so focused on competition at the time that I never spoke with Alex about his experiences leaving the Mountain View Motel and upgrading to the Holiday Inn. As a Black man with an eighth-grade education, he would have given me an entirely different take on life in the horse world. Knowing him, I would guess that he receded into the background while the white female grooms were standing up for their rights to better working conditions. He would have lived in worse, and several times while he worked for me I was hardly able to find suitable lodging for him. I think he would have slept outdoors, if that was what it took for him to have Henry in his care.

From the minute he saw him, and from that day forward, Henry became "tha Big Hoss" to Alex, who was devoted to him. He wasn't talking about Henry's size, although 17-hand horses are big enough. He meant his record, his abilities, and his wonderful, sweet personality. As I mentioned before, Alex didn't have much schooling, his speech patterns were unusual, and he went on the occasional bender, but he was a horseman through and through, and he loved Henry. That was enough for me, and my devotion to Henry was enough for Alex.

From Hayseed to "How 'Bout That!"

—— My knowledge of Henry's record—and my limited experience schooling and competing with him—were the sole basis for my quiet confidence about our next challenge, the U.S. National Championships at Myopia, Massachusetts. An examination of my own record wouldn't take long, and it would not impress anyone. I had ridden in two Nationals before, had a fall in one, and did not complete the next. I may have won a few classes in local horse shows, but I had won a grand total of one Classic and had probably completed fewer than 10 events. So I was just a redheaded hick from Kansas with no record, but with a nice horse, headed for Myopia in early June of 1967 to see if he could be successful at the next level.

My appearance with Henry at Myopia coincided with another major shift: New England was about to explode with eventing activity. Within ten years, the region would become the epicenter of eventing in the United States, and a great deal of that energy can be traced to the National Championships at Myopia. The dressage and show jumping were held on the practice polo field at the Myopia Hunt Club, a field you can still see on your right as you head north on Route 1A toward South Hamilton.

The facility is about 30 miles north of Boston, and a few miles inland from the Atlantic. The connection between foxhunting and eventing was firmly established by 1967, and the members of the Myopia Hunt Club were determined to make us as welcome in their community as the Essex Fox Hounds of New Jersey had done previously. One of the driving forces behind the scenes at Myopia was their Master of Foxhounds, Neil Ayer.

New to eventing, Neil brought to his efforts at Myopia the fervor of a convert, combined with as yet untapped skills as a course designer and an impresario. The Championships had attracted little notice when they were held in Myopia once before, in 1961, but this time would prove different, thanks to Neil and a small but dedicated group of supporters.

Within a few years, Neil was to become a worldwide expert, long-time president of the USCTA, Olympic and World Championship course designer, and eventually a member of the Eventing Hall of Fame. But all that was in the future; for now, we had a full-scale Classic on our hands.

The speed and endurance test took place on land owned by the Appleton and Winthrop families; more recently, the Groton House Horse Trials use much of the same ground that we galloped over in 1967. I had two rides and was fortunate that Atos came first. I knew him well, and could take what I learned about the course with me when I set out later on Henry.

I let Atos choose his speed on both steeplechase and cross-country, and got around safely with a few time and jumping faults. Atos was no racehorse; we were a bit slow and had one refusal on cross country. The course would be considered rustic and easy these days, but a tight turn in the Barnyard complex flummoxed us. Heavy rains the week before the event had flooded all the creeks and rivers; however, Atos was a former cow pony and swimming back and forth across the Ipswich River was no problem for him.

As I started my second ride of the day, I suddenly realized what a different sensation Henry gave me. He easily made the time on steeplechase and jumped clean with a few time faults cross-country, winding up in third place. When he show-jumped a clear round the next day, we moved into first place and were suddenly National Champions.

And that's how I went from hayseed to "How 'bout that" in one weekend. A great horse had changed my life. I had never won anything to speak of, being content to go cross-country, even occasionally finish, and to feel that my riding had improved. Now suddenly I was giving interviews and being asked for my opinion about all sorts of things, as if I were an expert.

Naturally, I was elated at my results, but felt a bit cynical about how people's opinion of me had suddenly changed. I was the same rider I had been the day before the event, still struggling with my technique, still hungry to learn. I had unshakeable confidence in Henry and was determined to be worthy of riding him. Our results were good enough that the following morning, Stefan announced that Kilkenny and I were named to the Pan American Games team, in Winnipeg, along with Mike Plumb, Michael Page, and Rick Eckhart.

We had planned on returning to Gladstone, but the local members of the Myopia Hunt Club had made stabling and facilities available to the Team while we trained for the Games.

This was welcome news, as it meant cooler temperatures and better footing. The bad news was that we would all have to uproot our lives for the next month and live on the road. This did not produce much grumbling, as we could all see the obvious benefits for our horses. Gail and I drove home to New Jersey, packed up a couple of young horses and Petunia, and headed north. I had more on my mind than my own athletic success, as the same morning I was named to the Team, war broke out in the Middle East, and the real world seemed darker just as my own future was brighter. I would report for basic training that November and might be more of a part of world affairs than I had anticipated. There was nothing I could do about it, so I concentrated on my upcoming challenge.

It wasn't long before we headed for Canada and my first international competition. I was comfortable with the schedule of activities at an event by now and completely believed in my teammates; all I had to do was ride. When we walked the course, however, we immediately noticed a significant shortcut on Phase A.

Unbelievable as it seems today, this was actually a recurring error by organizing committees of that era. In the 1960 Olympics, the Australian team found a shortcut on Phase C that cut the distance by about a third. This gave them a 10-minute rest period before starting the cross-country, an obvious advantage. (This mistake eventually led to a change in the rules, which mandated a ten-minute pause to allow for a veterinary examination.)

We mentioned to Stefan that there was a potential shortcut on Phase A. He told us the officials had decided we would have a "gentleman's agreement" that we would all go the long way, despite the mistake in flagging Phase A. Imagine my surprise, then, when on the morning of the speed and endurance test, I watched the first competitor—obviously no gentleman—gaily take the shortcut and arrive 10 minutes early for his steeplechase, thus gaining a slight advantage over the rest of the competitors.

In view of this development, the U.S. "gentlemen" all agreed to take the legal but shorter route on the second roads and tracks (Phase C). This decision seemed small at the time but marks a change in riders' attitudes toward competition. Since then, when riders find a legal means to make things easier on their horse, they take it. By using the new (but legal) route on Phase C, each of us would get to the vet box much sooner than our scheduled time. Combined with the relatively new 10-minute hold before cross-country, it meant we would wait 30 to 40 minutes after finishing Phase C.

I'd like to think this extended rest period explains why Henry and I had not one, but two rotational falls on cross-country. I don't have any other explanation for it. These days, I would have been carted off in an ambulance after my first fall to undergo the concussion protocol, which I would have failed, and that would be that. As it was, Henry and I just got up, shrugged it off, and continued. Because our first rider had a refusal on course, I was under instructions to have a few time faults, but jump clean. I started out at the same speed that worked for me at Myopia, and the next thing I knew, I had two rotational falls in two minutes. The rules were different in those days. We escaped unhurt. I suppose I "had my bell rung," in the casual, dismissive phrase of the day, but the bedrock attitude of a Classic team rider was to finish at all costs, and finish I did.

Not only did I finish, but the score sheet said that I had the fastest time of the day. The bonus points I gained (again, the complicated scoring—don't ask) offset most of the penalty points for my falls. I found myself in fourth place, and with a growing, although unintended, reputation as a swift cross-country rider. In addition, my team was in first place going into the show jumping.

I am always ready to brag about Henry's superlative capabilities—his speed, his courage, and on and on. But I haven't mentioned his physical and mental toughness. Henry was tough, and when you look at his record of completions, remember that record was compiled before we even knew how to pronounce the word "butazolidin."

So the next morning, after two crashing falls the previous day, Henry strutted down the jog strip for the vet check, jumped a clear show-jumping round, accepted his team gold medal (we had finished in fourth place individually), and quietly walked back to his stall, thinking it was all in a day's work.

For my part, I had a lot of thinking to do. My first thought was how pleased I was for Mike Plumb, who added two gold medals to his already impressive collection. He had always been the team captain in the past, turning in solid, dependable results—but an individual gold had escaped him until he found a horse who matched his talents. Plain Sailing seemed a worthy partner for Mike. I thought he totally deserved his success. In addition, Michael Page had finished in the silver-medal position with Foster, and our Olympic prospects were starting to look better. We had two wise veterans forming successful partnerships with new horses; now we had to find two dependable combinations. Both Rick Eckhart and I had gone well at Myopia in the spring, but had failed to live up to expectations; as we headed home, the jury was still out on us.

Naturally, I spent a lot of time considering the reasons for my falls. Knowledgeable onlookers said they had not seen them coming. My approach speeds were appropriate, and my takeoff spots were fairly accurate. My overall speed between fences looked about right. There did not seem to be any underlying cause; we just didn't jump high enough. After the cross-country, Alex, harking back to his flat racing background, was grumbling that someone had "done got to tha Big Hoss" in the vet box during our half-hour pause before setting out on cross-country. I dismissed the notion then, but later on started to think that Alex was right for the wrong reason.

I was supposed to have had the fastest round of the day, even with two falls. Chances are good that the course was measured correctly, because Colonel Frank Weldon, director and course designer at the Badminton Horse Trials, was the technical delegate at Winnipeg. However, our shortcut on Phase C had thrown the scoring system completely out of sync, and scores were being computed by hand. I'm convinced that a scoring error was the reason the scoreboard said I had turned in such a swift round. If the course was, as I thought, measured correctly, then I would have had to ride at an insane speed to make up for the time I spent on the ground. It just didn't compute. In my opinion, neither did the final scores. The complexity of the scoring system had created a situation that made me an inadvertent beneficiary.

That explained the errors in my cross-country times, but what about the two falls?

We had so much time in the vet box that I had laid down on a tack trunk and taken a nap. Was it possible that Henry had also "taken a nap," thinking that the long period of walking was the end of his workday? I finally accepted that as the reason we had not gone well and promised myself that next time I would ride better.

Life After Gladstone

——Spring and summer had been busy, and I was ready for a vacation. Henry and Alex returned to our rented farm, while Gail and I, plus Petunia and Squash, our new black Labrador, drove to Kansas for a week off. I realized that I was lessening my emotional connection with Gladstone and getting ready to move on with my career. When I returned to New Jersey, I would have no horses at Gladstone and no immediate plans to return. I knew I still had a lot to learn, but I wouldn't find it at Gladstone under Stefan's tutelage.

Our vacation was just right, but I was eager to get back to New Jersey. I was scheduled to ride in a few races and had to gallop a couple of sets every morning. I was more than busy enough, with plenty of work to do on the young horses, including taking them to local shows and hunter trials. I exercised Jill Slater's foxhunters and hunted them three days a week. The results from my new steeplechasing career did not show any unusual talent; I was usually listed down among the "also-rans." But the experience I gained in conditioning and caring for horses was invaluable, and the thrill of riding at speed over fixed fences was worth whatever effort it took to produce it.

USET president Whitney Stone called me that fall and asked if I could come in for a talk. I did not realize until later that he was considering a drastic change for the eventing team and wanted to talk to each team member before making up his mind. He asked me about my plans, and I mentioned the conclusion of my college career, and the opportunity I had with the U.S. Army Sports Program. I told him that I was not going to train at Gladstone before the Olympics, and he asked if I wanted him to fire the coach. That would be tough, he pointed out, considering that Stefan had coached gold and silver medal teams in the past. I replied that I did not have the standing with the Team to express any sort of opinion, but that my best chance of being selected for the Team was to develop a more consistent record. I had discussed this with Michael Page, who was returning to Badminton, and I felt my best option for improving my chances was to go to Badminton in the spring of 1968. Whitney made a non-committal response, wished me luck, and we left it at that.

I enjoyed my brief period of freedom. I was living a life filled with horses, and learning as much as I could, from whatever source. As my college reading lessened, I was able to able to expand my reading about horses. One of the most important horse books I ever read was not even about how to ride, but was entitled *The Mind of the Horse*, by veterinarian and author R. H. Smythe. He had a couple of important things to teach me. First, he discussed how to deal with a horse who spooks at strange objects. His advice was to desensitize the horse, rather than punish him for reacting. Punishment would only confirm in the horse's mind that the object was something to fear.

Before I read about this approach, I had already been practicing it by intuition. One of the USET horses I had ridden the previous winter was a devil to spook and frustrated several of his other riders. They had punished him for spooking, but I noticed that this did not prevent the next spook. When I was assigned to him, I instinctively softened my hands, closed my legs and rode a little farther from the object. Although Stefan quietly laughed when he noticed that the horse did not spook with me, he continued to assign him to other riders as well, in accordance with his mysterious rotational scheme that I mentioned earlier.

One of my major problems with the system in force at the USET during this period was how we were instructed to approach obstacles. Stefan wanted a direct application of dressage to our jumping, which meant he wanted horses to approach on the bit—that is, with the plane of their face vertical. I had difficulty with this, as it seemed to make my horses very resistant as they got closer to the obstacle.

When the young horses from Rimrock Farm arrived, I started taking them to local shows as part of their education. Most of the classes offered at lower heights were some version of working hunters. Bert de Némethy had recommended this, saying that local show hunter classes were "a charming introduction" for young horses. I showed my "green beans" as if they were really show hunters, meaning they were on long or loose reins in front of the obstacles. Much to my amazement, they were quiet as they cantered around; unlike my USET horses, they did not resist with their head and neck in the approach. Green as they were, they still managed to get some ribbons, which certainly improved their sale prospects.

I could not explain this difference, but fortunately Dr. Smythe had an answer. In his section on the anatomy of the horse's eye, he mentioned that although horses have wonderful peripheral vision, they see in focus roughly where their nose is pointing. As I read this, a huge number of lightbulbs went off in my chandelier. To my mind, it was a given that a horse should be able to see the obstacle. If that was true, then a rider needed to present his horse to the obstacle *in a frame that enabled the horse's vision.* In other words, the horse needed to poke his nose at the fence in order to see it in focus. If his vision were restricted, he would naturally resist the unnatural demands of the rider. Lightbulb! From that day on, I have brought my horses to the jump "on the contact," rather than "on the bit." I thank you, Dr. Smythe, and my horses thank you.

Unfortunately, it would be another 10 years before I had the same lightbulb moment regarding the eyes of the rider.

I Report for Duty

——As much as I enjoyed my brief period of freedom, this was about to change. Early on the morning of November 8, 1967, Gail dropped me off at the local train station, or as the U. S. Army would have it, I was to *"... report for induction 8Nov67."* Yup, I was in the Army now. At the induction center in Newark, New Jersey, I raised my hand along with the biggest collection of miscreants you can imagine and promised to defend the U.S. Constitution against all enemies, foreign and domestic—and thus was once more incarcerated. My platoon mates were mainly from places

33. ___ Mike Plumb was the Team captain when I joined the Team, and when I left 23 years later, he was still there. His record of eight Olympic Games is impressive, but people miss the rock-solid technique Mike has applied since his equitation days as a junior, when he won the Medal Maclay.

■ © Brant Gamma Photos

34. ___ My close friend Kevin Freeman, shown here on Morning Mac at the Maryland Hunt Cup, is one of the best all-around horsemen the United States has ever produced. He has Olympic medals to go with his successful exploits as a steeplechase jockey and a show jumper. Not many people have both jumped the infamous "thirteenth" at the Maryland Hunt Cup and won a show-jumping World Cup qualifier.

■ © Douglas Lees

35. ___ You can see why I had such utter confidence in Henry. Any horse that can produce such prodigious efforts makes a rider's heart sing—and believe there is nothing in the world his horse can't jump. Shown here in the steeplechase phase of the 1968 Mexico Olympics, Henry had the fastest round of the day and finished in sixth place. ■ *© Werner Ernst*

36. ___ My motto is that when the course designer gives you an easy fence, make it look easy. The ditch and drop at the 1969 Fair Hill Intermediate Championships was more a test of agility than of scope, and The Regent skipped over it and landed looking for the next fence. We would return to Fair Hill in 1971 and win the National Championships. ■ *© Gamecock*

37. ___ I'm lucky to have done so many different things on horseback. While stationed at Fort Sam Houston in Texas, I rode in a high jump contest on the U.S. Army's Galway Bay. These PVC rails were set at 7 feet, 6 inches, and while we jumped a couple of inches lower, the rails bent but stayed in the cups. Ever since then, I have bragged that I cleared 7 feet, 6 inches. ■ *© George Axt*

38. ___ Without meaning to, the Irish invented "frangible technology" at the 1970 World Championships. By the time Henry and I got to the infamous twenty-ninth fence, it had been broken by other riders so many times that Henry landed on the brush and walked out past the top rail. I had a rather more jarring landing but got up to finish with the fastest round of the day, and an individual bronze medal. ■ *© Peter Sweetman*

39. ___ When he completed the 1972 Munich Olympics, Henry became only the third horse in history to compete in three Olympics. To jump a clear show jumping round in front of a massive crowd and win a second Olympic silver medal brought his career as an eventer to a close. He would go on to foxhunt with the Piedmont Fox Hounds in Virginia for another six years. ■

40. ___ I had been "on the bench" for six years when Carawich found me. We formed an immediate partnership; when you see the ease with which he is jumping this maximum oxer, you can understand my unshakeable belief in him. Over my entire 20-year international career, my best years in the saddle were spent with him.

■ © Gamecock

41. ___ The 1978 World Championship cross-country course was already formidable, but the extreme heat on the day made it even more difficult. Carawich seemed to be unaffected by it, and at the halfway point on the course he was still jumping huge obstacles in stride. ∎ © *Alix Coleman*

42. ___ Carawich was capable of good dressage work, but his attitude toward it was affected by his fitness level. By the time we arrived at the 1978 World Championships, doing dressage on him was like sitting on a powder keg. At this point, I'm just trying not to light the fuse. ∎ © *Karl Leck*

43. ___ Classic events tested courage, scope, and agility, as shown here. The rails at the iconic 1978 World Championships "Head of the Lake" don't appear very large, but Carawich and I dropped 6 feet, 6 inches into deep water awaiting us. I kept my leg on him and slipped my reins to allow Carawich to work it out, while I braced myself for the shock of landing. ■ © Karl Leck

44. ___ Although there were 100,000 spectators at the 1978 World Championships, I'm standing alone, watching Carawich walk back to the stables, and thinking I had spent a year of my life chasing a dream of being the best. That dream had just disappeared. The highs and lows of the sport are extreme. ■ © Clarkson Lindley

45. ___ The 1978 World Championship team was the most experienced team ever entered to that date in an international event. Mike Plumb, Tad Coffin, Bruce Davidson, and I had all won individual medals at this level. Although Bruce won his second individual World Championship, a bronze team medal was the best we could do. The Culver color guard was a nice touch. ■ © Karl Leck

46. ___ This is one of my favorite photos—Carawich and I are out hacking in front of Badminton House on the Wednesday of the event, while the estate appears deserted. A few days later, Badminton would draw nearly a quarter of a million spectators, and this area would be completely covered with people. ■ *© Sue Maynard Photos*

47. ___ At Badminton in 1979, Carawich and I were a few feet away from the spot in the Duke of Beaufort's stable yard where, almost two years earlier to the day, he had picked me out of a crowd. I was reflecting on how incredible the last two years had been for me, and how he changed my life. ■ *© Sue Maynard Photos*

48. — Everybody is all smiles after a clean and fast round at Badminton. I signed and sent this photo to Jack Le Goff to thank him for all his help. It hung on his wall, but his family returned it to me as a memento after he passed away. "In the picture" refers to Jack's help in my return to elite competition.

■ © Sue Maynard Photos

49. — After an unfortunate experience two years before at the Badminton water, Carawich was uncharacteristically dropped out of the bridle early on the 1979 course. The moment he saw we were taking a different path this time, he went storming through the water and was his usual enthusiastic self the rest of the way around.

■ © Sue Maynard Photos

50. ___ Completing Badminton is a thrill, and placing fifth is a dream come true, but getting to meet HM The Queen is a once-in-a-lifetime opportunity. I received the Jubilee Trophy from The Queen as the highest-placed owner/rider. HRH The Duke of Edinburgh is over The Queen's left shoulder, while Colonel Frank Weldon, Badminton's longtime director and course designer, is over my left shoulder. ■ *© Sue Maynard Photos*

51. ___ Vita and Dick Thompson bought Rockingham for me to ride. He was one of the fastest horses I have ever ridden, but sometimes his feet would go faster than his brain. Being Irish, he would become intoxicated with speed and forget to jump the next obstacle. Although he was never a Team horse, I was able to win the Wylie, England CCI-L 4* with him in the fall of 1983.
■ © Brant Gamma Photos

52. ___ Alex had been a schoolmaster for the USET, and his idea of success was that his current rookie rider did not fall off. I saw Alex when he first arrived at the Team, loved him, and finally got a chance to ride him as my second horse to Carawich in the Olympic year. The disagreements we had about our speed were carefully concealed, but I put enough pressure on Alex to make the time on both the steeplechase and the cross-country at the 1980 National Championships at Chesterland. It was his only winning performance in his 10 years of service to the Team. ■ © Sue Maynard Photos

53. ___ I had always admired The Optimist, and with Karen O'Connor away at the 1986 World Championships, his owners, Diana and Bert Firestone, offered me the ride. The Optimist was a ferocious puller, and he jumped into water like a kid off a springboard. Although this is a spectacular moment, you can tell from my face I know he will recover. We went on to win my fifth National Championships. ■ *© Mary Phelps*

54. ___ Shown here at Burghley in 1983, Castlewellan was the only horse I've ever ridden who could have been equally as successful in a modern short format event as in a Classic. He was a threat to win every dressage class he went in, as judges fell in love with him the minute he entered the arena. Although not an easy ride, he won major competitions with three different riders—Judy Bradwell, Karen O'Connor, and me.
■ *© Findlay Davidson*

55. ___ Don Sachey and Landmark caught USET coach Jack Le Goff's eye at Ledyard in 1973, and Jack invited them to train with the Team. As my first working student, Don helped my new business model when he won a gold medal at the 1974 World Championships. Thanks to him, I had a wait list for the next 20 years.

■ © Courtesy of the Sachey Family

56. ___ Tad Zimmerman, shown here at Ledyard 1975 on Fine Tune, was one of the most talented students who ever came through my program. Reserve rider for the 1975 Pan Am and 1976 Olympic teams, he felt obligated to sell his horse in order to repay his family for his Princeton education. He went on to a very successful career at the International Monetary Fund. Not all of my program's success happened in the saddle.

■ © Howard Allen Photography LLC

57. ___ Jim Graham graduated from my program but worked below the international level for years until Easter Parade changed his life. His sparkling cross-country round at the 1994 World Championships in Holland was just the first of Jim's many successes.

■ © Brant Gamma Photos

58. ___ Bea di Grazia, shown here on Lad's Night Out,
was one of the youngest riders to ever complete Badminton.
Although her talent would have put her on every team for the
next 20 years, Bea found the call of marriage and family stronger
than competition. She made the right choice, but her love for the
sport still continues. ■ *© Sherry Stewart 2013*

59. ___ Ann Hardaway, shown here on her 1988 Olympic mount, Tarzan, comes from a world-famous foxhunting family. She took to the cross-country part of eventing naturally, and I could always count on her for an aggressive ride over any course. Tarzan lacked a little speed, but he made up for it with prodigious jumping ability. ■ *© Mary Phelps*

60. ___ With his impeccable technique, Derek di Grazia has been successful at every level, from Novice to National Championships. Shown here with Sasquatch at Boekelo 1983, he would go on to win Kentucky with Sasquatch and represent us at the 1986 World Championships. However, his career never matched what I knew in my mind was possible. He never found "the horse," one whose superlative capabilities would put Derek on the podium at the elite levels. ■ *© ASFO-OLD*

61. ___ I am proud of Karen O'Connor, who is famous for her multiple Olympic efforts, and rightly so. However, I am equally proud of the marvelous horsemanship she has displayed throughout her career, producing winning efforts on the widest possible range of horses, from 14.2-hand Theodore O'Connor, shown here at Kentucky, to 18-hand Biko. Regardless of her horse's size, Karen is at home in the saddle. ■ *© Brant Gamma Photos*

62. ___ Karen O'Connor and Wash Bishop, on Biko and Ask Away, attended by Paul Tait and Katie Strickland at the European Championships, are all smiles at the medal ceremony. By 1998, it was common to have more than one of my former students on the Team at the same time. My program was working.

■ © Brant Gamma Photos

63. ___ Wash Bishop, shown at the 1998 Pratoni (Italy) European Championships on Ask Away, was one of my best all-around horsemen. Blessed with a slight frame, he rode steeplechase and flat race winners as well as eventers. I was thrilled to join him for the 1980 Olympics, coach and student on the same team.

■ © Brant Gamma Photos

like Hoboken, Secaucus, and Jersey City. Some had been drafted, while some had "volunteered" at the urging of a local judge who had noticed a tendency toward violent recidivism on the part of the young men concerned. As a "white bread" college graduate, I was most definitely in the minority. During my "basic," my biggest success was that I hid my status as a "college guy" for most of the next 12 weeks.

U.S. Army basic training at Fort Dix in the winter of the late 1960s was no picnic. In addition to evil-tempered drill sergeants, we had cold weather, which only served to make this group of conscripts even more sullen. The political realities were that most of my platoon members would complete 12 weeks of basic, then would undergo advanced infantry training (AIT). Following that, they were bound for Vietnam, where their life expectancy would drop precipitously. I felt guilty about this, but not guilty enough to volunteer for combat service. I had a career path that would take me back to horses—and maybe, just maybe, to the Olympics.

I also had something else, and someone else, to live for in addition to the Olympics. Gail called me at Fort Dix one cold, dark night to tell me that we were about to have a family. I'd like to see a picture of my face when I hung up the phone. I kept this news to myself, as I had no friends in my platoon. Most of the recruits were in their late teens, so at age 23, I seemed like a grandfather to them.

I had a lot on my mind while I completed basic training. I was going to be the sole support of a family. I had one, and only one, chance to control the next year of my life, and that chance was called Kilkenny. If he and I continued the successful partnership we had begun by winning the Nationals, my Olympic dreams might become reality. However, if our performance at the Pan Ams in Winnipeg was any indicator, I was on the bubble. That was all up to me and my riding ability.

When you graduate from basic, the Army hands out your "orders." In my time they consisted of about 10 copies of a mimeographed page stating your MOS (Military Occupational Specialty) and sending you off to your next assignment. Most of the young men in my platoon were designated 11B. This was the MOS for an infantryman, which meant they were bound for two weeks' leave, then 12 weeks of AIT, then Vietnam for combat duty.

My orders told me that my MOS was now 70A, or clerk. I was promoted to PFC (which included a slight pay raise), and was assigned to Headquarters Company, Fort Dix, New Jersey. Once I translated the Army gobbledygook, my orders meant my files would be kept at Fort Dix. In the meantime, I was placed on indefinite TDY (Temporary Detached Duty) and would proceed immediately to the USET Training Center.

I took a deep breath after I read my orders; Colonel Mendenhall and the Army Sports Program had reached out from the Pentagon and set me on a path back to horses. I realized I was lucky: lucky in my family, lucky in the friends of my family, lucky to have Kilkenny to ride, lucky in my present career path—just plain lucky. Once again I was standing in the shadow of the rainbow.

I read my orders several more times just to make sure they said what I thought they said, marched in the graduation parade, put Fort Dix in my rearview mirror, and headed for Gladstone and horses. Gladstone wasn't my choice, but I was under orders, and at least Henry and I could go back into training.

Badminton on One Good Leg

——Gladstone in early 1968 was a very different situation compared to what it had been when I left it after the Pan Ams. We had a training center, but no trainer. I was surprised to hear that Whitney had let Stefan go; he had made no comment that would have tipped his hand. Looking back at Whitney's actions only increases my respect for him. It was a bold move on his part to let a successful coach go, and to bet on his riders instead. Now it was up to us to prove him right.

I planned to ship Henry to England in early March and stable in Oxfordshire with Lars Sederholm. At that time, Lars was the most successful eventing coach in the U.K., and I was excited at the prospect. I immediately went into training with the rest of the riders when I returned from Fort Dix in late January. In the fall of 1967, Gail and I had rented a farm just outside of Pluckemin, where we kept our young horses. I rode Henry first thing in the morning, stopped by Jill Slater's and galloped a couple of horses for her, then came home to exercise our young horses. Their quality varied, and we quickly sold several nice prospects, thus leaving us with the more difficult babies. One of them, Harty Manor, was a scrawny bay gelding with little athletic ability. He was narrow and low-fronted, and riding him felt like riding a toast rack.

What he lacked in athletic ability, he made up for by bucking me off every morning...*every morning*. I was sitting there on my backside one morning, watching Harty Manor disappear over the horizon once again, while Alex trudged over to pick me up. "Dammit, Alex, why does he do that?" In his inimitable Virginia cadence, Alex replied, "'Deed I dunno, Mistah Jimmy, he jus' takin' one ah hiz fits." One cold morning, Alex had to give me a little extra help getting up. Harty Manor had bucked me off one time too many, and I had broken my leg.

The doctor put me in a cast, said it was the small bone on the outside of my leg, and it should heal in about three weeks. Considering it was six weeks until Badminton and I had planned to leave in a few days, this was bad news. It didn't take long for me to call Colonel Mendenhall and explain my situation. He left it up to me, and I said that Lars had riders who could keep Henry in work while I was mending, and there was still time after I got out of my cast for a couple of smaller prep events before Badminton. Colonel Mendenhall had orders issued that allowed me to travel outside the United States, and in early March, Gail, Henry, and I headed for England.

Alex stayed in New Jersey to keep the young horses in work while we were gone. One of them, Malakasia ("Mac"), had been a problem in the hunt field the year before, continually running away. Jill Slater suggested that with an attitude like that he might make a point-to-point horse, and Gail had placed well in some of the local ladies' timber races. We told Alex to keep him in training and a friend of ours, Ben Griswold, was to ride him. (Years later, I would discover that Ben and I had both been passengers on the *SS America* coming home from the 1948 Olympics in London when I was three years old.)

While the horse world is small, my world was about to get larger, and the challenges greater.

One of my challenges was that I was on crutches, unable to travel on the cargo plane with Henry when he shipped to England. I remember how lonely I felt, and how worried. I had never seen this process before and realized that Henry had no headroom whatsoever—he was so tall his ears brushed the ceiling of the Boeing 707, which must have been claustrophobic for him. I was not a happy boy as they closed the cargo door and Henry left without me. Gail and I followed that night by a regular airline, and Henry had settled in nicely by the time we got to Waterstock House, Lars Sederholm's training center.

Fortunately for me, I was now in good hands. Training with Lars was one of the best things I have ever done. I explained to him as soon as I arrived that I had struggled with Stefan's methods. Lars said he had a very different attitude toward how horses and riders should be trained, and I was immediately comfortable with him. While I was to profit from his instruction in dressage and show jumping as soon as I could ride again, I especially enjoyed my cross-country lessons. Lars was a genius at explaining how your horse would react to various situations on cross-country, and my time at Waterstock House was one of the most instructional and beneficial periods of my career. After two long years of struggle, I finally felt my riding would improve. Henry would have to be trained by other riders until I healed, but Lars supervised carefully; while impatient, I realized it was necessary.

I could tell that Henry was going better and getting fitter, but I was slow to adjust to the fact that Gail was getting more pregnant. One morning at a local farmer's sheep field, Lars started very early, so that no one at the neighboring farm would know we were there. (We had permission, but it made Lars' life easier if the farmer didn't actually see us using the field.) He told Gail to give Henry a gallop, but by all means to avoid the herd of sheep that was sharing the field. It was a brisk spring morning and Henry, with an Irish sense of humor, sensed Gail's growing instability well before I did. He started out quietly, lulled her into relaxation, and then decided to take Gail and my unborn child for a gallop. Not a canter, mind you, but a full-speed, all-out gallop, which, considering Henry's capabilities, was an amazing thing to behold. In her struggles to at least keep Henry in the same field (at one point he had drawn a bead on a four-foot-high blind hedge), Gail circled several times. However, her circles and the herd of sheep finally intersected, producing a spectacular collision. Visualize sheep bolting for their lives, scattering in every direction, while Henry used them for cavalletti. Eventually, he subsided into a quiet canter and then walked back toward us; if ever a horse smiled, that was the day. After ascertaining that Henry had come to no injury, Lars mildly remarked that he had galloped enough for one day and perhaps in the future it would be best to have someone fitter gallop Henry, considering how much his condition had improved.

Henry's legs were fine after that experience, but my leg was not improving. Because sports medicine was still in its infancy, I had been told to keep the cast on my leg for three weeks, stay on crutches the whole time, and start my rehabilitation process once the cast came off. Naturally my leg atrophied and looked like an albino toothpick when it finally came out of the cast. As I gingerly stepped down onto the floor of the doctor's office, I visibly flinched. "Don't limp," the nurse barked at me. "It'll put your back out." She was such a harridan that I did exactly what she said, walked out of the office on my own two feet for the first time in a month—and kept myself from limping. I've often thought of that moment as a pretty good life lesson. Don't limp—it puts your back out, it shows weakness, and it draws the selectors' attention but not in a good way. I learned that I could use my mind to control my pain, a skill I would put to good use in years to come.

Looking back, I shake my head, but I was young and eager to get on with my competitive career. Only an idiot would think about riding around the biggest cross-country course in the world with one good leg, but it made perfect sense to me. Although I felt loose in the saddle, my prep events went fairly well. My main worry was Henry's fitness, as before shipping to England I had lost some conditioning time in New Jersey after my accident. Badminton was the same distance as the Pan Ams, but the jumps would be bigger and the ground much softer. This would be the most severe test I had yet faced. I wasn't sure I was ready, but I was going to do my best, and I knew Henry would take care of me.

There is a sense of relief when you finally move into the stabling at Badminton before the event. You have done your homework to the best of your ability, and it's time to see how you measure up against the best in the world. The vet check passed uneventfully and we got our first look at the whole course—roads and tracks, steeplechase, and cross-country. It was every bit as big as I had heard, but after walking around it again with Lars, I had a good plan in my mind as to how to ride it.

Returning from the course walk, several of us thought to walk into the village and have a beer. Taking a shortcut through the back of the stabling, we passed by Michael Page's stall, where he sat on a tack trunk, polishing his boots. The entire group immediately started teasing him, saying he should join the party. Michael never missed a stroke with his buffing brush as he looked up from his work and said, "No thanks; if you look sloppy, you ride sloppy." Something about the simplicity of his statement struck me. I made some sort of excuse, went back to my stall and polished my boots. I never forgot that moment. It might have been when I made the final commitment to excellence. I knew I wasn't a good rider yet, but I wasn't going to overlook even the smallest detail in my preparation.

I never got nervous before competitions. I was eager for the experience, and only worried about giving my horses the best possible ride. In those days, I had no trouble sleeping; when my head hit the pillow, I was out like a light. But I lay awake for a while the night before Badminton's cross-country, staring at the ceiling. I felt a bit nauseated and unsettled, and wondered if I was coming down with the flu, or had eaten something that didn't agree with me. As I finally drifted off to sleep, I suddenly thought to myself, "So this is what it's like to feel nervous."

There was plenty to make riders nervous that year, and the course was as hard as it looked. I stuck to my plan of accepting a few time faults while

I checked out Henry's fitness. I knew he was fast enough, but I didn't know if he was fit enough. Henry and I got around, but had a couple of refusals early in the course. It took a while for my leg to move when I thought about kicking, and I didn't give Henry the leg support he needed to jump big fences. Once we got past the first 10 fences or so, my leg seemed to wake up and join the party and the second half of the course proceeded just as Lars had predicted. Henry got tired at the end and I did not worry about the time, but rather allowed him to pick his own pace for the last few fences.

This attitude allowed Henry to recover nicely overnight, and we jumped well on Sunday, finishing just out of the money in thirteenth place. Although I was thrilled to finish as well as we did, it was also a mild disappointment, as the top 12 received their ribbons and trophies from Her Majesty the Queen. "Maybe next time," I thought. But in the meantime, I was headed back to New Jersey. ∎

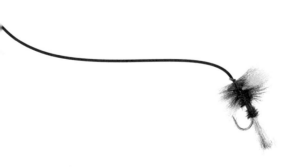

_Rain in Mexico

We are what we repeatedly do.
Excellence, then, is not an act, but a habit.

Aristotle

Badminton was a wonderful experience, but it showed me what I needed to work on in my search for excellence. When I got home to New Jersey, once again I had a training center, but no trainer. A few days after the riders got home, we learned that Lars had decided his business in England was too big to walk away from and had turned down the USET's coaching offer. I was sad about this, as I had learned a great deal from him, but my experiences at Badminton had reassured me that I was making progress; I wasn't the best in the world, but at least I was thirteenth.

After a week or so, we got word that the USET had hired Major Joe Lynch to coach us through to the Olympics. I thought this was good news.

In Ireland six years earlier I had taken some lessons from Joe, a lifelong cavalryman who had coached the Irish Olympic eventing team for a while. He was not systematic in the way that Bert de Némethy or Stefan von Visy were, but he was a shrewd horseman with an answer for any problem that came up during the training process.

The USET's plan was to name a "long list" of riders who were selected for further training at Gladstone. This list included Kevin Freeman, which was a relief; he was a team veteran. We would train during the summer, then travel to Canada in late August to compete at the Eastern Canadian Championships. After that, a "short list" would be named, and the team would be selected in September.

Joe's conditioning schedule was old-fashioned. We walked for hours on the roads around Gladstone. This suited me, as I remembered my father's advice about "pick-and-shovel" work for horses. I was riding quite a few horses every day, but the only one that really counted was Henry. If he stayed sound, I was in with a chance; if he broke down or got injured, I'd be back in the Army. Horses don't break down at the walk, so I was happy to do the pick-and-shovel work.

At the time, we considered a horse basically fit for a Classic event if he could slow canter for twice the distance of the cross-country course. In our case, the Olympic course would be about 4 miles, and would take about 15 minutes to complete; this meant we would gradually build up the duration of the canter sets until our horses could canter for 30 minutes. Joe added several brush fences for the final couple of gallops, and we jumped them as we went around the field. Joe stood next to one of them and bellowed instructions at us as we cantered by him.

I understood his reasoning for adding the jumps, but the weather was hot and the ground very hard. He could not see all the fences from where he was standing, so to save a bit of concussion on Henry's feet and legs I skipped the fences on the other side of the field.

The weather wasn't doing Gail any favors, either; she suffered through a hot, uncomfortable pregnancy that summer. It was a relief for her to finally head for the hospital. Hillary arrived August 4, 1968, and when I held her for the first time, I thought I had never seen anything so perfect. All these years later, I still think so. Gail's mother, Vivian, had come back east to help us, and I don't remember going through the sleep deprivation that many young parents suffer. Whatever needed doing, I was "shooed" out of the room, so Gail and Vivian could minister to the young princess. When Henry and I shipped to Canada with the other horses and riders at the end of August, I doubt the ladies even noticed I was gone.

We shipped to Montreal for the Canadian Championships, which would be a factor in our selection process. Once we had been named to the Team's list, the USET started to pay for our horses' stabling and provided grooms for us. Alex had been running back and forth between our farm and Gladstone, maintaining two operations. It was a relief for him when I connected with Duffy Smith, who had served in the Marines, somehow wandered into horse care, and was now in charge of Henry's well-being. Alex could now stay in New Jersey while Henry and Duffy went to Canada, and then (hopefully) to Mexico.

The training squad that gathered in Gladstone was small but represented most of the U.S. event riders with any international experience. The USET would eventually ship five horses and riders—a team of four plus one non-riding reserve—to Mexico. When that plane left the ground, there would not be another five horses left in the country that could conceivably compete in the Olympics.

Compared to some of the teams I was on in my later years, there was surprisingly little jealousy or tension between us that summer. Mike Plumb on Plain Sailing, Michael Page on Foster, and Kevin Freeman on Thunder Road were such established veterans that the rest of us regarded them as a certainty for the team. I thought I had a slight edge, based on my horse, but my performances at the Pan Ams and Badminton were not shining examples of horsemanship; I still had a lot to prove.

Rick Eckhardt's 1966 World Championship mount, Gallopade, had finally succumbed to age and infirmity, and retired to pasture. His replacement ride, Chalan, was very experienced. Captain Carlos Moratorio of Argentina had ridden Chalan to the individual silver medal in the 1964 Tokyo Olympics and the individual gold medal at the 1966 World Championships. Billy Haggard purchased him in the fall of 1966 as a possible ride for 1968. While he achieved some initial success in 1967, he did not go well in 1968.

Billy, who had been on the USET training squad with both of my brothers, was a very successful steeplechase jockey and a longtime family friend. After a discouraging experience at Badminton in 1968, he suddenly retired, soon walked back out on the course after finishing his round, and first announced his decision to my mother who was sitting by the first cross-country jump at the time. (She said she always sat there because no matter how well or badly the rest of the day went for riders, at the competitors' party that night she could always say how good they looked at the first fence.) "Dot," Billy said, "I have decided to retire, and let these younger riders have a chance."

"Oh, Billy, I'm so sad to hear that," she replied. "Yes," Billy elaborated, "All my life I have been used to jumping steeplechase and cross-country fences and hearing the crowd yelling 'Aaaah!' but every time I jumped today the crowd went 'Uuuuh!' so I decided it was time. I'm going to donate Chalan to the USET."

Assigned to ride Chalan at the beginning of the summer, Rick had yet to develop a partnership. Like Rick, Mason Phelps had a new horse to ride, Char's Choice; like the rest of us, he hadn't much record to brag about yet.

Sally Ike (née Lord) had a lovely young gray Thoroughbred gelding, Evening Mail, to ride. Like the rest of us, she had some experience, but no record of consistency, nor did Brad Smith, Carol Davidson (née Hannum), or Charlotte Robson. The Olympic eventing teams that year were composed of four riders, with the three best scores to count. In the lead up to Canada, I'm sure Joe Lynch and the selectors were thinking that potentially they had a team consisting of three dependable veterans, but they needed an insurance rider in case of accident or injury to one of the three veterans. The final place on the team was still up for grabs.

Henry jogged out sound on his return to Gladstone from Canada, which was a tremendous relief to me. If I had won, I'd probably feel differently about it. You're either first or nowhere. I did not realize until years later how much my training practices, for myself and others, would be shaped by those six long months of waking up each morning, worrying about my horse. I knew that I had a chance with Henry, but without him—*nada*. Ever since then, I have trained every horse in my care as if it were the only horse available.

Our final selection trial was a combined test: dressage and show jumping. The ground was rock hard, plus we were too close to the Olympics to ask anything strenuous. Afterward, all the riders were called into the upstairs trophy room at Gladstone and the team was announced: Mike on Plain Sailing, Michael on Foster, Kevin on Chalan, and me on Kilkenny. Mason Phelps and his new acquisition, Argonaut, would be the non-riding reserve. I was excited but kept it in check. I had been left off a team before, so I knew how some of my friends felt. They were very good sports about it, but there is no way that they didn't hurt terribly inside.

I went home and called my mother to tell her we were going to Mexico. Then I called Colonel Mendenhall to ask him about orders/permission to leave the country, and to continue on TDY. He promised to arrange it, congratulated me, we hung up, and I sat back in the kitchen and thought for a moment. I actually was one step closer to riding in the Olympics. But there was too much that could go wrong for me to celebrate, so Gail and I went out to the movies on a double date with Sally and Rick. Looking back, I am impressed by their grace as they dealt with their massive disappointment, and I'm pleased that Gail and I were thoughtful enough to be there for friends in need—and 50 years later we are still friends. They both went on to outstanding careers in the horse world, and I was starting to apply an old adage from the Country and Western music world: "Be real nice to people on the way up, 'cause you're gonna meet the same people on the way back down." I was on the way up right now, but I knew how it felt to be on the way down, and I didn't want it to happen right now.

We left for the Olympics a month early, due to the high altitude of the Olympic venue. But there was one more social function we had to attend. The night before we left, the USET threw a big going-away party for us, basically inviting the entire horse world. People were eager to say goodbye and wish us good luck, but I think the real reason for the large crowd that showed up is that the USET held the gala at the Brady mansion. If you stand with your back to the main stables at Gladstone and look straight down the long drive, you just get a glimpse of a huge white columned building at the other end of the drive. By the time we got there that night, that entire lawn area was covered with cars, with a steady stream of more cars pulling up to drop people off at the main door.

Denny and Ailsa Mosely Crawford, descendants of James Brady, the original owner of the estate, were living there and were eager to make this a memorable occasion. Denny and Ailsa were notorious hosts: on their twentieth wedding anniversary they gave each other miniature motor bikes, and we held motorbike races up and down the long hall in the main part of the mansion. Despite their long dresses, the ladies more than held their own that night. That was some party, but it couldn't hold a candle to this bash; of course, the open bar probably helped.

We got lucky with the weather, a lovely soft early fall evening, and the party spilled out the back steps and down onto the lawn. This didn't slow things down much, as Ailsa had skillfully placed a couple of bars there as well. I spent most of the evening saying hello to people I hadn't seen for a while, greeting family friends and well-wishers, and reconnecting with Army Dutch Uncles and Aunts.

Longtime friend and Dutch Uncle Tubby Tuckerman stepped out of the crowd late in the evening and we immediately fell into a long conversation about the impending Olympics, family reminiscences, and the horse world in general. Tubby was more properly Major General Alfred G. Tuckerman, U.S. Army Ret. He was about 10 years younger than my father, and had looked up to him as a mentor. A former polo player and member of the Army horse-show team, Tubby had lovely stories to tell. I'll never forget the last one he told me, as the party started to dwindle.

Tubby said, "Hell, Jim, I was a soldier all my life, but I never wanted to go to war. The only reason I stayed in the Army was so I could ride. Between the wars, we spent most of our time playing polo, foxhunting, and showing horses. I wasn't much of a soldier, but I loved horses." Major

General Tuckerman must have been more of a soldier than he would admit. Serving with the 1st Cavalry Division in the Pacific during World War II, he was awarded a Silver Star for gallantry in combat.

He loved to have a few drinks and tell how he became a general. According to him, when his unit had their last mounted Division Parade at the outbreak of war, he disobeyed orders and rode his private mount rather than the charger the U.S. Cavalry supplied him.

I will let Tubby tell the rest of the story. "By God, I'm telling you, Jim, that army charger was just too damned ugly for me to ride. We knew the days of the cavalry were numbered; I figured this would be my last mounted parade, so I rode a gorgeous four-year-old that I had just imported from Ireland. There were nearly 10,000 mounted troopers on that parade. Although I was only a major, because I was on the General Staff, I rode up toward the front. Everything was great—until the band struck up 'Garryowen' [a famous marching song for cavalry parades]. Jim, the moment the band played the first note, that four-year-old spun back, ran sideways through all 10,000 horses and riders, and scattered them from hell to breakfast. Naturally, I was court-martialed and had to appear at a military judicial proceeding. The generals and colonels chewed me up one side and down the other, but let me off with a reprimand. Then, as I saluted and started to leave the room, the general in charge stopped me as I got to the door. When I turned, he said, 'By the way, Tuckerman, that was a hell of a ride you gave that four-year-old.'"

Tubby said every time he came before a promotion board after that, they would all agree he gave that Irish four-year-old a hell of a ride and promote him to the next grade. I discounted his modesty because his record in the war spoke for itself; at the same time, his affection for horses shone through every word he spoke. I never saw Tubby again; he died a couple of years later, but wherever he is, I'll bet he's giving a four-year-old a hell of a ride.

For my part, I had a hell of a headache the next morning, but at that age coffee cures hangovers, and Kilkenny, Duffy, and the whole USET contingent—show-jumping team, dressage team, and eventers—all headed for JFK to be crammed into the same Boeing 707. The loading process was long and complex, so Henry and I waited while the shipping agents sorted out the details of loading the horses, grooms, and eventing riders. Eventers were the stepchild of the USET at the time, so the jumper riders went commercially, while we eventers helped with the loading process and rode in the back of the plane. I had mixed emotions about the obvious stratification but was relieved I could be there to make sure Henry had the easiest possible experience.

It was dark by the time we landed in Mexico City. I can't remember if it was a Sunday, but it certainly felt like it, as the airport seemed deserted. We taxied to the freight area, shut the engines down—and nothing happened. After an interminable wait, the rear door opened, and a loading platform appeared out of the dark. It was obviously an improvised procedure: raised and lowered by a simple forklift, the platform was nothing but a flat area, slightly larger than the horses' pallets, with no guard rails. This was hair-raising enough, but it soon got worse. The operator of the forklift was learning on the job, and the first pallet proceeded down by dropping precipitously several feet, jolting to a sudden stop, and repeating this erratic progress until the loading area banged down onto the pavement. The horses involved were badly upset by this, scrambling and kicking the walls of the shipping containers.

Kevin Freeman and I were first out of the plane and were naturally alarmed. Kevin and his family ran a farm implement manufacturing company, so he understood how to run machinery. Leaping up onto the seat behind the operator, Kevin grabbed him by the collar, forcibly ejected him, and took over the controls. The unloading process went smoothly from that point forward. Eventually, we settled the horses into their stalls and were taken to the Olympic village. Although we arrived weeks early, we had expected things to be close to completion. This was not the case; for example, our rooms had beds, but no sheets, pillows, or doorknobs.

We stayed in the main village for several days, hand-walking our horses twice a day, while waiting for the rest of the eventing teams to arrive. The plan was for all the teams to ship to the competition venue, a golf club and resort a couple of hours north of Mexico City, in a giant convoy. The cross-country course followed the outlines of the golf course, while the steeplechase and roads and tracks took place in the mountains above the club. The altitude was a serious factor, as we would be 7,000 feet above sea level. Some research on the effects of altitude on horses showed that they needed 30 days to acclimatize. We had just that amount of time when we arrived at the Valle de Bravos and moved into the Avandaro Golf Club.

This was a lovely club, with a nice restaurant and sitting areas, all attractively landscaped and presented. Our living facilities were a bit cramped, as all five U.S. riders plus Joe Lynch were in a bungalow designed for four people. It says a lot about our team spirit that the close quarters never caused any personnel problems. I think we had each decided that we were sharing the space and would make the best of it. The large plate glass window of our bungalow looked out at the cross-country course, where we could see several jumps still under construction. As the time for the event drew closer, there was a lot of concern that things would not be ready.

There was nothing we could do about it, so the whole experience became an extended eventing camp, with the best horses and riders all in the same place for a long period of time. We could watch each other train, learn from each other, and—as you might expect—party together. There wasn't anything to do *except* ride and party.

The training facilities were limited, so we had to base our schedules around arena availability, but Joe continued his practice of conditioning with long walks, followed by long, slow canters. Our daily schedule usually included a two-hour walk in the morning. We would watch the other teams train, then break for lunch. These walks were really pleasurable, as the mountain air was clean, with sunshine every day. Just after lunch we would get a quick thunderstorm. This rarely lasted, and everything dried out quickly due to the low humidity. This was handy, as all the riders were serious about their own physical conditioning. In addition to my riding and some running, I played tennis, which led me to become friends with the Australian riders.

I grew especially fond of Brien Cobcroft; he and I had some wonderful matches against Barry Roycroft and Jimmie Scanlon. We might not have invented "trash talking," but we got pretty good at it. Our routine was that we went for a swim after the tennis match, changed for dinner, and then headed for the bar. We were far enough back in the mountains that TV and radio could not reach us and there were no movies; the only thing left for us to do was to have a few drinks and talk about horses. These were almost exclusively stag functions; out of the 30 or 40 riders up there, most were male. Women had only been allowed to compete in Olympic eventing since 1964, and three ladies showed up this time: Jane Holderness-Roddam (née Bullen) rode for the British, while Juliet Jobling Purser and Penny Moreton were on the Irish team.

By mid-October we were more than ready. Cabin fever was setting in, and it was time to compete. For the past month, we had been like kids with our noses pressed against the pet shop window, looking at the puppies inside. We had been gazing out our plate glass window at the jumps, and now we would be allowed to walk the course and decide our strategy. After our first look, we decided it was not as big as Badminton, but the altitude would be a factor, and we would have to "ride smart."

When determining the order of go for their riders, most teams followed the same strategy: the first rider out was the pathfinder. His job was to get home at all costs, in order to tell his teammates about the course. If he got around, the next rider could ride a little closer to the maximum bonus time, and so on. Remember, this was before the era of cell phones and closed-circuit TV. Teams needed elaborate "spy systems," to gather as much information as possible.

I was named first of the U.S. team, on the basis that Henry was our most experienced horse, and my performance at the Pan Ams had at least shown that I could take a licking and keep on ticking. I wasn't supposed to worry about the time, just get around and set the table for Michael, Kevin, and Mike, who would follow in that order. Henry had a phenomenal trot and could easily cruise at nearly 400 meters per minute (mpm). I had learned that rather than holding him to the required speed of 240 mpm on roads and tracks, I was better off letting him trot at his pace, and then walking when I could. He would walk on, take a few breaths, then strut off with me, obviously as eager as I was to see what the competition had in store for us.

I followed the same strategy on the steeplechase, allowing Henry to cruise along at a pace that was comfortable for him. I started my watch but didn't check it until the finish and was surprised at how easily he had made the time. I mentioned to Joe in the vet box that the first three phases had no surprises for us, got a leg up, and after all those years of effort I was on course at the Olympics. Once again, I started my watch, but did not refer to it again.

My strategy remained the same—to accept time faults, but to make sure I finished. Henry settled into a rhythm quickly, and things were going well until I jumped a simple ditch and rail at fence number seven. The landing was level, and covered with gravel, and we had not thought much of it when we walked it. However, the gravel was only a top dressing, and it quickly gave way to deep mud when a horse landed on it. I have a video of our efforts there—Henry jumped the rail in stride but punched through the gravel halfway up to his knees. The abrupt halt pitched me forward onto his ears, and the next thing I knew, I was hanging on Henry's off side, with my left spur caught in the wither pad, and hanging on the left rein, which was crossed over the top of Henry's head. My eyes were level with Henry's right eye, and he stood like a statue while I laboriously pulled myself back into the saddle by using the rein as a rope.

Extricating myself, I got my stirrups back, gathered my reins and set off again. I made no attempt to ask for speed, but every time we jumped onto a gravel landing, you can believe that I had my legs in front of me, anticipating another serious peck. There was an open ditch at the far end of the course; looking ahead, I could see a crowd gathered to the side, and a rider standing next to a form covered with a tarpaulin. I later learned that the first Russian horse, Ballerina, had broken her neck when her legs got stuck in the mud on landing over the ditch. I understood the situation, but I had my hands full and had to concentrate on getting home. I did not have any further dramas and finished about 30 seconds slow, a very acceptable performance for the pathfinder. I quickly shared my information about the footing with Joe Lynch, then ran up to our bungalow to change clothes. Michael was on course with Foster, and I missed watching his round, but could catch Kevin and Mike.

As I looked out the window, a sudden rainstorm obliterated the scene. The weather had been perfect for me and Michael, but the footing changed dramatically as the course's volcanic pumice soil turned to soup in the heavy rain. The competition was proceeding normally up to that point; however, the deluge changed the competition from a normal cross-country event to a fight for completion and survival. Kevin's horse slid into a jump in rain so heavy that Kevin could not see it until the final strides; he had been staying on course by following the footsteps of earlier horses. A heavy fall there shook Chalan's confidence and he had two more falls before completing, thus being eliminated. This put enormous pressure on Mike to finish, as by now we knew that any team that finished was in with a chance at a medal.

Mike and Plain Sailing had a fall at the first water. By the time Mike got to 5AB, the gentle stream underneath the rails had become a torrent, and the water was so high that only the top rails of the in-and-out were visible. The water was moving so fast that it knocked Plain Sailing off his feet when he landed. Fortunately, Mike was able to remount and complete the course, thus assuring us of a team score. Mike told me that Plain Sailing was the bravest horse he ever rode; knowing he would fall if he jumped into swiftly moving water, he jumped anyway. Given the rough-and-tumble attitude of eventers in that era, I then thought that Plain Sailing was the model of a Classic horse, one that would fall rather than refuse or run out.

Later that evening the scores were posted, and several things became apparent. Despite our difficulties, the U.S. Team was in second place behind the British, and I was in second place individually. Henry had the fastest round of the day by 30 seconds, with Michael the next fastest. For the second team competition in a row, Henry and I had the fastest time of the day, and we were developing an international reputation for speed.

As we studied the scores, it was clear that there had really been two separate competitions—before the rain, and during the rain. Except for two fatalities (Ballerina and a horse name Loughlin that inexplicably suffered a rotational fall over one of the simplest fences on course), the first two riders from each team managed to complete because they had acceptable conditions. Once the rain started, the competition became a debacle. The only good outcome of the downpour was that it shorted out the generators needed to run the television cameras. Fortunately for the sport, no broadcast recorded the deaths of two horses, or displayed the extreme conditions.

There would be time enough to learn from our experiences, but the vet check came next. Henry jogged out very well, a testimony to the care that Duffy and Dr. Jacque Jenny, our treating vet, gave him after the cross-country. We walked the show-jumping course, which was on one of the golf course's main fairways. The footing was, in a word, horrible. Boggy in some places, hard and slick in others, it was going to increase the difficulty for horses who were already tired. I finished dressing for the show jumping, only to learn that Duffy, so nervous that Henry was in contention for a medal that his hands were shaking, had broken the outside caulk of Henry's left hind shoe.

There wasn't enough time for our farrier, Seamus Brady, to reset the shoe; we would have to go, while being extra careful on the turns. I went into the show jumping in second place but finished in sixth.

Henry's left hind slipped underneath him as he turned left toward the final line of obstacles, and I had a fall, thus losing my chance at an individual medal.

While terribly disappointed at my individual results, I was proud to get a silver team medal, standing on the podium during the Olympic medal ceremony with three of my heroes. I have experienced all sorts of emotions in my life—marriage, the births of my two daughters—but I would have to add the emotion of watching the Stars and Stripes being raised in a foreign country, and knowing I had a part in making it happen. We stepped off the podium, remounted, took part in the victory gallop, left the arena, and just like that my Olympic experience was over.

The atmosphere immediately went flat. Gail, my mother, and my mother-in-law all left for Mexico City, while I stayed behind to pack six weeks of laundry. I had permission from the Army to stay for the duration of the Olympics, so I would follow the family to Mexico City next morning. In the meantime, there was a competitors' party to attend. Many of the riders and officials had left, but the rest of us more than made up for it. The Australian team was gone, but the British had stayed to celebrate their team gold medal. I had made friends with Mark Phillips and Michael Tucker while in England for Badminton, and we had remained friends ever since. We celebrated as hard as we could, with Mark showing that he was able to walk through a plate-glass door, emerging out of the shattered remnants unscathed.

After several cups of coffee next morning, we piled into a Team car for the long drive down to the city. I had plenty of time to think, and plenty to think about. My first thought was, "Now what?" What came next in my life, where would Gail and Hillary be, how would I handle going back to a sort-of Army prison after a year of living a life of horses? I was not comfortable allowing others to define the parameters of my behavior, but I owed the United States two more years of my life, and that was that.

I also had a lot of eventing to think about, while studying the final Olympic scores. Surely the debacle must have taught our officials something; it was their rigid attitude that had started the cross-country day two hours later than it should have begun. Although no one predicted the torrential downpour, we all knew it would rain after lunch. If we had started sooner, the entire disaster would have been avoided. However, the original schedule called for a late morning start, and the ground jury stuck to the schedule. The United States had once again won a silver medal at the Olympics and was now firmly established as an eventing force to be reckoned with. On the other hand, with less than a thousand members we didn't exactly look like an eventing superpower at home—and if our membership numbers were thin, our horse numbers were absolutely skimpy. Just as when the Team's plane left JFK on its way to the Tokyo Olympics in 1964, when our flight left for Mexico in 1968, every qualified Classic horse in the country was on it. If we wanted to stay close to the top of the international eventing tree, we needed to undertake a major building program.

I vowed to continue to improve; if I ever had a chance at a medal again, I would be a better rider. In the meantime, after missing this shot at an individual Olympic silver medal, I had Seamus Brady pull Henry's left hind shoe and had it silver-plated. It has hung on my wall ever since.

Many of the friends I made at the Valle de Bravos stayed in the sport the rest of their lives as riders and, later, as officials, administrators, and organizers. In years to come they would rise to prominent positions in their various organizations and were all very effective agents of change. I attribute this to their conscious decision that we must learn from such an unfortunate outcome as Mexico in 1968, where horses were abused by the organizers and half the field of competitors were robbed of a chance to compete on a level playing field. Years later, Jack Le Goff told me that after the medal ceremony, Jacque Guyon, the French individual gold medal winner, wanted to return his medal; he felt he had not won it fair and square. Jack talked him out of it, but said it took him several bottles of red wine to settle Jacque down.

The next week passed in a whirl, with parties every night and dressage and show-jumping competitions every day. For me the high point of the second week of the Olympics was watching Bill Steinkraus win the individual gold medal on Snowbound, over the biggest show-jumping course that will ever be built. The individual course was so big that the FEI subsequently changed the specifications to prevent show-jumping course designers from building "unjumpable" obstacles.

Gail left midway through the second week, but we went out to dinner with Brien Cobcroft, Kevin Freeman, Richard Meade, and several other eventing types the night before she left. Brien and I had become good friends, and I had arranged for him to retire his Tokyo veteran Hutano ("Nemo") in Kansas, rather than ship him all the way back to Australia only for him to undergo six months of quarantine. (Nemo was his best horse, but had broken down in the final preparatory gallop, and Brien had ridden his alternate instead.)

At the end of a very boozy evening, Brien rolled up his sleeves, and said, "Here, Jimmy, I want you to have these." Brien had first ridden at the 1964 Olympics; as a present, his father had given him a set of cufflinks engraved with the Australian kangaroo symbol, plus the five Olympic rings. I protested that I could not take such an heirloom, but he insisted, saying that whenever I wore them I would think of Nemo, of him, and of the good times we had in Mexico. I have kept them for more than 50 years, and I have been as good as my word. Brien is gone now, but I have worn a little bit of him every time I put on those cufflinks and thought of him. I have worn them in castles and palaces, to weddings and funerals, and have taken them off and hidden them in my pocket when I went into bars that warned you to take out your false teeth before going through the bat-wing doors. Brien's grandson never knew him, but he will be 21 in a few years and I am going to send the cufflinks back to him, back to Australia, where I have always known they truly belong.

But all that was in the distant future; right now, I headed back to Gladstone, and checked in with Colonel Mendenhall. I could almost hear his smile over the phone line, when he told me to stay at Gladstone another week "to take inventory." I immediately caught his drift, thanked him profusely, and promised to check with him next week.

In the meantime, Kevin was staying on the East Coast to foxhunt, gallop racehorses, and generally enjoy himself. I was glad to have the company, as Gail and Hillary were in Colorado, staying with Gail's parents while I waited for my orders from the Army. It didn't take Jill Slater long to find out that two keen foxhunters, eventers, and extra men for a party were living in the dormitory at the Team. Next thing we knew, we were living at Jill's farm, joining her and her husband, "Sonny" Slater, for dinner every night, and generally living the life of Riley. A week of this passed far too quickly, but as instructed I called Colonel Mendenhall again, and he directed me to the First Sergeant at Headquarters Company, Fort Dix.

The Army Reclaims Me

—— Changing into my Army uniform, I set out for Fort Dix. Reporting in, I was immediately chewed out by the First Sergeant (aka "Top"—First

Sergeants are often referred to as "Top," meaning the top sergeant in the unit): I was "out of uniform" and badly in need of an army haircut. In Top's opinion the civilian haircut I had recently obtained at great expense left a great deal to be desired, my posture badly needed improvement, and he didn't know what this man's Army was coming to, promoting a sorry-ass sad sack like me to the exalted rank of corporal. I meekly agreed with all this but asked about the "out of uniform" part. Concealing a smile while he continued his harangue, Top informed me that I had been promoted to corporal while on TDY, and that after getting a "real haircut" and having my new stripes sewn on, I should stop at the paymaster; his records showed that my pay had been held while I was on TDY. He suspected I had been able to support myself during this period either because I was a richie-rich, or a drug dealer—he left it to me to decide which he thought was worse. After tending to all these details, I was to report back for my next orders and, I suspected, for further ass-chewing.

All of this happened as directed, and I reported back as a Specialist 4 (aka a corporal), with several thousand dollars in cash on my hip. Once I underwent the usual negative criticism from the First Sergeant, it appeared that because my "slot" had not yet opened up, the Army was not yet ready to send me to my next post. Translated, it meant the Army didn't really know what to do with me. Top handed me new orders that *"auth two weeks TDY, will report HqFortDix NLT 10NOV68. No per diem auth; travel by POV auth."*

It took me a moment to understand that my new orders meant I was back on TDY for another two weeks. I wouldn't get any extra per diem but travel by personally owned vehicle was okay. I had heard, and now came to believe, that the powers of a senior NCO were close to God-like: "I say to that man 'go' and he goeth, and to this man 'come' and he cometh."

It didn't take me long to "leaveth" Fort Dix, stopping in the nearest phone booth to see if Jill Slater needed an extra hand for the next couple of weeks. I explained the situation, she laughed, and I headed back to Gladstone. I had arranged for Henry and Nemo to be turned out at a local farm, while I stored most of my clothes in my two-horse trailer. Kevin had left for Portland, and the stables at Gladstone were empty; once again we had lost a coach, and the Team riders were scattered across the country. The next couple of weeks passed uneventfully, but I grew increasingly anxious. I missed my family, and I was ready to come to grips with whatever life and the Army had in store for me. Our parents and in-laws were wonderfully generous, but Gail and I needed to set up our own place.

When I reported back after my extra two weeks of TDY, I was greeted with yet another two weeks of TDY—the army still didn't know what to do with me. When I checked back in early December, I was assigned to the post gymnasium. I swept the floor of the basketball court about four times a day and waited impatiently for my orders. On December 16, they finally came: I was authorized two weeks of leave, and would "*rpt for duty USMPTC FT SAM HOUSTON MOS desig 91T40 NLT 2JAN69.*" I was headed for Texas to work as the assistant riding coach at the U.S. Modern Pentathlon Training Center. My MOS was now that of a veterinary technician, and provided for my next promotion, when I would be NCOIC (non-commissioned officer in charge) of the stables.

I didn't know it yet, but a lot of old Army friends were waiting for me.

Top said that to "clear post," I needed to get my records checked at the medic, the paymaster, the provost marshal, and several other offices, and then I'd be good to go. He said this would take several days, as I was to make sure I got a signature at each office. That was not music to my ears, but I quickly found if I slid my 201 file over the counter with a five- or ten-dollar bill inside and explained my situation, I could get a signature without bothering the officer involved; the NCO at the counter would sign it for me. I was beginning to understand the Army. Returning to HqCo in record time, I presented my file, got my final orders, and said goodbye to Fort Dix.

In the early evening of December eighteenth, I loaded Henry and Nemo into my two-horse Hartman, closed the storm flap, and headed west on the Pennsylvania Turnpike. Stopping for coffee and gas a couple of hours later, I was contemplating how far I could go before I would need to find stabling for the night. Looking up, I noticed a few snowflakes sifting down and decided I would drive on for a while. Thus began a non-stop, 36-hour, 1,300-mile adventure. I was just ahead of a blizzard that was coming down from the Great Lakes, bringing snow and record cold temperatures. If I stopped at a fairgrounds to rest, I might be stranded for several days. That was not in my master plan; I was due to meet Gail and Hillary in Colorado Springs, then to go skiing for a few days in Aspen.

It was dry every time I stopped for gas, and snowing by the time I had fueled up, gotten another cup of coffee and come back outside. If I stepped on it each time, I could drive out from underneath the storm, so I persevered. My only companion was AM radio and I was a prisoner of whatever local stations I could find when I drove out of range of one and searched through the static until I found another. I repeated this process for the two nights and a day I spent driving. Most AM radio stations were limited, but WLS in Chicago had a 50,000-watt transmitter, and once the atmosphere cooled enough my first night, I could get it on my radio dial.

The next day, I was subjected to an array of listening experiences, from cooking advice, to the local mayor's daughter singing, to an amazing number of preachers, all telling me they would show me the way, if only I would put my hand on the speaker and trust in Jesus. I admit I put my hand on the speaker, but I was really praying, "Jesus, please keep me awake, I got a long way to go." I lost the signal from WLS my second night on the road, but "KOMA, your 50,000-watt tower of power" reached out to me from Oklahoma City. The Rolling Stones and the Beatles kept me going all the way across Indiana and Missouri, and the local news on KJCK greeted me as I drove due west past Leavenworth, heading for Rimrock Farm.

Poor Henry and Nemo stayed cooped up in that trailer for a day and a half, while I fought my way halfway across the United States. They were warm enough, with double wool blankets and the windows closed. Experienced travelers, they both drank water, munched on their hay nets, and unashamedly peed at the gas stations when I stopped. I pulled into the stables courtyard at Rimrock Farm 36 hours after leaving New Jersey, unhooked the storm flap, and dropped the ramp, expecting to let the boys unload. Instead, I found a wall of frozen manure nearly as tall as the ramp. Dan and I had to batter the wall down to unload these two unfortunates. I led Henry into his stall, where he drank a bucket of warm water and promptly lay down for a nap, groaning as he stretched out. I knew how he felt, so I checked on Nemo (who had drunk a similar amount and was napping while standing), then drove over to the main house and slept for a few hours. The weather was no longer a factor, but I was in a sweat to see my family. Leaving the trailer and horses behind, I was in Colorado Springs by 10 o'clock that night. A lovely few days skiing in Aspen followed, but I had my orders. I soon left via Colorado Springs for Fort Sam Houston, driving south toward my new career in the Army, and a whole new world. ∎

10

__The Eyes of Texas

This is the Army, Mister Jones.

Irving Berlin
Composer

D riving from Colorado Springs to San Antonio gave me an impromptu tour of the southwestern United States. Gail would follow later with Hillary, and I was alone with my thoughts for a couple of days. The Olympics were now safely on my resumé, and I had time to think about both my future and our future. I was just coming to grips with my new role as a father. In addition, I was nervous about my new role in the U.S. Army, and my new responsibilities.

I was assigned to the U.S. Modern Pentathlon Training Center (USMPTC) at Fort Sam Houston for the next two years. All I knew about my new job was that yet another old Army friend, Colonel Johnny Russell, would be my boss.

My family connections stretched from Johnny to Colonel Mendenhall at the Army Sports program, and then back to Johnny. By a strange coincidence, my father had been Johnny's coach at the 1952 Olympics, and now Johnny would be my coach. Although self-awareness was not my strong suit, I was beginning to realize how lucky I was in my family's involvement with horses and with the Army. The shadow of the rainbow extended all the way to Texas, and my good fortune with it.

My family had been arranging the next chapter of our lives behind the scenes while I was training for the Olympics. Colonel Billy and Helen Greear, my brother Warren's godparents and close family friends, had just retired from the Army and Billy had accepted the position of City Manager for Terrell Hills, a nice suburb just outside the post at Fort Sam Houston. Gail and my mother reached out to the Greears, and made a quick inspection tour on their way to Mexico for the Olympics. This was news to me; they did not bother me with the details. By the time I heard of it, we had rented a lovely house at 913 Ivy Lane in Terrell Hills, about 10 minutes from USMPTC. While they were at it, Gail and Mom arranged stabling for our horses at Johnny Russell's civilian stables and found a wonderful babysitter for Hillary.

Basically, all I had to do once I got to San Antonio was report in to *"HqCo, Fort Sam Houston, Tx nlt 2Jan69."* In obedience to my mimeographed orders, not later than the morning of January second, I presented myself to the Headquarters Company First Sergeant (aka "Top"), gave him my orders and my 201 file, and was told to get a haircut. Based on my Army experience, this command was a reflex for all senior NCOs (non-commissioned officers). It was usually partnered with constructive criticism about my posture, general appearance, and dismal prospects for future success in this man's Army. I replied that I completely understood the First Sergeant's helpful comments and promised to improve every aspect of my Army performance. Mollified by my obsequious response, Top directed me toward the USMPTC stables and dismissed me.

FNG Learns the Ropes

Some people at the stables were glad to see me. Johnny showed me around, first introducing me to another old Army friend, Master Sergeant Harry Cruzan. He was the NCOIC USMPTC Stables in Army parlance, Stable Sergeant to the rest of the world. I was knee-high the first time I met him, when he was Fuddy Wing's groom at the 1948 Olympics, and our paths had occasionally crossed since then.

Johnny's plan was that I would take over from Harry, once my promotion to "Specialist 5" (sergeant) came through. There was a slight hitch in his plan: I needed another couple of months as a corporal before I would be eligible for promotion. This all sounded fine with me; I was just happy to be in a situation that involved horses. If I had the chance to ride all day, I didn't much care if I was a private or an NCO. However, I changed my mind about that after a few days.

I expected a certain amount of hazing whenever I got to a new post. The Army term is "FNG"—most of the acronym stands for "New Guy." So, I was the FNG. Johnny introduced me and left me to get acquainted. My reception was definitely chilly, which I understood. Most of the stable crew had been there for a year or more and were counting the days until they could return to civilian life. The stable operation consisted of six to eight riders, a farrier, a carpenter, and a civilian night watchman. For the most part, crew members were assigned because they could ride well enough to re-school the Pentathlon horses.

Compared to the small operation Gail and I had been running in New Jersey, I was going to be in charge of a much bigger organization. It occurred to me later that Johnny might have been worried about our relationship, as I had been on a first-name basis with him since I could remember. But I had also been raised with the Army, and during business hours I stood up when he came into the stable office, called him "Colonel Russell," replied with "Yes, sir," or "No, sir," and tried to be a model NCO. After business hours at his facility north of town (Johnny was effectively running two programs at the same time), we were on a first name basis, but there was an invisible line between us, and throughout my time at the USMPTC I was careful never to cross it.

The USMPTC was the Olympic center for modern pentathlon, much as Gladstone was for the equestrian team. Officers from the various services sent likely candidates to us for training. It was possible, but rare, for civilians to participate. Young officers who could either run or swim at a near-Olympic level were assigned to the USMPTC on a trial basis. There they were coached in all five pentathlon disciplines—running, swimming, fencing, shooting, and riding. The riding part is where the stable crew came in; we rode the horses that developed bad habits. Most of the athletes who came through the program had no experience with horses, which was the reason for the bad habits our horses developed, yet within 90 days these young men had to be able to draw a horse's name out of a hat and successfully complete a 3-foot, 6-inch show-jumping course with it—*90 days!* Think of that the next time you struggle with improving your riding skills. The pressure on these aspiring pentathletes was enormous; if they washed out of the pentathlon program in the late 1960s, most were destined to be reassigned as platoon leaders in Vietnam. At that point, their life expectancy would be measured in hours and days, not in years. All elite athletes are motivated, but these guys were *really* motivated. By the time these first or second lieutenants arrived at USMPTC to begin their riding instruction, they would have recently set NCAA records in running or swimming. (The theory was that the three "skill sports"—fencing, shooting, and riding—could all be taught, while the ability to run or swim at an elite level was determined more by pure athletic gifts than by practice.) Working at the USMPTC was my first experience with teaching on a regular basis, and I was learning faster than the pentathletes.

I noticed immediately that these super-fit athletes, who had recently won big college running or swimming competitions, quivered with fatigue after only a few minutes in the saddle, and I realized that riding fitness is different from running and swimming fitness. Another insight: the runners made better riders than the swimmers. It made sense to me, as runners were typically long and lean, used to relaxing their arms while their legs did all the work. Swimmers, on the other hand, were usually shaped like a wedge, and tended to move their arms and shoulders rather than their legs. Both could learn, but it helped to have the right physique to begin with.

My early exposure to Colonel Chamberlin's style of teaching now came in handy. Colonel Russell had been brought up in the cavalry tradition, and his teaching, based on Chamberlin's writings, reflected it; therefore, I spoke his language immediately, and was able to impart it to my students. Soon after I arrived, I was designated as the assistant riding instructor.

I'd like to think my students improved, but Colonel Russell was the driving force of the program. When the athletes reported to the stables daily, he assigned two horses for each to ride. In addition, the stable riders were assigned horses who needed remedial jumping before being put back on the athletes' list. We schooled these horses along with the athletes, sometimes acting as visual role models, sometimes bringing up the rear of the session if our "schoolies" had behavioral problems. The athletes rode two sets, then continued their training in the other four disciplines. For the rest of the morning, we schooled the rest of the horses on the flat or over fences as required.

Colonel Russell had an uncanny knack of knowing which horse to select for each rider. As horses rotated on and off the re-schooling list, I knew after a while which ones just needed some negative reinforcement to get them jumping again, and which needed to canter over small fences for a day or so to rebuild their confidence. Although some of the other crew members resented riding such an amazing array of stoppers, buckers, runaways, nappers, and general equine miscreants, I regarded it as a graduate degree in how to ride. If I could learn to deal with all the problems these poor horses presented, I could do anything with horses. The analogy I used with the crew members was that if we were graduate psychiatrists, we would want to work in a mental institution; while there, we would see a little bit of everything. As riders at the center, we would meet every kind of problem a horse could present and have Colonel Russell to guide us through the rehabilitation process. Thanks to my experiences in Texas, I'm rarely surprised by a horse's misbehavior; chances are I've seen it before.

Mornings were busy, considering that we had between 55 and 85 horses in work year-round. Their care was rudimentary. After riding we untacked each horse, put a halter and lead rope on, and tied it to a picket line that ran down the middle of the outside asphalt apron. Once we had 20 horses or so tied to each side of the picket line, we got out the fire hose.

My eyes bugged out the first time I witnessed this process. I had come from Gladstone, where meticulous horse care was a religion, yet now we were going to wash an entire herd of horses at once. It was not as barbaric as you might think; the trickiest part was turning the fire hose on to the required water pressure. Not enough pressure, and you could not reach the entire herd from one spot; too much pressure and the hose would escape. This set the nozzle swinging wildly back and forth across the pavement like a scythe of death until several brave crew members tackled and subdued it while the other crew members adjusted the pressure. Once correctly focused, the hose was directed skyward, creating an instant rainstorm. The horses, used to this treatment, shut their eyes and pinned their ears back until the downpour subsided.

At this point the hose was shut off and several crew members started down the line with sweat scrapers. Each horse was scraped, then the trustworthy ones were released and told to get back to their stalls. After a few days I accepted this as an efficient means of getting a large number of horses cleaned off; if the horses were okay with it, I guess I was too. Possibly the horses involved knew that most of them were one step ahead of an Alpo can when their owners donated them to the USMPTC, and thus accepted their lot in life as high-level school horses for unschooled riders.

And my goodness, were these riders unschooled! Some of the stunts they got up to on horseback still make me laugh. My very first day, Johnny was showing me around, and took me down to see the large outdoor sand arena. Two athletes were riding around in it. Stopping at the gate, Johnny watched them for a second, then with an evil smile said, "Watch this." These riders had been trotting, but they soon switched to cantering large circles that increased in speed and size until both horses had built up a good head of steam. The riders were locked in the reins, desperately looking down at their horses' necks, paying no attention to each other. You guessed it: In less time than it takes to tell, those two had ridden from a wide-open gallop into a perfect head-to-head collision. It sounded as if a watermelon had dropped out of a second-story window, and both horses were a bit wobbly as they staggered away. Johnny mildly remarked to the two miscreants they should look where they were going and told them to carry on. "Stuff like that happens every day around here," he muttered to me as we walked back toward the stables.

"I can hardly wait," I thought to myself.

FNG Takes the Reins

—— Soon after I arrived, Harry Cruzan retired, having served for 35 years, and a master sergeant was brought down as a placeholder NCOIC while I waited for my promotion to come through. I kept my head down, my mouth shut, and rode the horses assigned to me. The schedule at the stables started when we mucked out at six in the morning. Pancho, the night watchman, would have already fed the horses and had a 5-gallon urn of coffee ready for us. This was noteworthy for two reasons. Except for me, most of the crew would be suffering from the effects of either alcohol or marijuana and needed a stimulant to get them going. I was older than most of them, married, and still considered myself an athlete; I only needed coffee to help me wake up. In addition, Pancho's coffee was not just bad, it was spectacularly awful. Such was the crew's typical morning condition that in order to get some caffeine they gagged it down. Johnny showed up just before the pentathletes arrived, stopped by the office, poured a cup of coffee, shuddered, and stepped out to the assignment board to match riders with horses.

Before my promotion came through, I noticed that most mornings an Army staff car with a driver pulled up to the stables at seven. A middle-aged man dressed in old-fashioned "bat-wing" britches, highly polished three-buckle brown riding boots, and a khaki shirt with no markings stepped out. He would select a bridle and saddle from the tack room, throw the saddle on a Thoroughbred chestnut gelding called Upland, step aboard, and ride away. He returned just before eight, untacked Upland, left him in his stall, hung up his tack, and stepped back into his car.

All this went unremarked by the crew, who seemed to accept it as a normal procedure. After observing a few repetitions, I asked Johnny about it. He told me that the man in question was Major General Francis Murdoch, recently assigned to Fort Sam Houston as the Deputy Commander of the U.S. Third Army. General Murdoch liked to ride, and two-star generals, like 500-pound gorillas, went wherever they wanted. I filed away the crew's lack of attention and put it on my list of things I wanted to change once I was given a chance.

Change was certainly coming to the Center; several malcontents left, and several FNGs were assigned to the stable crew. They were all good riders, including Mason Phelps, Trip Harting, Gould ("Peanut") Brittle, and Mike Hunter.

We also got a new farrier, T.R. Smith, and a new carpenter, Mike Klepzig. Meanwhile, I had to put on my full green army uniform (we usually reported for work in fatigue jackets, blue tee-shirts, rust-colored britches, and black boots) in order to report to a Promotion Board.

I didn't get the same reaction from my Board as General Tuckerman used to get. (If you recall, he told me years earlier that each of his promotions resulted from his having given a spooked four-year-old "a hell of a ride" through a scattered military parade as a young officer.) But

I seemed to satisfy the Board that I could be *"promoted E-5, designated MOS 91T40, and assigned NCOIC USMPTC."* All this Army jargon meant that I was now the equivalent of a sergeant, "Specialist 5," which meant I got a pay raise, an increase in my housing allowance, and could officially take over at the stables with my new veterinary technician MOS designation.

I had been looking forward to this, as the crew had gotten pretty slipshod in their attitudes, and the two "lifer" sergeants before me had just been putting in their time until retirement. I wanted a new attitude around the stables and explained to the crew at my first staff meeting that although Colonel Russell had a friendly, relaxed way of conducting himself, he was still a colonel, and we would observe the correct military courtesies around him: stand up when he came in the office, hustle when he "suggested" something, ride the horses he said to ride in the way he said to ride them, and life would be good. If he decided you were not pulling your weight (and by implication, if I thought the same), you could start practicing Vietnamese as a second language. The gist of my message to them was that this was a sweet assignment. If they would shine their boots, salute, and say "Yes-sir-no-sir" they would get away with murder for the duration of their Army career.

Part of the laxity in our program was caused by the Texas heat. We started early, riding while it was cool. The horses were washed and put up before lunch, and several stable crew members could quickly knock out the tack. This left little to do in the afternoons, and most of the riders drifted away for a siesta in the barracks adjacent to the stables. Some of them came back, but there was no roll call, and not much going on at the stables; usually, afternoon attendance dropped off considerably. If I needed someone, they could usually be found in the bunkhouse. It had rudimentary kitchen facilities, a lounge with a television set, hot showers, bunk beds upstairs, and little else to recommend it beyond proximity.

Another source of the laxity was a growing misconception among the crew that our daily six o'clock starting time was a suggestion, not a rule. One of the crew, Mike Hunter, started sleeping in later and later, and the previous NCOIC was disinclined to climb the stairs and roust him out of bed. Once I took over, I told Mike it was a new day and a new way, and he was to start with everybody else. Naturally, he slept in, so I walked upstairs and dumped a large bucket of cold water on him. Mike went from a deep drunken sleep to a burning rage in no time and came out of the sodden mess of bed clothes, promising to whip my ass for me. Considering I was not still drunk, and had him by 4 inches and 50 pounds, I wasn't too worried. However, it never got that far. When he jumped out of bed with his fists clenched, he stepped into a puddle, both of his feet shot out from underneath him, and he landed flat on his back, knocking his wind out of him. I reminded Mike we all started at six and walked out. He slept in again the next day but heard my step on the bottom stair plus the clank of my water bucket and leapt out of bed, promising to be at work immediately. I had no more trouble with Mike, and the rest of the crew smiled and went about their business. But as long as I was there, we all started on time.

I had not been warned by my predecessors about Colonel Whiting. While Colonel Russell was the USMPTC Head Coach and Head Riding Coach, Colonel Whiting was the Commanding Officer of the whole operation. He had a four-thirty golf tee-time every Friday. He told his office staff that he was going to inspect one of the five training facilities, left work early, made a cameo appearance at a facility, and drove on to the Officer's Club in time for his weekly golf game. A week or so after I took over, it was my turn to entertain Colonel Whiting. He rolled up, got out puffing a big cigar, and asked to "see Private Klepzig," my newly assigned carpenter, who was usually employed in repairing jumps, fences, and seeing to general maintenance around the stables. I stammered and stuttered a bit, saying I was sure he could be found if I went looking for him. Colonel Whiting delivered a stern lecture to the effect that every man needed to do his military duty right up until five o'clock, even on Fridays, and I had to be there, supervising all of them. Thus suitably reprimanded, I assured him it would be done, and I would personally see to it.

One of the first items on my list of "things to change" happened at seven in the morning most days. The change was obvious immediately: when General Murdoch appeared for his morning ride, Upland was tacked up and standing in the cross-ties. His mane was pulled, the hoof oil on all four hooves was correctly applied, and his saddle and bridle showed the loving application of elbow grease and saddle soap. While the crew was mucking out, I was in the office, dealing with the unending stream of Army paperwork. When General Murdoch walked through I stood and said, "Good morning, sir." He replied absentmindedly and continued through to his morning ride. Occasionally his office called to say the general would not be in the stables until such and such a date. I would seize the moment; I had already assigned Mason to Upland on the days when General Murdoch didn't ride, and Johnny did not assign the horse to a pentathlete.

Upland—as I've mentioned, a gorgeous bright chestnut Thoroughbred—was 16.2 hands, with no chrome. He carried 90 percent of his considerable weight on his forehand and had a mouth like cold iron. In addition, jumping higher than 3-foot fences on him was a potentially lethal exercise; he had as little jumping talent as any Thoroughbred I have ever seen, thus Johnny rarely put him in the athletes' string. I handed Mason, who was a super rider, a double bridle and told him to "put a mouth on that son-of-a-bitch." Knowing the situation was in good hands, I then put it out of my mind.

As part of the pentathletes' training, we took them to horse shows. Right after I assumed responsibility at the stables, I got to the office early to make plans for shipping horses to a show the coming weekend. Sitting at the desk, I watched as Pancho poured water into the coffee machine, sprinkled some Folgers in, put the top back on, and flicked the switch. I turned back to my paperwork, then paused.

Calling Pancho back, I asked him if he had dumped yesterday's grounds and rinsed the machine. Pancho looked at me as if I had crawled out from under a rock, replying that he *never* rinsed it out; that took too much time. He just filled it up, sprinkled more coffee on top, and it was ready to dispense coffee to the crew. He dumped the basket when it got full; otherwise, "saving money on coffee, by not using so much."

Finally, an explanation for the vile potion inflicted on the crew.

Upon lifting the lid, I was greeted by a substantial green crust on top of used grounds, with small green sprigs of some volunteer plant sticking out. The entire inside of the container was completely black. I sternly explained that from now on the machine and basket were to be cleaned until spotless every morning, and only new coffee grounds were to be used. Pancho took the machine away, grumbling about the expense.

A few minutes later I sampled a fresh batch of coffee. It wasn't nectar and ambrosia, but it was a huge improvement. Colonel Russell arrived, reached for a mug and poured himself a cup, almost visibly preparing to be poisoned. A smile came over his face after the first sip. He nodded to me and went out to the aisle. I smiled too, thinking that the prospects of my keeping this job were improving, and turned back to my shipping list; we had a show to go to and I wanted to be ready.

It's a good thing to be ready, because Colonel Whiting showed up en route to his golf game the next Friday, smoking his usual cigar, and asked me if I knew "where Klepzig is." I knew Klepzig had earlier been on the rooftop of the barracks, fixing the television antenna. Truth be told, I had no earthly idea where he was now, but knew I could track him down quickly if need be. Quick as a flash, I said, "Sir-he's-up-on-the-rooftop-fixing-the-antenna," all in one burst. Rather than asking to see him, Colonel Whiting nodded vaguely and stepped back in his car, saying something about never mind, it could wait until Monday. As he drove off for the golf course, I realized he hadn't really heard what I had said but had been impressed by the tone of absolute certainty in my voice. I heard strangled laughter coming from around the corner, where several crew members had listened to this exchange and were cracking up. Thereafter, "up on the rooftop, fixing the antenna" entered the lexicon as shorthand for anyone who was MIA. It taught me a valuable lesson: if I was going to BS, I needed to be definite.

The Old Army...Again

——What with personnel transfers and retirements, by the early summer the crew was a congenial group. They did a good job with the horses, kept the stables in apple-pie order, and usually vanished for the rest of the day. One of the hardest-working FNGs was T.R. Smith, who had been assigned as our farrier. I was a little worried when he showed up, as all the Army farriers I knew were older sergeants with years of experience; what could a 20-year-old kid know about shoeing horses? We were so backed up on the shoeing list, however, that I handed him the work order, figuring that if he was okay with Colonel Russell, I'd better give him a try.

With too much on my mind, I inadvertently added Spare Time to the list. The USMPTC horses did not come to us because they were model citizens, and Spare Time was a case in point. A gray 16-hand Thoroughbred foaled on a ranch in southwest Texas, he'd missed the annual roundup for several years and grew up feral; he didn't see anything in trousers until his fifth year. Rough-broken by cowboys, he had wound up at the Center because he was no use to normal riders.

"Snorty" does not begin to describe him. We left a halter and a short rope with a "monkey fist" knot at the end on him all the time so that we could reach into his stall with a chicken hook and capture the rope. Cowboys had taught him to respect the rope and halter, so once he felt the halter we could tack him up and ride him safely. Neglect this part of the process, however, and you were taking your life in your hands; given the opportunity, he would strike you with his ears up, or kick your lights out. He carried his notorious "Leave me alone" attitude over into his jumping. Anyone who drew his name out of the hat at a pentathlon competition could be sure of jumping a clear round. As long as you left the reins alone, Spare Time would take care of business.

But I forgot to tell T.R. Smith that he had to be heavily tranquilized for shoeing. When T.R. came up for lunch he described the horses he had shod so far, including conditions, changes, and the other usual details. He then mentioned he needed to talk to me about Spare Time. Suddenly realizing my error, I turned white, and was about to ask how many people had been hurt when T.R. said, "Jim, Spare Time gave me a little trouble, so I put him down, hobbled him, and got him done while he was on his side—I hope you don't mind." I gaped at him for a second, then asked if the horse was skinned up or injured. T.R. replied, "Nah, I spread a tarp before I laid him down," adding he would be back after lunch to finish the list.

Later on, I learned T.R. came from a family of farriers who shod horses on the Standardbred trotting tracks of the Midwest. Once I saw how skilled he was, I asked him to shoe my own horses. I had been in touch with Colonel Mendenhall about riding in the U.S. National Championships in Pebble Beach, California, and he agreed to issue the necessary TDY orders. The spring and summer shows were just tune-ups for Henry before we started serious conditioning work. I wanted him shod with caulks for the horse-show season, and (hopefully) Pebble Beach. T.R. had never heard of screw-in caulks, but took one look at an old pair of Henry's shoes and remarked laconically that he could do that—and he could, too. That was one more detail taken care of; I was learning to take care of small details before my competitions.

Meanwhile, Back at the Barn...

—— Showing was good for the pentathletes, and handy for Gail and me as well. By now, we had several Rimrock Farm horses stabled at Johnny's facility. I had Kilkenny back in work and was showing him lightly as a jumper to keep him interested. Gail had two homebreds and was extremely successful in the Green and Working Hunter divisions. While Happy Plate did not have perfect hunter form over fences, Gail had a knack for covering this up, and Happy Plate had what Daddy used to call "winning ways." Judges took one look at Gail and Happy Plate and signed their judge's card over to her; she was usually champion or reserve champion at the shows. I had started out riding Dr. Fuji but gave up on him, pronouncing him "not worth the powder to blow him up." Gail took one look, fell in love, and told Mom she wanted to keep going with him. A year later she was the runner-up high point First Year Green Hunter in the entire country—tells you what

I know about horses. I'm the one sitting in the corner wearing a dunce cap.

One of the shows we attended our first summer in Texas was a four-day affair at Fort Sill, Oklahoma. Mom decided this was a good excuse to drive her brand-new Winnebago down from Kansas. She planned to watch her horses, see her granddaughter, and visit old friends at Fort Sam Houston. I showed Henry and Malakasia ("Mac") in the jumper divisions, but it was obvious that Mac was not cut out to be a show jumper; his future career was as a timber racer. We shipped him to New Jersey for Jill Slater to train, thinking that we would run him in some timber races on the East Coast. I also rode a horse from the Center named Galway Bay, a great jumper, but stone-cold crazy. Johnny hoped that I could settle him enough for the pentathletes to ride. I was never able to accomplish that, but later that fall I cleared 7 feet, 6 inches in a high jump contest on him—and he stood off to do it.

Mom brought us good luck, as Gail and I won every hunter class we entered at Fort Sill, including First Year, First Year Green Conformation, Second Year, and Open Working Hunter. Needless to say, Mom was a happy camper as we drove back to Fort Sam Houston. She had casually mentioned we were invited to dinner with some old Army friends when we got home. Busy with shipping both the USMPTC horses and our own, I had not completely registered our social program. We were in the car and headed for the dinner party when it finally dawned on me that we were dining with "...that nice Frank Murdoch and his lovely wife and daughter." You know, Frank Murdoch who had been a plebe at West Point when Daddy was Master of the Sword, was a favorite young officer of Daddy's who had stayed in touch with Mom and Dad all these years—and was now Deputy Commander of Third Army. Yeah, that Frank Murdoch who rode Upland from the USMPTC stable many mornings. Small world.

The Murdochs couldn't have been nicer. They were delighted to see Mom, and very welcoming to Gail and me. The subject of General Murdoch's morning rides didn't come up, and after a nice evening we parted with best wishes and an open invitation for them to visit Rimrock Farm soon. The only change I noticed in my relationship with General Murdoch afterward was that when he passed through the stable office in the mornings, he replied to my greeting with a vague smile and "Good morning, Wofford."

General Murdoch's visits were irregular due to his Army duties, and whenever he was away, Mason continued his efforts to improve Upland's manners. He was resorting to draw reins by now, as the double bridle wasn't getting the job done. A few months later, General Murdoch mentioned to me that he had looked up his old riding books by Colonel Chamberlin, and while riding on the parade ground was starting to apply Chamberlin's suppling exercises—shoulder-in, counter-canter, and so on—to Upland. "By golly, Wofford, Colonel Chamberlin knew his stuff. I really feel like Upland is going better." Straight-faced, I replied soberly that Colonel Chamberlin did indeed know his stuff and I was glad the General was making progress. I mentioned this to Mason, and he walked away, muttering something about "Old Lockjaw."

By now I had gotten accustomed to the summer heat at Texas horse shows. The show would start in the cool of early morning and run until midday, when everyone took a siesta. Most of the show facilities had lights, and evening classes were run in lighted arenas after it had cooled down. Uvalde and New Braunfels had public reservoirs, and after a morning session these were nice places for a quick dip before retiring to an air-conditioned motel room to beat the heat.

Although this was good experience for our younger horses and kept Henry in work, I was getting restless to event with him again. Mason Phelps was already developing his organizational skills, and we decided to put on a full-scale Classic event, using the post facilities. I don't know how he talked Johnny into it—or, more importantly, how he got funding from the Army to help with the costs—but Mason did all the organizing, while I designed the cross-country and laid out the roads and tracks and steeplechase. This was the first Classic event to be held in the Midwest since the 1951 selection trials at Fort Riley. I was proud of that connection, and of my contribution to the development of eventing. The project also confirmed my suspicion that I would much rather ride in events than organize them. Johnny assigned me a horse to compete, and I won the Fort Sam Houston Three-Day Event, on a horse whose name I can't remember.

On My Own at the Nationals

——I knew that Kilkenny had completely recuperated from his exertions in Mexico and was looking for a job. The U.S. Eventing Nationals were scheduled for early September at Pebble Beach, California, and I had permission from Colonel Mendenhall to take a week's TDY to compete. This was a big step for me, as it would be the first time I was completely responsible for getting Henry into peak condition. Others had trained him for me in the past; now I was on my own. Classic competitions take much longer to prepare for than short format events, so I started planning in June for a September competition. I drew up a daily schedule that included two hours of walking almost every day. Johnny had good help at his barn, and I could trust them to do the hacking, while I did the technical work in the afternoons.

Johnny did not have any large fields suitable for conditioning gallops, but a short distance from the barn I found a mile-long straightaway on a state highway with acceptable footing on the shoulder. In the afternoons when I planned to canter, I drove to the start of this makeshift galloping lane, then jogged down and back on foot, throwing bottles, cans, and all sorts of trash aside as I inspected the footing. (Texans had an unusual means of gauging the amount of time required to go from one point to another. I asked a cowboy how long a drive it was from San Antonio to Dallas. "About a six-pack," he replied, meaning if he drank one beer an hour—tossing the empties out on the shoulder—he would get to Dallas in six hours, and yet would not get a DUI if he were pulled over. Texas is different in a lot of ways.)

My cousin Bill Wofford was showing signs of being as horse-crazy as me. He came to San Antonio to spend some time with us, and to accompany Henry out to Pebble Beach. Some of the tales that Billy tells about his trip might even be true; like me, he has never let the facts get in the way of a good story. Early September in Pebble Beach during the late 1960s was an enchanted time and place. I had been there in 1959 for the Pan American Games selection trials and was thrilled to return, this time with a chance to ride along the Spyglass Hill golf course, on the shores of the Pacific Ocean.

I thought Henry was fit enough for the challenge, but my plan was to slow down and nurse him home if he showed signs of fatigue. It worried me that he was subdued during the last stages of training in Texas, as he had been quite sharp before Mexico. I needn't have worried. Late August weather at Pebble Beach is wonderful—cool and crisp in the mornings, with a fog that soon burns off to leave the skies bright blue. Henry stepped off the trailer, took one sniff of cool air, and became an idiot. The heat in

Texas had been suppressing his usual personality, but he was back and he was bad. I spent the next couple of days trying to settle him down by taking long hacks through the Del Monte Forest.

Although the Nationals speed and endurance phase was not as long as Mexico's, it was a full-scale Classic, totaling about fifteen miles. When we walked the roads and tracks, however, it was once again immediately apparent that Phases C and D had not been flagged correctly, creating the possibility for shortcuts that were technically legal. After this was pointed out to the organizer, Dick Collins, he called a meeting of all the riders and said we needed a "gentleman's agreement" (even though there were several female riders—it was the 1960s, what can I say) that everyone would cover the measured distance, despite the lack of mandatory flags.

I had seen this movie before and pointed out that Dick was assuming everyone present was a gentleman. I didn't say it, but I knew the other riders, and suspected several of them would nod and smile—then take the shortcut. Classic events were tests of endurance, so any shortcut was a major advantage. I had been burned by an earlier "gentleman's agreement" and wanted to make sure it didn't happen again. Dick Collins was furious at my comment, partly because he knew I was right, and partly because he had been working too hard and had not had time to flag the course properly.

The upshot of all this was that Dick and Kevin Freeman went out early Saturday morning (cross-country day) and flagged Phase C correctly. However, they forgot to flag the *other* shortcut—yup, the one that cut across the fairway of the famous seventeenth hole of the Spyglass Hill golf course, the scenic one by Seal Rock that ran along the coast of the Pacific Ocean. *That* shortcut. We were supposed to gallop along the fairway, turn behind the green, and so on. It had not occurred to me they would forget to flag it, but by the time Henry and I got there, there were already several sets of footprints straight across hallowed ground. I thought, "In for a penny, in for a pound," as I cut across the fairway. (After this debacle, Dick inaugurated a fine of one hundred dollars per footprint on a fairway or putting green. I would be long gone by that time.)

I finished with a good cross-country time, and Henry felt as if he had been out for a stroll, rather than completing a Classic. I was disappointed not to be in first place at the end of Saturday afternoon, but I felt a growing confidence in my program based on Henry's condition at that point. Classic results in those days were almost entirely determined by performance in the speed and endurance phases. Historically, if you could produce a brave and fit horse, you were in with a chance, no matter what your dressage and show jumping looked like.

As we know now, however, the sport was about to change.

Henry was his usual irrepressible self when I showed up early Sunday morning, which was always a relief. Walking back toward the stables, I turned a corner and bumped into Dick Collins, the technical delegate, and the ground jury, all having a meeting. In front of the whole group, with no warning, he launched into a furious tirade against me for causing so much trouble and for cutting across the fairway. From my own experiences with organizing Classic events, I knew how much work went into them, and how tired organizers got by the time the event took place. I understood both his motivations, and his anger that things were not perfectly organized, so I replied mildly that I was following other footsteps and walked away.

I finished in fourth place. Mike Plumb was second and third, and a cute young girl from California named Hilda Gurney was first. Hilda was following in the footsteps of another female eventer from England. By winning Badminton in the late 1950s, Sheila Wilcox had shown the eventing world that dressage would become more and more important. You could only go so fast on cross-country day, and only jump so clean in the final show jumping phase, but you could always get better in dressage. The news had been slow to reach the United States, but Hilda was showing us the way. I was not sorry to learn later on that she had moved on to a spectacular career in the Grand Prix dressage world; I already had enough competition without Hilda and Flag's Elf, who would usually be close to the lead after dressage.

I Become Essential Personnel

——I returned home to Fort Sam and soon placed a call to Colonel Mendenhall. I had been asking him about several future competitions, and to date he had been a bit vague. Basically, he was saying, "Go well at the Nationals, and then we'll see." Fourth place in the Nationals wasn't as good as first, but as they said in Texas, it was "better'n a dry, hacking cough." Colonel Mendenhall said that things were going well for me and agreed I could take a catch ride at the fall Intermediate Championships in Fair Hill, Maryland.

Joe Lynch had called me earlier in the year, looking for a rider at Fair Hill on The Regent. The horse had some experience in England, then in 1968 was loaned to the USET, probably as part of Joe's compensation package. I was glad for any chance to ride cross-country and relieved that Colonel Mendenhall was sold on the idea. In addition, he agreed that I could take a long weekend in October, come back to Virginia, and ride Malakasia in the Chronicle Cup, the feature race at the Middleburg Fall Races. Feeling my luck was good, I pressed him for permission to attend the 1970 World

Championships, scheduled for Punchestown, Ireland. "We'll see," was his reply. I figured I was ahead of the game so far, thanked him, and hung up. Once again, my future would be determined by my results.

However, a few days later, that future took a decided turn for the worse when I got a call from the HQ CO First Sergeant: "You'd better come up here right away." This didn't happen every day. "Top" viewed the soldiers assigned to the USMPTC as perpetual irritants; we wore boots and breeches to work, not Army fatigues; we did not live in his barracks; we were excused KP and Guard Duty—and we always, but always, needed haircuts. When I reported in, I knew things were serious. Top did not stop to criticize my personal appearance; he just said, "Wofford, you've come down on a levy. I'm required to give you your official 30-day notice of transfer to a combat zone."

Maybe I wasn't going to escape overseas duty after all. The war in Southeast Asia was grinding up men and material, and the strain on Army resources was starting to show. The Pentagon would regularly "levy" various posts in the United States, seeking manpower for the conflict. Men who had at least thirteen months of eligibility remaining before their discharge were sent to Vietnam. It took the army two weeks to out-process personnel. The soldier was expected to spend twelve months serving abroad, then return state-side two weeks before separation from the active Army.

I had 15 months remaining in my enlistment, and thus a target on my back where the Personnel Office at the Pentagon was concerned. The army decided that they needed a replacement 91T40 (me) in Cambodia, where my new duties would be to inspect the meat going through the Quartermaster supply department. You can imagine this proposal did not blow my skirts up, and I hotfooted it back to the stables. I called Gail first, and told her my news, then reached out to Colonel Russell, who said, "Leave it to me."

Two days passed, and Colonel Russell was getting nowhere, so we asked Colonel Whiting to see what he could do. He likewise took a couple of days, then called and said it looked as if I was bound for Cambodia; he couldn't get me off the levy. I had one more card to play. I called Colonel Mendenhall but got the same response and the same results. Gail and I had just started to have discussions about what we would do next when I got another call from Top the following Monday, with the same message: come to his office soonest.

"Wofford, you must have friends in high places," he said when I walked into his office. I replied something along the lines of "Huh?" Top said, "I just got a call from the G-1's office at the Pentagon." (The G-1 is the General in charge of Army personnel anywhere in the world.) "The G-1's assistant told me you have just been declared 'Essential Personnel to the post' and your name has been removed from the levy." He went on to say that due to my new classification, I would be at Fort Sam Houston for the duration of my Army career; I could not be transferred. While I wandered out of his office in a daze, it didn't take me long to snap out of it, call Gail, then let Colonel Russell know my news.

Although I never followed up to identify my "friend in high places," I had a pretty good idea. You can bet Upland was glistening in the cross-ties whenever General Murdoch's office called to say he was going to ride that day. Once again, my family's circle of friends had reached out and touched my life. The kindness of a long-dead father to a young plebe at West Point 30 years earlier was repaid by a quiet word between two generals at the top level of the army. Once again, I could turn back to my riding career with renewed focus. Once again, another young man would go in my place, this time to Cambodia, and I would have to deal with my guilt at not going in person. Once again, I was standing in the shadow of the rainbow.

Destination: World Eventing Championship

——People had gone to a great deal of trouble on my behalf, and my results had to show those efforts were not wasted. With my immediate future secure, I could turn my efforts toward riding and competing. In late September, I had a successful ride on The Regent at the U.S. Intermediate Championships, placing third. As always, I was disappointed not to win, but thought third wasn't bad for a catch ride on a horse I had never ridden before. (At least it had turned out better than my 1966 catch ride on Duck Soup!)

My competition results were good enough that Colonel Mendenhall approved a trip to Virginia in October 1969 for me ride in a timber race, the Middleburg Bowl. Malakasia had been in training with Jill Slater, and she thought he had a good chance. I could (barely) make the weight of 154 pounds, and had dreams of defeating King of Spades, who was the best timber horse around. Mac was not the best jumper in the world, but he could go to the front and gallop away from the field. He had no finishing "kick," so I planned to break off sharply, get to the inside rail, and go as fast as we could for as long as we could.

My plan worked really well for the first two fences, but my stirrup leather broke landing over the third fence, sending me sprawling onto Mac's neck, desperately working to get back in the saddle. By now the field was galloping past me, going around a turning beacon and heading out toward the back side of the course, leaving me finally wiggling back into the saddle. Before I could get my reins organized, Mac turned inside the beacon, and galloped after the rest of the horses. By now, I was hundreds of lengths behind, so I retired in disgust. I had come a long way to pull up. (But I had a ball over the first three fences. Jumping solid timber at 800 mpm was a dream come true for me. That's about 30 mph, the next time you happen to glance at your speedometer.)

That evening, I got my first taste of Virginia hospitality when Erskine Bedford, the local MFH, invited riders, owners, and trainers to "Old Welbourn" for ham biscuits and hard liquor. I called Gail and Mom to reassure them that both Mac and I were fine, if disappointed. Mom decided to leave Mac in training with Jill Slater and try again in the spring. I called Colonel Mendenhall when I got back to Fort Sam Houston and he finally agreed that the World Championships were a good idea. In addition, he authorized six weeks of training in England ahead of the Championships, in order for me to compete in some horse trials and shows. Gail agreed this was my best possible chance at getting ready, and patiently agreed to stay in Texas until just before the event. When I told Mom of my plans, she decided to send along one of her young horses—Happy Plate—with Henry. It would be good experience for him and would give me a second horse to ride.

Coincidentally, Joe Lynch called me to ask if I would be interested in coming to Morven Park in Leesburg, Virginia to serve as the Director of Administration once I got out of the Army. This seemed like a good idea; I had gotten along well with Joe before the Mexico Olympics, he knew Henry, and he seemed pleased with the ride I had given The Regent and wanted that to continue. However, there was one big problem: money. I was an amateur in the eyes of the IOC, and I needed to retain that status if I wanted to compete in the Olympics.

AMATEURS AND "SHAMATEURS"

Here's the background (yes, another digression coming up): The modern Olympic Games were founded in 1896 with the motto of *citius, altius, fortius* ("faster, higher, stronger"). From their inception, the Modern Olympic Games were dedicated to the ideal of sport done for its own reward, and not for profit. This attitude can be attributed to either a high-minded attempt to speak to all the noblest and purest aspirations of the human spirit, or a shoddy attempt by upper-class white administrators and officials to keep lower-class athletes in their place. In 1961, when I first tried out for the USET, one had to maintain amateur status in order to retain eligibility. I made the squad four years later, and immediately became concerned about my status. I would need to keep an eye on it going forward, because I could only ride in the Olympics as an amateur.

In order to comply with the IOC rules, I became a "shamateur." Joe agreed to rent a small house for us and provide stabling for four horses. In return, I would ride and teach in the morning, and take care of administrative details. This was acceptable to the IOC—barely—so we agreed this was a good deal for both of us. I would be a shamateur for the rest of my riding career.

Joe owned a small training establishment in the U.K., in Kent near Gravesend, and would make that available to me while I was in training for Punchestown. With our plans for 1970 made, Gail and I could relax, take

Soon thereafter, legendary show-jumping rider Frank Chapot explained to me how to deal with the amateur rules. Riders could not be paid for riding horses or teach lessons for money—end of story. But riders could be reimbursed for their expenses, could buy and sell if they were quiet about it, and could run a facility where generous sums were paid for boarding, but lessons or training were no-nos. The availability of loopholes were immediately obvious to me.

Frank continued, saying that it was a bad rule because it encouraged people to cheat. There were really only two times my status could be called into question: my status could be challenged if I rode in a recognized competition as an amateur (for example, Amateur Owner hunters) or actually at the Olympic Games. The answers were simple: don't ride as an amateur and don't worry about my status at the Olympic Games. If I got there, they would not challenge my status, because we would then challenge their status; it was sort of the Mutually Assured Destruction détente of the IOC amateur rules.

Once I got out of the Army, I never again rode as an amateur. When I started my "working pupil" training program in 1971, I charged more than the going rate for boarding, which included lessons that were included in the board bill. I did not charge for lessons at competitions, but my expenses were generously reimbursed. I did not charge a fee for the few clinics I taught during that period, but once again my expenses were considerable. I wasn't getting rich, but I was paying for my own riding, and that was my goal at the time. Thus, I spent 20 years of my life as a "shamateur." ■

our young horses to shows, and generally enjoy life in Texas. I had a "personal best" that fall, when Johnny let me ride Galway Bay in the high jump class at the San Antonio Shriner Charity Horse Show. The show offered a $10,000 bonus for anyone who could break the world high jump record for horses, at that time 8 feet, 1¼ inches. Historically, horses could jump higher over purpose-built "high jumps" than they could over puissance walls. The high jumps were constructed with the top rails at an angle away from the horse, thus allowing more speed in the approach. There were several very good jumpers in the class who jumped 7 feet, while the rest of the class retired or withdrew. The horse with the best chance to break the record was a horse named Dear Brutus.

My horse, Galway Bay, was equally talented, but nearly unrideable in the ring. I had to get lucky with the takeoff stride, because there was nothing I could do to arrange the outcome. Dear Brutus and Galway Bay both cleared 7 feet, 6 inches, and I started mentally counting that $10,000. I didn't realize that my horse had taken advantage of the fact we were jumping PVC pipe, which would bend before it was knocked down. According to the photo, although he probably jumped an inch or two less than the measured height, the top rail bounced but stayed up—and I had officially jumped 7 feet, 6 inches. That's my story and I'm sticking to it. Things were going my way beginning the next attempt, until Galway Bay stood off a stride at 7 feet, 9 inches. He jumped 7 feet, 6 inches again, but hadn't noticed the top rail had been raised. It was a heck of a try, but not quite good enough. Brutus was the only horse left in the class; he got the prize money, but his rider wanted a chance at the bonus, so they raised the bar to 8 feet, 2 inches, which would be a new world record. Brutus came as close as any horse can. He rubbed the rail—it bent, but this time came down.

Anyway, it was a great night to be at a horse show.

By the fall of 1969, Gail and I were starting to think about life after the one more year I owed the Army. We had a family and several horses to plan for; the job at Morven Park sounded great, but it wasn't something we wanted to spend the rest of our lives doing. Meanwhile, I had it in the back of my mind that if Henry went well at Punchestown, the 1972 Olympics were not out of the question.

I knew Henry had been bought as a schoolmaster for me, but he was becoming far more than that. I did not show him a great deal during this period. I had plenty of other horses to ride, and I did just enough with Henry to keep him fit and interested. He would be 14 at the next Olympics, which at the time was considered too old for Classic competition. Only two other horses in history, Grasshopper and Paket, had ever competed in three Olympics. I resolved that if any horse could join that very exclusive club, it would be Henry. But to make that dream happen, I needed a good area for training. We talked about places that were suitable, including Far Hills (New Jersey), Unionville (Pennsylvania), and Middleburg (Virginia)—all "horsey" areas, with plenty of open country for hacking and galloping.

We decided on Middleburg because of my new connection with Morven Park. With our future plans made, I could concentrate on Henry and our trip abroad. Both horses shipped to Morven Park and had a couple of days' rest. I joined them in mid-July for a series of lessons with Joe Lynch before shipping out for England.

Making plans to ride in the World Championships was a much simpler process at that time than it is now. I called Fuddy Wing, executive vice president of the USET, and told him of my plans. He replied that my plans were fine with the USET, and that he would see me there; he had been invited to be on the Championships ground jury. Next I called the AHSA, which was the National Federation for the sport. Each Federation had to give permission for the international riders, and the AHSA office immediately agreed to send a letter to the organizing committee in Ireland. Once I made travel arrangements, I was good to go.

It's hard to imagine making arrangements to ride in the World Championships today with three or four phone calls, but eventing in 1970 was a different world. The USCTA had about 250 members, and once I left with Henry there would be no—repeat, no—upper-level horses in work anywhere in the United States. Henry was it. Mason Phelps would join me in Ireland, but his horse was at Lars Sederholm's yard in England. Mason would train there, then ship to Ireland with me. When the 1968 Olympic team had disbanded, the Team closed the eventing stables. Once again, eventers had no coach, no horses, no facility, no selection trials, no procedures, and no funding. Whatever happened in the eventing world would be privately supported. Fortunately for me, my mother was behind my efforts, and agreed to fund my trip.

I was able to accompany the horses to England, to make sure they had as good a trip as possible and arrived in good condition, but I was startled by a blast of warm air when the cargo door opened at Heathrow, near London. Part of the reason I wanted to ship to England so far in advance was to avoid the Texas summer heat. Naturally, England was stuck in a heat wave of its own, and I had to change my conditioning plans. Preparing a horse for an old-fashioned Classic championship was a serious endeavor; you had to start well ahead of time, and your horse's fitness was paramount. Any change in the temperature or the footing was a big factor.

Fortunately, the area where we stayed was quiet and suitable for hacking. I could trust my groom, Catherine Rowland, to do the hacking, while I did the technical work. I was spoiled for choice when it came to finding jumper classes and events to enter, and I soon took Happy Plate to a Novice event at Stoneleigh, England's national training center. It didn't take me long to find out I was under-schooled for the level. We had a couple of refusals but completed. Happy was green, but I persevered the rest of the summer, adding more cross-country practice at home. I planned a couple of events for Henry and was able to show in jumper classes at Hickstead. I never showed in the main arena, which was for international jumpers, but Happy was perfectly suited for the Novice series, and Henry thought the 3-feet, 9-inch Intermediate jumpers were made to order for him.

I could tell that both horses were going better and better over these courses. Curious about this, I went in search of Hickstead course designer Pamela Carruthers. She was world famous, having designed the signature Hickstead Derby course, as well as designing for well-known shows around the world. She was also good friends with my brother Warren and couldn't have been more accommodating. She explained her design theories, pointed out the differences in the height, spread, the distances between and the shape of her fences, then explained her reasons for various questions. I was intrigued with all this, and she enhanced my lifelong interest in course design.

At the time, Spillers, a horse feed company, sponsored a Novice jumper series in which Happy Plate was competing successfully. He was an attractive horse, and I got several offers to buy him, but Mom liked him and wasn't interested in selling. This meant I could keep showing him about once a week, which helped me get ready for Punchestown. Happy Plate went so well that he qualified for the Regional Finals, to be held a couple of weeks after the Championship. When I called Colonel Mendenhall and told him I was qualified for a big competition on my second horse, he readily agreed to extend my TDY to cover the extra time and wished me luck.

Another Debacle

—— Once we arrived at Punchestown and walked the World Championship course I would be tackling with Henry, I gulped and thought I would *need* luck to get around. The course was big, it was long, and Ireland was getting its usual share of rain, so the going was soft. This event was a serious test of horse and rider: 22 miles total, starting with Phase A, the 6,000-meter roads and tracks, lasting about 25 minutes at 240 mpm. This was followed immediately by a 3,450-meter steeplechase using the Punchestown race fences. These steeplechase "brush" fences averaged 3 feet, 7 inches high, and the horse could only brush through the top few inches. There were 10 of these fences, and at 690 mpm they would take a lot of jumping on soft ground.

Phase C, 15,600 meters, would take 65 minutes, and finally there was an 8,100-meter cross-country course, with a time allowed of 14 minutes, 12 seconds. (You can see why veterans of the Classic era smile when modern riders complain their horses got tired after eight minutes.) Our steeple-chase phase was almost as long as a modern cross-country course, and we would be on the cross-country course for almost twice as long. Although the times allowed for the Punchestown steeplechase and cross-country were 5 minutes and 14 minutes, 12 seconds, respectively, riders knew this was a nearly impossible standard. Most horses would take 15 to 17 minutes to complete the cross-country course. Each competitor wanted to ride as close as possible to the time allowed, but we knew we would have time penalties; the trick was to have as few as possible. My plan was the same as at Pebble Beach: I would let Henry choose his speed and concentrate on finishing rather than competing.

The 1970 World Championship cross-country course would look plain to the modern observer. There was little in the way of decoration, the materials used were skimpy, and the design was unsophisticated and, in a couple of instances, actively dangerous. The sport was growing and changing, but we still had a lot to learn. The ground juries were usually retired military officers who took an inflexible attitude toward the rules.

(For example, the Olympic jury in 1968 had refused to change the time schedule, even though they knew it would rain during the competition. The result was the Olympics were a debacle. Punchestown 1970 would be another debacle.)

At that time, courses were designed according to the terrain and used local materials. These are good design features, and still in use today, but the limits of horses' mental and physical abilities were still being explored. When those limits were exceeded, the results were disastrous; Punchestown is a good example.

The soft footing, combined with the extreme distance, guaranteed horses and riders would be tired by the time they got toward the end of the course. This explains some of the mistakes horses made. However, the course designer made mistakes as well. The entire course was big, but the difficult fences were in the last mile, and the *most* difficult was a quarter of a mile from the finish. Fence 29 was an oxer...with no perceptible height. The approach was through a dark wooded lane, with a guard rail at the lip of a drop. The oxer rail was suspended 6 feet away, with a maximum drop behind it of nearly 7 feet.

Horses did not read this question correctly; they had banked an obstacle a few fences before this, and the front part of the oxer was in the dark, while the back rail was well lit. To horses, it looked as if this were another bank jump, one that could be safely stepped on. All this is easy to understand in hindsight, but at the time our sport's learning curve was vertical. As soon as the cross-country started, it became obvious that 29 was a "bogey" fence. According to the final results, only 29 horses got that far—and 26 of them fell.

By the time I trotted into the vet box, Punchestown was shaping up to be the biggest disaster since the 1936 Berlin Olympics with its infamous water jump, where most of the competitors fell in deep water. Lars Se-derholm walked the Punchestown course with me and came across the vet box to give me some last-minute advice about footing, striding, and so on. (This was before the age of closed-circuit TV, so any information about how the course was riding was invaluable.) While Lars was briefing me, Simon Wallford, an individual Irish rider, approached with his left arm in a sling and his right hand offering me a bottle of port, cheerfully explaining he had fallen at Fence 29. In a wonderful Irish brogue he said he had broken his collarbone, but I would be all right, because "Kilkenny has been well and truly hunted." This did nothing to ease my mind, as the only time Tommy Brennan had taken Henry hunting, he had kicked the lights out of two cars passing him on the road and in general behaved like such an idiot that Tommy took him home.

Lars and Simon left me alone for the last few moments before I started. I mentally adjusted my approach at various fences, but resolved to stick to my overall plan. I would let Henry tell me how he felt, and take whatever time it took in order to finish. Besides, I wasn't so worried about Fence 29; it was Fence 28 that gave me the chills. A vertical with a drop behind, it was similar to fences where we had fallen in the Pan Ams, and I wanted to make sure we got over it safely. I would let 29 take care of itself.

Once on course, Henry was jumping well and my plan was working—but about two minutes from home, I could tell he was getting tired. This was not good news, and we still had to survive Fence 28. Suddenly a course controller stepped out, waving a red flag. Lorna Sutherland and Popadom had demolished Fence 29 and the crew were repairing it. The course was on hold, and he would tell me when they were ready for me to continue. In a vain attempt to make the fence safer, the jump judge had been stuffing branches and gorse into the fence each time horses landed on it, thinking this would make them jump over it instead. Naturally, horses saw the green filling, thought it was yet another bank, stepped on it, and wrecked it even more thoroughly.

The hold meant we got a 10-minute break, Henry caught his breath, and when we started again he grabbed the bit and set off even faster than before. Somehow, we slithered over Fence 28, and I turned into the path toward 29 convinced that Henry could jump anything in his path. I was correct about that, but unfortunately Henry made the same mistake as other horses in thinking he could bank the fence. Photos of my fall are spectacular, but I have never had a softer landing. Henry stepped onto the filling, which cushioned his arrival 6 feet below, and he calmly walked out through the shattered remains of the back rail of the jump. This fence had taken such a beating that the jump judge had been repairing the back rail with baling twine and his belt—thus, the Irish were the first to invent the frangible pin.

Meanwhile I had jumped to my feet and gotten a leg up into the saddle. None the worse for wear, Henry decided that as we were so close to home, we might as well jump the last three fences at a flat-out gallop. He threw in such a tremendous leap at the last fence that I was left behind, expecting another stride. My mother had been sitting nearby and asked me later if I had been hurt by my fall. I replied I was okay, I just could not believe Henry would stand off as far as he did, at the end of 22 miles. We both smiled and just shook our heads at being associated with such a magnificent creature.

I have already mentioned that the scoring system in use at the time was very complicated. When almost every horse has a fall, and an obstacle has to be rebuilt, the other competitors on course must be held. This causes mayhem computing the time scores, and I'm sure a lot of educated guessing was going on when they got to mine. The scores were so late in coming out that we all went back to our hotels, changed, and headed for the local golf club, where a black-tie competitors' party was in full swing. When we got there, the party had become a legendary brawl. We were having so much fun that nobody cared that the scores were late. At about eight-thirty, a damp mimeographed sheet was passed around that showed Henry and me in third place, with the fastest round of the day. What a horse!

Henry jogged out on Sunday morning as if he had been for a stroll in the park, and we jumped clean that afternoon with a couple of time faults to win the bronze medal. I had to stay and make sure Henry got back to England safely, and Gail and I (along with all the international riders) had been invited to foxhunt by the Master of the Scarteen Hunt, Thady Ryan. However, the real world had interfered with our activities: news arrived that Hillary had come down with some childhood malady, and Gail left for Colorado Springs early the next morning.

I only feel slightly guilty that I over-imbibed that night, and literally "woke up" as I pulled my head out of a drainage pipe, calling to Thady Ryan that I did not see a fox at my end. Standing up, I suddenly realized I was in some farmyard in the middle of Ireland, dressed in boots and britches, holding a nice-looking young Irish hunter...with no recollection of how I got there. It must have been some farewell party the night before; I'm sorry I missed it.

I could have gladly missed the hangover I suffered the rest of the day, but we shipped home safely, and I started a quiet period. This was welcome; I had been training and dieting intensely and felt I could take the next couple of weeks off before I took Happy Plate to the Regionals of the Spillers show-jumping competition.

My Brief International 'Chasing Career

____No sooner had the thought of relaxation—and a big, juicy sirloin—crossed my mind, when the phone rang. It was John Harty, calling from Ireland, asking me if I could "do 11 stone?" This was jargon from the steeplechasing world, meaning would I weigh 154 pounds with a racing saddle? (One "stone" is 14 pounds. Our eventing mandatory weight was "11 stone 11," meaning 165 pounds.) John, a leading jockey at the time, had broken his collarbone. Could I ride a handicapper named Ronald's Boy in a 3-mile 'chase next week in Northern Ireland?

I said "yes" quick as a flash. John told me to fly into Belfast, gave me an address to meet him the morning of the race, the deal was done, and I was back on my diet, thinking that John must have been impressed by my recent exploits at Punchestown.

Just as with eventing internationally, I needed permission to ride "under rules," that is, at a race held under steeplechasing regulations where public betting was allowed. My experience with the U.S. racing body was similar to my recent experience with the AHSA; I called the ruling body, the National Steeplechase and Hunt Association (later the NSA), explained my situation, and a voice at the other end said that would be no problem and good luck. I didn't realize how much luck I was going to need.

Landing in Belfast that morning, I hailed a taxi, showed him the address, and asked him to repeat his answer. I am comfortable with an Irish brogue, but the accent in Northern Ireland defeats me. It transpired my route would take me through downtown Belfast, where there was violent rioting on a daily basis. I had arrived in the midst of the "Troubles"—armed conflict between the Irish Republican Army and British troops. I told the driver to take the safest way, and he glanced at his watch. "Agh now," he said, "da boyz will still be in the pubs, won't dey? Sure an' we'll be safe enough." With that he took off like a rocket, straight through the "war zone" part of Belfast. Emerging safely the other side, he deposited me. John soon appeared, and we set off to meet Ronald's Boy, a 16.1-hand, roly-poly bay with a stripe and a cold, small eye. Then we walked the course.

The course was no joke: about 20 fences right-handed, over 3 miles of lovely Irish turf. I asked John how he wanted his horse ridden, and he simply told me to follow the leaders, and if I was in touch after the last I should hit him and try to win. This sounded sensible and I set off to change and check my weight. A jockey's weight is a serious consideration because the handicappers' rule of thumb is that a pound of weight equals a horse's length in a mile. The more weight assigned to a horse, the harder that horse's task. In addition, people are betting on the outcome, and officials guard against any transgressions. This suddenly became a problem. The scales I had been using in England to check my weight were "light," meaning I weighed more than I thought I did and was 5 pounds overweight. At that amount, the stewards would take me off the horse; this would cause a minor scandal, as one didn't accept rides if the weight allowed was too light.

"Not to worry," John reassured me, as he hastily handed me a 2-pound flat racing saddle, with one stirrup showing and no girth. Draping my number cloth over this, he said, "Try this." I made the weight, barely, and stepping down off the scales, asked John if I were to ride in a 2-pound postage stamp of a saddle. "Not at all," was his reply. Ronald's Boy appeared in the paddock wearing a proper steeplechase saddle. "In for a penny, in for a pound," I thought, as I threw my leg over and settled into the saddle.

You may have heard the famous advice about playing poker for money: If you sit down at the table, and don't see a sucker, you are the sucker.

As I sat on the saddle, quaking with nerves (I never got nervous before events, but racing elevated my pulse), I didn't realize my role in this little drama. *I* was the sucker. As we cantered down to the start, Pat Taffe, the leading steeplechase jockey at the time, came up alongside me and asked, "Nah den, Yank, what'll ya be gettin' up ta?" I replied that I was going to break off quietly, follow the leaders, and see what happened at the last fence. Satisfied I would not be a menace to the others, he headed toward the start line and circled under starter's orders. Ronald's Boy knew what was up, but was well schooled and waited his turn in the circle until we flattened out the line, approached the start, the tape lifted and the track announcer said, "An dey are auff."

An instant later I was nearly off in real time, as Ronald's Boy had blundered through the first fence like never before. Pushing myself back into the saddle and regaining my stirrups, I thought I had taken the wrong hold on him, and I would kick into a softer rein at the next. That didn't work either, and we hit the next fence almost as hard. I resolved to sit quietly and hold him to the base, so naturally he threw in a prodigious leap at the next. I was left behind so badly I think I felt my helmet hit him on the croup, but I'm not sure.

Thinking I could replicate the huge stand-off, I repeated my signals to Ronald's Boy, but this time he put in a horrible short stride, twisting like a corkscrew to stay up right. No matter what technique I tried, I could not get Ronald's Boy to jump well. What followed was nothing but a struggle for survival while I covered every hair on his body over at least one fence. This was the longest seven minutes in my life, one bad fence succeeding another, until finally we staggered through the last fence, crossed the finish line and pulled up. I collapsed on his neck, wheezing with exhaustion, while John ran up, grabbed his bridle and told me, "Don't get down yet." This was good advice, as I probably would have fallen on my ass if I dismounted right away.

Leading me in a circle, John kept up a running conversation, meanwhile with one eye on the clerk of the scales. My wind had come back, and eventually he stopped and told me it was okay to dismount. We unsaddled Ronald's Boy, who was still gasping for air, and I headed for the scales to weigh in. Just as I stepped on the scales, I remembered I was going to be over the announced weight, and thought, "Uh-oh." Sure enough, the balance beam on the scales went "clunk," announcing in no uncertain terms that I weighed 5 pounds more now than when I had weighed out.

As soon as the scales registered my weight, John grabbed my elbow and dragged me off the scales and around the corner. As we left, I heard the clerk of the scales yell after us, "That'll be enough of you, Harty," meaning the clerk knew John had fudged my weight when weighing out onto the course and would have him up on charges if he tried it again. All of this barely registered on me. I was weak and dehydrated from dieting to try to make 154 pounds, exhausted by my recent debut as an international steeplechase jockey, and adrenaline-depleted from the seven minutes of fear I had just lived through. Keeping up a lively chatter, John administered several glasses of port in an effort to get me rehydrated and stuffed me into a taxi headed back to the airport. By the time I truly woke up, we were landing at Heathrow.

So here's what I *think* happened. I say think, because we'll never know the truth.

The plot that had (unbeknownst to me then) begun with my ill-fated ride on Ronald's Boy thickened 10 days later, when I glanced through the racing newspapers and was amazed to notice that Ronald's Boy had won a big handicap steeplechase by several lengths—at odds of 30 to 1, with a well-known jockey aboard. I immediately called John and asked him if he had "put a bit down" for me, as a sort of courtesy. "Not at all," John replied; he didn't want me to lose my amateur status! Irish logic. My take on the situation is that John had a horse that obviously had a "key" to jumping well—one he had not shared with me. My guess is that without knowing it, I had been involved in a betting scam. John knew the horse would not jump well for me and would be lucky to finish at all. He had not counted on my weight problems, or on my "stickability," but both played into his scheme.

Ronald's Boy was coming back from a layoff but had run well in his last few outings before his break. After my ride, however, the next day's racing newspapers commented laconically on my efforts: "Ronald's Boy jumped erratically, never featured, finished seventh of 14 starters." After that display, what were Irish punters (bettors) to think? They would think, the horse is obviously not going well, so not worth a bet. Then the smart money comes in, those with insider knowledge. John, still with a broken collarbone, would have told the jockey, "Do this or that at your fences," and Ronald's Boy was a sure thing. At the last moment, John's brothers would have hustled to the window to make a sizeable bet, too late to affect the odds. (This was before pari-mutuel betting.) If they put down a thousand pounds at 30 to 1, well, you do the math.

You know what bothers me? It's not losing money I never had in the first place. There was little chance the stewards would set me down for overweight, especially after the clerk didn't call me back, thinking correctly that my weight had been a handicap, not an effort to ride too light. I am mildly chagrined at being involved in a betting scam but would have pleaded ignorance. What irks me the most out of all of this is that

I never learned the key to Ronald's Boy. John died a few years later of Lou Gehrig's Disease without ever discussing my experiences with me, and he took the key with him. I'll always wonder what it was.

But I was too busy to dwell on this. Happy Plate was getting ready for his big chance in the Regional Finals, and I was making reservations for all of us to go home.

My summer season ended anticlimactically: Happy Plate and I had two rails in the Regional, not the success for which I had hoped. I shrugged as we loaded the horses on the plane; he was young and there was always next year. Mom had arranged for Happy Plate and Henry to spend the winter with some Virginia friends of hers, Brigadier General Bryan and Ethyl Conrad. They had a farm near White Post and were glad to help. I should have looked into this situation more closely, but in the rush of returning to San Antonio, I overlooked the arrangements. This was storing trouble for me; I just didn't know it yet.

By now it was early October, and I returned to Army duty. However, I had saved up two weeks of leave, and checked out almost immediately. (Top made a mistake: he told me to get a haircut *after* he handed me my leave papers, not before. I skipped that part.) Gail and I drove Dr. Fuji, two Labradors, and all our possessions to Rimrock Farm. I showed Dr. Fuji at the Kansas City Royal Horse Show for a week, although not as successfully as Gail. She was losing her interest in horse shows, however, while her interest in raising Hillary grew.

We relaxed at Rimrock Farm for our second week of vacation, then I returned to Fort Sam Houston and prepared for civilian life. A quiet week or so of packing was followed by my "permanent separation" from the Army. Just as at Fort Dix, I had to make the rounds of various departments, but this time Top sent me off to get a haircut before he would sign the final papers. When I returned, newly shorn, he grunted and said at least I was rejoining the civilian world looking like a soldier. Then he handed me my final orders, and thus on *"7Nov70"* I rejoined the civilian world and left my Army career behind me.

Gail and I planned to spend Christmas at my sister and brother-in-law's house in Aspen before leaving to start a new chapter in our lives. ∎

__Horse Politics and International Competition, a Heady Brew

*I wasn't born here,
but I got here just as quick as I could.*

Anonymous

E very new chapter of my life seemed to start with one of my family's friends reaching out and taking care of us. That's why I wasn't at all surprised when my mother casually mentioned she had arranged for Fuddy and Neva Wing to take care of us in Virginia. I arrived in Virginia in early January 1971, driving a station wagon and pulling a Hartman two-horse trailer stuffed with worldly goods. Gail and Hillary arrived soon thereafter, and we became part of Fuddy and Neva's life for the next couple of weeks.

The Wings had bought a small horse farm just outside of Leesburg when Fuddy retired from the USET. This was handy for me, and I started work at Morven Park right away. It never occurred to me that a retired middle-aged couple wasn't in a big hurry to put up with a young married couple and a highly mobile two-year old. Dot and Gyp's hospitality and generosity at our farm in Kansas from years past were being paid forward.

As soon as I could, I drove the trailer over to the Conrads' farm in White Post to pick up Henry and Happy Plate, and encountered an unwelcome surprise. When the horses were led in from the pasture, I barely recognized them. Each had lost several hundred pounds, their ribs were showing, and their feet were in terrible condition. They were lethargic, their coats dull; they had obviously not been wormed, nor cared for in any way. General Conrad was embarrassed and explained that Mom had been explicit that the horses were to be completely turned out, with no grain to "get a good rest from a strenuous season." My plans for competing with these two horses had just changed; in fact, I was worried I might never get them back in shape. This was a terrible situation, but I had to make the most of it. I thanked General Conrad, loaded them and took them to Morven Park.

I explained what had happened to Joe Lynch, who agreed with my new plan. I would do my best to get Henry and Happy Plate back into shape, but any thoughts of riding in the National Championships that spring were on hold. I planned to feed them as well as possible, worm them, check their blood work, and generally nurse them back to health. Once they were shod they started a program of walking out, following the same general schedule I had developed in years past. They walked for increasing amounts until they could easily do two hours of walk six days a week. I then cut the walking back, but added some trotting on good footing, and mild canter exercise. After a couple of months of this, both horses started to look good again and my morale improved.

I had assumed a program such as Morven's would have a good black-smith available; this was another failure of my stable management, and I would pay a price for my lack of supervision. Happy Plate was only seven, and soon bloomed into full health again. Henry was now thirteen, and although his weight, coat, and general health improved, his feet were bothering him. I finally took him to New Bolton in Unionville, Pennsylvania, where staff farrier Jack Anderson restored him to soundness and I was able to put him back into more serious work. The USET eventing squad and its new coach, Jack Le Goff, were planning a trip to Burghley that fall. I was on the list—if Henry was sound and fit by then.

That Shortcut Thing AGAIN

___ I was busy at Morven—teaching in the morning, then riding my own horses. Gail had found a daycare center for Hillary and was able to ride a couple as well. I enjoyed teaching and felt a growing confidence in my methods. At the same time, however, I gradually realized Morven was not a good long-term fit for me. Mom was about to send more young horses back to Virginia, and we would need more stalls than Morven could provide. Despite the uncertainty, Gail and I had a good spring. The students at Morven (mostly late teens and early twenties) were great, and all were keen to learn. I competed The Regent for Joe, and another horse, Blue Moon, that spring. Happy Plate joined in the fun midway through the season.

The culmination of the spring eventing season was held at Fair Hill in early June 1971. Both the National (Advanced) and Intermediate Championships were offered, and I aimed all three of my horses at it. The distances were less than other Classics where I had competed due to the June heat, but the climate and the venue's hilly terrain would provide a severe test.

Once again, when we walked the course, we found a shortcut, this time on Phase B, the steeplechase. At the time, we used the racecourse in front of the grandstand for this phase. There were no mandatory flags at one end of the circular track, and if I jumped the infield I could cut out most of the distance, yet jump all the fences and go through all the mandatory flags involved.

Taking shortcuts was still a controversial practice and I knew there would be an uproar if I did this. When no flags had appeared at the north end of the course by Friday afternoon, I went to see Jack Fritz, the technical delegate, and explained there was a shortcut on Phase B, and I intended to take it. He asked if I was "going through all the flags," and I replied, "yes." "Well, okay," he replied. I knew that wasn't going to be the end of the affair. Fortunately, Johnny Russell had come back to watch, and I asked him if he had his international rulebook with him. When he said he had it, I said, "Good. Bring it with you and be at the end of the steeplechase when I finish with my first horse tomorrow morning." Johnny loved stuff like this and asked, "Why, what's up?" I replied, "Never mind, just be there."

Years later, I went back and walked the line I took to jump across the infield with all three of my horses. I must have been crazy. The inside rail of the racecourse was a white plank about three feet nine inches high set on top of black posts with no filling and no ground line; all in all, the thought of jumping it was a chilling prospect. I was a lot braver then; I jumped it on Blue Moon, finishing the course in half the allotted time. Sure enough, I looked back at the finish line as I gradually pulled up and the ground jury was standing in a group, obviously having a conference about how to eliminate me. My intent was to keep them from declaring me eliminated for "not following the track of the course." This had happened to another competitor a few years earlier in a different situation. The rider had won the appeal, but only after the competition was over; I didn't want to go through that, and Johnny was my ace in the hole.

I almost burst out laughing as I trotted by the group. The judges were waving their arms in the air and obviously agitated, but Johnny had his rulebook open to the relevant page and was vigorously tapping it with his finger. Jack Fritz, whom I had told the night before that there was a shortcut, hated disagreements. He was headed for his car, carrying his briefcase and walking like a two-year-old with a load in his diapers. He obviously had remembered an important meeting in "Somerselse."

I had expected a furor, and I wasn't surprised. Jack Le Goff approached me in the vet box while I was waiting to ride my third horse in what had quickly become 100-degree heat. He explained that the organizer (and benefactor) of the event was upset, and would I go and have a word with her. I replied, "Jack, I'll tell her anything you want—except that I was wrong." Jack visibly flinched and said maybe it would be better if he talked with her. I said that was a good idea, stepped up on my third ride of the day, and rode off to once again take the shortcut.

By the time I finished, I had ridden nearly 50 miles in heat that reached 100 degrees. Horses do not deal with heat and humidity as well as humans, and there were several overheated horses at the end of the cross-country. This was the first year that riders and vets used ice therapy—soaking the horse's neck, back, loins, and chest with ice water, scraping it off and repeating without letting the water stand on the skin—to cool horses off. I have no doubt the technique saved several horses' lives. Once again, the guiding powers had organized an event at the wrong time of the year under conditions that guaranteed horse abuse.

I was coming in for a good deal of abuse myself and was eventually declared a moral degenerate in an editorial in the *Chronicle of the Horse*.

I thought this was a serious misunderstanding of the nature of competition, but "Never complain, never explain" became my rule for dealing with the media, one that would be useful to me over the next few years as my life took some strange turns.

My moral degeneracy had earned me first and third place at the National Championships, along with the grand total of $750 in prize money, won on two very different horses. The Regent was a genuine little guy, basically a 16-hand pony. Blue Moon, a 16.3-hand Canadian three-quarter bred, had never evented before the spring of this year, and had been in one Preliminary horse trial, one Intermediate, and one Advanced before the National Championships. (We didn't go in for much in the way of qualifications in those days.)

Before I move on, I want to share one funny story from Fair Hill 1971.

I mentioned earlier that the heat on cross-country day was a problem for the horses. It affected riders as well. Kevin Freeman and I both had to diet in order to tack 165 pounds, which meant that by the time of the Saturday afternoon wine-and-cheese party we had not eaten since the night before and were both dehydrated, despite drinking gallons of Gatorade during the day.

We solved this at the party by skipping the wine and cheese and going straight to the rum and tonics, with limes for vitamin C. We were tucked into our third in 30 minutes and having a wonderful time. We were alive! I have enjoyed both the psychic payoff from success in an upper-level, big-time short format event—and the ecstatic joy one feels after completing a Classic. They are not even close. There is no sensation like completing a Classic cross-country phase. And when your horse has come out on top of the placings? Indescribable. Kevin was also feeling pretty good at Fair Hill because this was his only chance to qualify for the 1972 Olympic short list, and he and Good Mixture had come through under pressure.

Kevin and I were both veterans by now; both of us had won team and individual medals, yet both of us had also been at the bottom of the heap. We knew how lucky we were to be successful while riding nice horses—Kevin leading the Intermediate Championships and me standing first and third in the Nationals. We had done this on our own (Kevin coming all the way from Portland, Oregon), and neither of us had gotten any coaching to speak of. We were responsible for our own efforts, and now we were going to celebrate.

I mention all this as context for what happened next (and it's possible that alcohol also played a part). Jack Le Goff, our new USET coach, approached us with a glass of wine in his hand and a scowl on his face. "I need to speak with you two boys," he said. Remember, at this time Jack had not yet attained the mythic status his later results would produce. Kevin and I knew him slightly from our time together but to us he was a guy with a funny accent and a cigarette dangling from his lower lip, just another USET hired hand. Sure, when Jack coached the French team in Mexico, his rider had won the individual gold, but Jacques Guyon had ridden before the deluge, and even a blind pig finds an acorn. The U.S. team had beat Jack's team by a mile. We didn't feel we had anything to prove to him.

Jack pitched into Kevin first: "Kevin, you are riding terrible, your reins too long, you too fast are riding, and God for damn you are standing off too much!" This tirade was delivered in a French accent, with clouds of smoke surrounding us, and heightened by Jack's faulty use of American idioms. (His translations of French idioms into English weren't much better. We never did find out what "you are bicycling in the sauerkraut" meant.)

Kevin is the mildest of men. He held a sheet of paper in one hand and with his other hand he quietly tapped Jack on the chest, saying, "But, Jack..." Undeterred, Jack continued his rant. Kevin tried again, "But, Jack..." to no avail. Kevin finally grasped Jack's shoulder and firmly said, "But, Jack…!" Stalled in mid-sentence, Jack said, "What is it, Kevin?" Kevin pointed to the score sheet in his hand. "But, Jack, I'm in first." In a split second I was doubled over with laughter, and Kevin was waiting with a small smile of satisfaction. "I will talk to you two boys later," Jack blustered, and stormed away. Our first critique had not gone well. I didn't realize it, but more was to come. I didn't worry about that, because I had so much change going on in my life.

Unintentional Trendsetter Me

——Change was my only constant at this time. Gail and I moved 10 times in the first 10 years of our marriage, so she and Hillary had been dragged around the country. Yet wherever we were, whenever I was through in the stables for the day, I came home to a well-ordered household, with Hillary running down the steps to tell me about *her* day. I was adjusting to my new role as a father, and her youthful voice helped me settle into my life with a family.

I needed to adjust to other roles too; my increased exposure in the sport led to increased involvement in the world of horse politics. Neil Ayer's election as president of the USCTA in 1971 was like a bolt of lightning to U.S. eventing. He energized every aspect of our sport, and certainly deserves his place in the Hall of Fame. He asked me to serve as secretary of the Association shortly after his election, and I agreed. Jack Fritz (another future Hall of Famer) asked me to serve on the AHSA Events Committee about the same time. He was determined to start a "youth revolution" on the committee, which—like the USCTA—had become moribund. The other "youth revolutionaries" who were to serve with me were Roger Haller, Denny Emerson, and Denis Glaccum.

These commitments launched my career as a horse politician, a long and complicated career that paralleled the changes going on in the horse world. I was to spend the next 30 years of my life arguing on conference calls, reading and answering memos and minutes, and enduring endless committee meetings. My involvement in what Gail called "the alphabets" (AHSA, USCTA, USET, FEI, USOC, IOC) was lengthy, tangled, and time-consuming. But at this point, I was about to introduce a new concept into the U.S. eventing scene—without even knowing it.

Gail and I did not feel "at home" in the Leesburg area, despite Fuddy and Neva's best efforts. Gail was unhappy with Hillary's daycare situation, and my young horse operation was about to expand to an extent that exceeded my arrangement with Joe Lynch, who was growing disenchanted with me anyway. He viewed me as a threat to his job and was under increasing pressure to have his horses ridden by someone other than a moral degenerate. We agreed to part ways, and I moved our horses to Colony Farm, a facility east of Middleburg recently known as Fox Chase Farm.

Colony Farm was a barebones boarding operation: you rented stalls by the day, week, or month for a dollar a day, and provided your own bedding, hay, and grain. I had been intrigued with Lars Sederholm's "working student" business model in England and started to take in working students. This sort of financial arrangement was okay with the IOC, as I wasn't getting paid for riding or teaching, but rather for boarding horses. To me it was a distinction without a difference, but as long as I could be a shamateur, I was good to go.

This working student concept was new to the United States, and word quickly got out about my new program. Don Sachey, who had just graduated from Morven Park, signed up to become my first working student.

(Don won a gold medal at the World Championships three years later, and I have been bragging about him ever since.) Unbeknownst to me, in the summer of 1971, I had tapped into a coming trend. I rented seven stalls when I moved into Colony Farm—for Henry, Dr. Fuji, Happy Plate, Harty Manor—yes, *that* Harty Manor, who since you saw him last had broken Gail's knee and given her a serious concussion—a new young homebred named Clodomir, Don's horse, Landmark, and a tack stall. (I've been asked why Harty Manor was still in the picture, given the trouble he caused. The simple truth was, we couldn't sell him; he hung around like a bad cold.) A year and a half later, I had 36 horses in training. If it's better to be good than lucky, it's even better to be lucky and first. When you are in the shadow of the rainbow, stuff like that happens.

Both good and lucky depend on organization, and I flunked my first test in that regard. The afternoon of my first day at Colony Farm the horses were fed, the tack room was organized, everything was spick and span, and Don had left to find some dinner. All alone, I stepped up to the brand new whiteboard I had mounted outside the tack room, picked up the erasable pen, looked at the board—and had no idea what to write down for the next day's exercises. My stomach sank as I realized I was now on my own, and responsible for other people as well as myself.

I spent several hours at my kitchen table that night, and when I showed up early the next morning I had plans for today, this week, this month, and the entire season for each horse. I might not be a very good trainer, but I would be well-organized. I was going to need that organization, as the number of horses and riders I was responsible for shot up. Meanwhile, my riding workload increased when Gail told me we were about to have another baby, and she needed to cut back on her time in the saddle.

U.S. Eventing Explodes

—— I also had to organize both my green horses and my working students in order to attend the new events that were springing up in the Mid-Atlantic region. Lana du Pont was organizing the Middletown Pony Club Horse Trials in Middletown, Delaware, and Trish Gilbert was putting on the Blue Ridge Horse Trials in Boyce, Virginia.

While still at Morven Park, I had attended the inaugural horse trials at the Radnor Hunt Club in a driving rain in the spring of 1971. Mom drove her Winnebago from Kansas, and I parked it on the hill where she could sit, smoke, and—when the rain lifted—watch the dressage. Radnor had not yet installed any rings, and the grass field where the dressage was held quickly became a sea of mud. I finished my test on Clodomir and ducked back into the Winnebago to get out of the rain for a minute. I soon had plenty of company. (You never know how many friends you have until you show up in a mobile home stocked with beer, wine, and booze—and the weather at the event is horrible.)

Mom said, "Well, when I watched your test, I didn't think it was very good. But then I saw a few others, and maybe yours wasn't so bad after all." This was the first of several events I won at Radnor over the next 20 years. The members of the new Radnor organizing committee—Vita and Dick Thompson, Ann and Art Zimmerman, Marilyn and Anson Taylor, Sheila and George Hundt, Charlotte Thayer, and Kate Jackson—all became ardent supporters of eventing, and helped make the sport what it is today.

Although my own responsibilities were expanding even as the sport was exploding, the growth was in its early stages at this point and I was free to plan for a Team-sponsored trip. Jack had gotten USET funding for a training squad to spend a month in England, preparing for Burghley in

September. The five riders named to the list included four international rookies—Roger Haller, Jimmy and David Powers, and Bruce Davidson—plus me as the supposed steadying influence. We were scheduled to leave the first of August, compete in a couple of horse trials, and wind up our trip at the Burghley Horse Trials. At the time, Burghley was not built to the same standard as Badminton, so it was a good introduction to international competition for young or inexperienced horses and riders. I was thrilled at the prospect; I had heard a great deal about the event, and definitely had it on my bucket list.

This plan went out the window when my phone rang early one July morning. It was Jack telling me to pack myself and my horses. I replied that I had indeed started packing and was excited about our upcoming trip to England. Nope. The U.K. had reacted to the Venezuelan Equine Encephalitis (VEE) epidemic raging throughout the United States by suddenly closing its borders to all horses from the Americas (North, Central, and South). The Canadian authorities were closing their borders tomorrow—and Jack wanted us over the border by then. I had to have Henry and Clodomir at Gladstone before Hennessey Van lines left at six that evening. Jack was determined to take a team on the road, and if I wanted to make the training session, I had to hustle.

Bill Wofford, who had helped me at Pebble Beach two years previously, had rejoined me. I started him packing the horses and tack while I called Gail to tell her about the sudden change of plans. I came back to the house we were renting on Edwards Ferry Road (just beyond where the Leesburg Costco is now located), packed, and returned to the stables. Six hours later we were loading our horses and trunks onto the Team's van at the USET. Six hours after that we cleared the Canadian border and headed for the shores of Lake of Two Mountains, west of Montreal in Quebec, where somehow Jack had miraculously arranged stabling for the horses, plus housing for the riders and grooms.

Our Unplanned Canadian Interlude

——Our horses were in a nice stable in the country, with miles of hacking on sandy soil (without stirrups, of course), and a rudimentary ring for technical work. We didn't need much in the way of facilities, as Jack planned an active competitive schedule for us. Over the next four weekends we would alternate weekend dressage shows with jumper classes, and finally ride in a one-day event two weeks before the Eastern Canadian Championships.

This was a very productive summer for me. I got lessons each day on Clodomir and Henry with Jack, and felt much more confident about my dressage work. Jack's English was improving, although he ran into a roadblock when he went to a local farmer to buy hay for the horses. We were in French-speaking Quebec, and Jack had assumed he would be able to converse in French with the locals. He showed up in a while, asking me to come with him. "Jimmy, I can't understand his God for damn French accent, and he can't understand my English. You come interpret for me." After a while we got it worked out.

The hardest part of the whole summer happened two weeks before the Canadian Championships when Jack entered us in the Eastern Canadian Dressage Championships, a four-day show. We rode each of our two horses in four classes a day—by memory. Jack would not let us have the test read aloud, which provoked grumbling acceptance from us. There was method to his madness, and I noticed that Henry was a little bit more rideable each day until, cantering down the center line on the fourth day, I no longer felt as if I were sitting on a powder keg with a lit fuse. Henry was back to himself, healthy and bursting with energy, seemingly recovered from his horrible experiences of last winter. Punchestown had provided soft going the previous year and this summer the sandy Canadian soil suited his footing preferences.

Once we got to the Canadian Championships, Jack gave me little direction about how I was to ride the cross-country course, remarking that he was more concerned that we jump well than if we made the time. This suited me, and I resolved to follow the same plan I had used in every event to date: I would let Henry pick the pace, and nurse him home if he got tired. I was interested in Henry's fitness. We had competed over much the same Canadian course as a preparation for Mexico, and he had gotten tired about half a mile from the finish. When I finished this time, Henry's breathing was easy, and he was still full of run. This gave me confidence in Jack's new "interval training system." A good placing didn't hurt, either, and I felt good about my chances for the 1972 Olympic team.

The rest of the U.S. horses finished well, with a skinny young rookie named Bruce Davidson showing his extraordinary talent by winning his first international event riding Plain Sailing ("Sam"). Jack, already feeling the pressure of producing a team for the Munich Olympics, was determined to accelerate the learning curve of the rookies on this Canadian trip and drove them relentlessly, Bruce especially.

Bruce's ride was a great gentleman, but Sam also had a sense of humor. When practicing dressage, he stood like a statue at the halt for Jack but invariably pranced, piaffed, and passaged with Bruce. Jack verbally abused Bruce unmercifully, but nothing improved the situation until, in desperation, Jack had Bruce feed Sam a sugar cube each time he halted correctly. Bruce would canter down the center line of our practice arena, halt, and—instead of saluting—reach down and hand Sam some sugar.

This produced a miraculous change in Sam's behavior. However, the improvement only lasted until the big day, when Bruce halted and saluted to begin the first international dressage test of his career. As Sam saw Bruce's right hand go past the corner of his eye, he ripped the reins out of Bruce's hands, looking for sugar. Neither Jack nor Bruce ever thought it was as funny as the rest of us did. Although Jack grumbled about Bruce's halt—and about everything else—he had to be secretly pleased at the progress we had made, and confident that the United States would have a competitive team for the Olympics.

Jack Le Goff: A Worthwhile Digression

Jack's training system had certain weaknesses at this stage in his career. His show-jumping advice was rudimentary, and his cross-country insight was limited. I had been so impressed with Lars Sederholm that I rarely listened to others. In addition, the show-jumping advice I had gotten from Bill Steinkraus, Johnny Russell, and Bert de Némethy suited me well. However, Jack already displayed two of the traits that would put him in the Hall of Fame a decade later. He could get horses fit while keeping them mentally and physically sound, and he could train fit Thoroughbreds to do dressage. Jack trained during the era of the Classic format, and most of our horses were Thoroughbreds or nearly so. Given the scoring system in use at the time (with its emphasis on cross-country), this was a formula for success.

Admittedly, Jack had excellent credentials, having ridden in two Olympics (1960 and 1964) himself, and then having coached the individual gold medalist in the 1968 Olympics. He had been a successful steeplechase jockey earlier in his career, then spent ten years at the Cadré Noir, the French national military riding academy.

AN INTERMITTENT SYSTEM

Jack Le Goff's interval training system should really be called an intermittent system. He had devised a way of giving his horses more exercise than in other methods, but the work was broken up into shorter periods. Other trainers (notably Noel Jackson) had experimented with an interval system, but had based it too closely on human research, which used short periods of maximum effort to produce fitness. A true interval training system was guaranteed to make horses lame. Humans will "self-monitor,"

Most people do not know that Jack was also a combat veteran, having fought in the Algerian war during the early 1960s. It was only in the last few years of his life that he spoke of it to me; he was obviously moved and changed by his experiences and tortured by his memories. Combat survivors whom I knew rarely talked about their experiences. Bill Steinkraus, who had fought in the Pacific during World War II, once mentioned to me the only thing that combat taught him was that no matter how tired you were, you could always put one foot in front of the other. Art Zimmerman, a U.S. marine who also survived World War II in the Pacific, kept a photo of the beach at Iwo Jima by his shaving mirror, where he could see it every morning. When asked about it, he replied that he kept it there to remind himself how lucky he was, to have one more day and the chance to do something good that day. A fellow combat survivor, Jack had much the same attitude—every day was a gift, and he would live it to the fullest. To Jack, this meant that he trained and rode all day with indefatigable intensity and then ate, drank, smoked (like a chimney), and partied well into the evening.

meaning if they feel something wrong in their muscles or joints, they will ease themselves. Horses do not self-monitor—and the better the horse, the less likely he is to hold himself back. A good horse will hurt himself trying to do what you ask. The old-fashioned description of a Thoroughbred was that a true Thoroughbred would never quit; he would gallop until he died. Jack avoided the potential for lameness by intermittent, rather than maximum, exercise.

As I trained with Jack over the next decade, this system became more sophisticated and specific. The gallops he used to train the Team horses in 1971 were very different from the works we utilized in 1981. Jack was never satisfied with his riders' performances, and he was hard on us. What I came to realize was that he was secretly as hard on himself and was continually changing and improving his techniques. ∎

I am sad that video was not in general use while Jack was still riding, because in a film of him on horseback you would have seen an exemplar of the lightness and sensitivity of the classical French system. Jack expected you to solve your own problems, but occasionally he would ride your horse for a few minutes. When he stepped down and you got back on, you were sitting on a different horse. Karen Stives once complained how difficult her Advanced horse, Silent Partner, was to ride. In his inimitable accent, Jack replied, "Oh, daahling, I vould put him in passage and piaffe in one week." She jumped down, handed him the reins and said, "I bet you a case of champagne you can't."

One week later and one case of Moët & Chandon champagne poorer, she watched as Jack rode a 20-meter circle around her with the snaffle reins in one hand and a cigarette in the other, and alternating between passage and piaffe with invisible aids. I later asked Patrick Lynch, the Team stable manager at the time, about this story. He confirmed that Jack worked the horse for six days behind closed doors in the indoor arena, and that Silent Partner was not sweating and bore no spur or whip marks after an hour of schooling. I was not surprised by this, as years before I had ridden Foster at the USET after Jack had taught Foster to passage and piaffe. Jack just did it to amuse himself, and to have a horse his Advanced students could ride in order to feel truly elevated gaits.

Looking back, I don't envy Jack the situation he found when he arrived in the United States in late 1970. The Gladstone eventing stables were deserted, and veteran U.S. riders were running their own programs in various parts of the country. Mike Plumb had already ridden in three of his eventual eight—yes, eight—Olympics. Kevin Freeman and I were successful Olympic and World Championship veterans, but I was starting a program in Virginia and Kevin was helping his family run J.A. Freeman and Sons in Portland, Oregon. As far as we were concerned, Jack had to prove himself to us. This attitude guaranteed some spectacular clashes behind the scenes, but Jack gradually realized as we trained together that he had a few experienced riders who wanted to win as badly as he did, and we realized that Jack was a consummate horseman. Thus began what some refer to as the "Golden Era" of U.S. eventing.

There are many reasons for competitive success; certainly, good horses and good riders are a part of it. But Jack was a rare mixture of sensitive horseman, ruthless human disciplinarian, shrewd sports psychologist, and classical dressage trainer.

You cannot point to one element and say, "That's it." This is especially true of Jack Le Goff, who may have been the most complicated person I have ever known. His ability to train a horse to a high level in dressage was a skill missing in the U.S. eventing world when he first arrived. His steeplechase experience gave him unusual insight into working horses at speed. Jack was a severe taskmaster. One of his favorite sayings was,

"I am not your friend; I am your coach." This was difficult for some to understand, but my military upbringing made me comfortable with it; I had just been through that sort of relationship with Johnny Russell. When Jack was through training for the day, he would revert to informality and would once again show you how to take the top off a champagne bottle using a cavalry sabre, and let you practice until you too learned the skill. Some 50 years later, I can still do it.

Jack remained my coach after I had trained with him for a few years, but he also became my friend, and remained so until the end of his life. We had some rough times and some hard words ahead of us, however, before we came to an understanding.

After the Canadian Championship I went back to Colony Farm, a new shipment of homebreds from Kansas, and my growing working-student operation. Mom's homebred Malakasia, who appeared in this narrative earlier, had come sound after some time off, and Jill Slater said he had a good chance in the New Jersey Hunt Cup. Encouraged by this, Gail and I drove up to Moorland Farm racecourse, near Gladstone. This was a bit of a homecoming for us, as we had lived in the vicinity for two years and had made a lot of friends. Jill was a marvelous trainer, and Mac looked to be in peak condition; the race would be competitive, but we were joint favorites with Johnny Fisher aboard Island Stream. I came as close as I ever will to winning a big-time timber race that afternoon. Johnny Fisher and Island Stream beat Mac and me by a length. Johnny was a better jockey than I was, and Island Stream was faster than Mac, so I was satisfied with our results.

Unfortunately, the next morning Mac once again jogged out unsound and Mom and I decided to retire him. He was too big and too much on his forehand to withstand the speed of timber racing; he did not owe us anything, so he lived out his days at Rimrock Farm. Soon afterward, we had Thanksgiving at the farm, then Gail and Hillary went on to Colorado Springs to await our new addition with Gail's parents. I flew back to Virginia for the next few weeks, then joined them for Christmas and a week of skiing before returning to Virginia—and the New Year. This was the last vacation I would have for some time, as I was about to go into training for the 1972 Olympics.

International Sport and Epidemics

——Jack's plan was shaped by the still problematic VEE epidemic. Horses could travel to the U.K. once again, but the borders would close March 1. (VEE is insect-borne. Horses could travel while the weather was cold, but we would not be allowed to travel abroad once insects came out.) If the USET wanted to get its dressage, show jumping, and eventing horses to Munich, they would all have to be in Europe by the end of February.

Jack was ready to make lemonade out of this particular bag of lemons. His plan involved five riders and as many horses as he could scrounge up. Beginning in March, the eventing squad would be based in England and take advantage of several horse trials there. The spring training season would culminate at Bramham, a full-scale event in Yorkshire.

There was only one problem with this plan: I didn't agree with it. Henry had gone very well in Canada, but I could sense a diminution of his energy and a lessening of his interest. He was still wonderful, he could still jump the moon, but he was fourteen. Only two other horses had ever participated in three Olympic games, and they had not competed as much overall as Henry. In addition to his Olympic record he had done two Badmintons, two World Championships, and two National Championships, plus innumerable horse trials and shows. He was still sound after all this and had a fair chance of getting to Munich. However, it wouldn't do to arrive there with a horse that was burned out. I decided I wouldn't compete with Henry that spring, but would keep him in light work, with an emphasis on his dressage. I felt that he only had one big effort left in him, and I wanted that to be at the Olympics.

I explained all this to Jack in a telephone conversation and added that the Gladstone training session was not working for me because Gail was due in late January. She was in Colorado Springs with her family, and I would join her there.

It wasn't my first disagreement of this type with Jack. He and I had gotten off to a rocky start in 1970 about my participation in the 1971 Pan American Games in Cali, Columbia. I had dug in my heels, refusing to go to Cali as an individual representative, and Jack finally gave up on me. Our latest confrontation was a continuation of that argument, with Jack accusing me of not being a team player, and me accusing him of abusing my horse for his purposes.

The battle lines were drawn. For my part, I was about to become a father for the second time, and I needed to be there. If I had to go to England and compete during the spring as part of the Olympic selection process, I would withdraw my name from consideration. I knew Henry needed careful management to get to Munich, and part of that management was to save him until late summer. If Jack wasn't on board with my plans, he would have to go on without me.

Jack replied that this was exactly what would happen: the team would go to England as planned, and I could kiss my Olympic dreams goodbye. My final statement was that I had already been to the Olympics, and would like to go again, but I knew my horse better than anyone alive, and he had one big competition left in him.

I hung up thinking that my dream of Henry going to the Olympics for a third time was dead. I was sad, but strangely accepting of the situation. I had done everything I could. If I used him in the spring, I was sure that Henry's competitive career would end before the Games, and I would have spent a good part of the year engaged in an effort that was doomed to failure. That wasn't written down anywhere in black and white, but I knew my horse.

None of this mattered, because Jack called me the next morning with a compromise. First, I would attend the two-month training session at Gladstone in January and February. As Jack pointed out, Gail was in Colorado Springs and well taken care of by her family. If anything went wrong, or if the baby started to arrive, I could be on a plane immediately. When the team shipped to England, Henry would be on the plane with the other horses. The other members of the training squad—Kevin Freeman, Mike Plumb, Bruce Davidson, and Jimmy Powers—would travel to England with the horses and participate in the spring events. Jack would keep Henry in light work during the spring. I would join the squad in early July and go into training for the Munich Olympics, which would take place in late August and early September. If Henry was still sound at the end of our training, there was a good chance he would go to his third Games.

I had discussed my thinking with Gail throughout this process, but she had left all the final decisions to me. After talking Jack's proposal over with her, I called him back later that day and signed on to the new plan. Gail and Hillary moved to Colorado Springs, where she could be close to her family—and her doctor—that winter. I kept the horses in light work and made progress with my working student program. Early in January I shipped Henry, Happy Plate, and Clodomir to Gladstone for the winter training session.

Kevin and I claimed the corner room, and settled into the strangely monastic existence of the Gladstone era. Because we were always dieting, we skipped breakfast, grabbed a cup of coffee, and scrambled downstairs for the first set of the day. We shared access to Nautical Hall with Bert de Némethy and the jumping team, as Bert was holding a training session for the jumpers at the same time—and we were all cold. (As I've mentioned before, don't believe your local weatherman; Gladstone is one of the coldest places in the world in January and the indoor arena, Nautical Hall, is the absolute deep freeze of the horse world.)

We rode two sets in the morning and one set after lunch. Then Kevin and I went for a jog and started planning dinner. Because we also skipped lunch every day, by now it had been a long time since dinner the night before, and we made extravagant plans for a steak and baked potato. It is possible a bottle of red wine figured in there as well. We got a *per diem* from the Team because we were at an official Olympic training session, and Kevin and I figured that if we skipped two meals, had a nice dinner, then the next day skipped two more meals and had some wine with cheese and crackers the second night, we could make the per diem work out financially.

What can I say? We didn't know much about proper dieting, and we were willing to do anything it took to lose weight. Being hungry was worth it, if it made life easier for our horses. Our lifestyle meant we had no trouble falling asleep at night, so it took our stable manager, Patrick Lynch, a while to wake me up in the middle of one night; my sister was calling to tell me I had reservations for Colorado Springs on the next plane out of Newark. Gail was at the hospital, and our next addition to the Wofford family was on the way.

Leaving it to Kevin to explain my absence to Jack, I landed in Colorado Springs on February 12, 1972, to meet Jennifer, who by that time was sleeping contentedly in her mother's arms. Just as with Hillary, and her mother before her, I fell instantly in love, and that has never changed.

I spent a few days in Colorado Springs, but Jack was leaning on me to get back to Gladstone. I flew back, leaving my family behind, because I felt guilty about the deal I had made with Jack (that I would train with the team until the horses left, but then skip the entire spring session). Meanwhile, the other riders were going to spend months away from home, chasing their Olympic dreams, while I slept in my own bed. The least I could do was return for the rest of this training session.

By the end of February, the Team horses were ready to ship out and the trunks were packed. Only one thing remained: a going-away party in the Gladstone trophy room. Like his riders, Jack had a "work hard, play hard" attitude, and it was time to play. This entailed copious amounts of wine, an indifferent casserole, paper plates, plastic glasses, and loud music. There were probably fifty people packed into a room not designed for large groups of rowdy riders and friends. The only answer was for the

MY RED-HAIRED TEMPER

Kevin picked me up at the airport when I returned to Gladstone after Jennifer was born, and he set the scene for me: he had a practical joke ready, if I would play along. The jumpers were training at the same time as we, and one of the rookies, a young kid named Robbie Ridland, had the dorm room directly across from us. He knew why I was away and had put a "Zero Population Growth" poster on my door. At first he was very pleased with himself, thinking it was a huge joke, but then had second thoughts and anxiously asked Kevin if I would think it was funny. Kevin played it glass ceiling of the ground-floor rotunda to become a dance floor. In a flash the ceiling was subjected to forces the architects had never envisioned. We had a disco apocalypse going on, with a potential 30-foot fall to the floor of the rotunda below if the glass broke. It's a good thing Bert de Némethy wasn't there; he would have had heart failure.

Late in the evening, I looked down through the dance floor/rotunda ceiling toward the door to the men's room on the main floor and got sober in a hurry. I had noticed some time ago that Jack was no longer around, and now saw his faithful dog lying with her nose to the men's room door, obviously waiting for him to come out. Jack had tried to keep it quiet that winter, but he had a little problem with his heart, and the doctor told him to take it easy. Jack's idea of taking it easy meant he would only drink red wine, no white wine or hard liquor. With this on my mind, I hurried downstairs and went into the men's room to find Jack sprawled out on the

perfectly—"Yeah, Woff has a great sense of humor, most of the time...of course, he can be a little strange, with his red-haired temper and all, but he'll be fine. Probably."

Thus forewarned, I entered the staircase swearing at Kevin in a loud voice, telling him what a bad flight I'd had, how rude the airline staff were, and so on, all interspersed with profanities and obscenities. My volume increased until I got to my room at the end of the hall; standing outside my door, I went silent. Into the pregnant pause that followed, I dropped both my suitcases,

which made loud noises that echoed down the hallway...boom...and then... boom! "All right," I asked Kevin in an enraged voice. "What sort of person would think that was funny?"

Kevin, already doubled over with laughter, mumbled an unintelligible reply. I continued in this vein long enough to grab Robbie's door, wait until Kevin caught up with me, then we both burst into his room, roaring at the top of our voices. Robbie turned white until he realized we were laughing hysterically at his reaction. He laughed and admitted that the prankster had been pranked! ■

cold tile floor, sound asleep. I asked him the usual questions about what's up, how ya doing, and so on. When I got him to his feet, I realized that he was way beyond inebriated. In a thick French accent, he stated, "Dis eees a restroom, I came down to rest." I agreed with this logic, loaded him and his dog into the other seat of my two-seater, and took him home.

The rest of the team was under the weather the next morning, and I didn't feel so good myself, but Jack appeared on time and continued preparations for shipping out. I went downstairs to the eventers' stables, patted Henry one more time, explained the situation to him, and headed back to Virginia, where Gail, Hillary, and Jennifer were waiting for me.

Our growing family made it clear that the small log cabin we rented in Leesburg was too small, and we had to move again. Our horses were in Middleburg and the childcare resources in that area suited Gail much better, so we rented a house south of Middleburg. By now we were experts at moving, and we quickly settled into Gone Away Farm, where I busied myself with our young horses and my growing working student program. I rode a few point-to-point races, but better riders got to ride faster horses, and I had to content myself with the experience of riding at speed over fixed fences, rather than winning.

I heard little from Jack during this time. International phone calls were expensive, email had not yet been invented, and he and I were both indifferent letter writers; I figured that no news was good news. Gail and I were selling just enough of the Rimrock Farm young stock to keep the stable operations moderately profitable, and my students were becoming successful. I'd like to think this was due to the brilliance of my work, but it certainly helped to have the first operation of this type. Where prospective students were concerned, I got the pick of the litter for the first couple of years, which gave them a leg up on their competitors.

Because my operation was more of a training facility than a show barn, the competition horses ran in an early June Classic at the Potomac Horse Center, then my program went quiet for a while. They needed a break, and I was headed for England.

It's England, so the Weather Is Bad

———Flying into Heathrow Airport near London, I met Kevin, who had been on vacation in Oregon and was eager to get back to work. We traveled by train to York, in Yorkshire, where Patrick Lynch picked us up, took us to the stables, then showed us where we would be living for the next month. Knowing that Kevin and I were comfortable rooming together, and being short of beds at the stables, Jack had put the two of us at a farmhouse a couple of miles away. This gave us some privacy; even better, Jack gave us the team's car to drive back and forth to work.

We soon developed our routine. First day: ride all morning, take care of building jump exercises for the following day, skip lunch (yes, we were "dieting" again, if starving yourself is dieting) drive back for a nap, jog a few miles on the back roads of Yorkshire. Then we would gnaw on some hard cheddar cheese wedges and take a hot bath, accompanied by a stiff jolt of single malt whisky. Combined with the exercise we had taken that day, the whisky and warm water had us in bed and snoring before long.

The second day in our routine was our favorite. Once again, we had done a "cost-benefit" analysis of the *per diem* we got from the Team and realized if we subsisted on cheese and tea with no milk or sugar for a day and a half and then pooled our resources, we could go down to the Black Swan, order two large sirloin steaks with small salads, and split a nice bottle of *Chateauneuf du Pape*. (The same bottle would cost us a week's *per diem* today.) All this largesse would consume two days' worth of *per diem*, but we figured it was worth it. Besides, we needed to lose the weight, and this is what passed for scientific dieting at the time.

Kevin and I were living large that summer. We drove the Team's used Range Rover back and forth to the stables and used it for transport to our occasional visits to the Black Swan. The Range Rover was fun to drive and we fought over who got to drive it through the winding country lanes of Yorkshire to the pub. Two hours later, and each of us half a bottle of red wine for the worse, we fought to make the other guy drive home. This was even more complicated if there was a night fog as we sometimes forgot where we had parked our car and wandered the streets of Bedale until we stumbled across it. Simple pleasures for simple minds.

This was the third time I had trained in England, and each time the weather had been extreme. In 1968, it was cold and wet. My summer preparing for the World Championships was hot and dry. This summer was equally hot and dry. Jack knew he had to be careful with the horses, because our backups were not the same quality as our first string. Once again, when the Team left for an international competition, we took all the qualified horses with us. The cupboard back home was bare. Our Team looked good on paper, but that would change if we lost any of our main horses.

Back home, all the pieces were in place but the eventing scene in the United States had not come into focus. Although new USCTA president Neil Ayer and his leadership team were busy the results of their efforts were not yet visible. Our entire membership probably totaled a thousand, and our fundraising efforts still consisted of several wealthy individuals pulling out their checkbooks. We'd had success at the last two Olympics, winning silver team medals in 1964 and 1968, and I had contributed an individual bronze medal at the World Championships, but we were not (yet) a powerhouse.

The Olympics at Last

_____ Late August finally arrived, and we shipped to Saumur, France, where we met up with the U.S. dressage and show-jumping teams. The extra horses from all three disciplines were shipped back to the United States, while our Olympic horses went by horse van to Munich. The eventing team would be Mike Plumb on Free and Easy, Kevin Freeman on Good Mixture, Bruce Davidson on Plain Sailing, and myself on Kilkenny, with Jimmy Powers and Foster as the reserve.

The Munich stables were lovely and close to the stadium, but the cross-country course was about ten miles away. This made it difficult to inspect, as transport was limited.

The German organizers were extremely sensitive to the atmosphere they created. When Germany hosted the 1936 Olympics, the Nazis were in power and eager to flex their muscles; this time, Germany was determined that the Olympics would show the world a friendly face. (That relaxed attitude toward rules and regulations would contribute to tragic results in a few days.) At the competitors' briefing, the organizers announced that each sport was allowed to decide how much drug testing would be performed, and eventing horses would be tested according to the rules in place. As for the riders...the organizers paused...and a bevy of attractive young ladies dressed in dirndls marched in carrying trays of champagne. The point was made that eventers had not lost their work-hard, play-hard attitude; we all drank a toast to the success of the Games, secure in the knowledge riders would not be tested. (This would, however, be the last time riders escaped testing.)

After walking the course, Jack called a Team meeting and announced our order of go. I would be the pathfinder, followed by Bruce and Kevin, with Mike to provide the anchor round. Jack wanted me to ride slowly in between fences and make sure I completed the course so that I could report back to the rest of the team. I was startled by this, as Jack had not discussed it with me before the meeting. It differed from Joe Lynch's instructions to me at Mexico, where he had said to let Henry "run his race" while I made sure to get around. This had worked well for me and was the same approach I had used in 1970. However, I accepted my role and said I would do my best. Jack and I'd had a frosty relationship all that summer. He was still secretly angry that I had not trained with the rest of the team and suspected me of not being a team player. Determined to prove to him that I had acted in Henry's best interests, not mine, I would try to fill any role assigned to me.

I was lucky throughout my career that I did not get nervous before competitions—with the exception of Badminton 1968. I was eager, and impatient to get started, but knew what I and my horse could do, and looked forward to it. When I woke up the morning of the Munich cross-country I didn't feel nervous, or agitated—I just felt blank, almost numb. I have never felt that way before or since, I have never ridden worse than I did that day, and I have never completely gotten over it.

I came out of the start box cautiously, and Henry quickly picked up on my new attitude. A horse who had never stopped on cross-country in his life now had two refusals early in the course. I started attacking the fences more, desperate to get around and at least tell the other riders what I had learned. Once I reverted to my usual style of riding, Henry jumped well—until a few fences from home. We jumped the last combination on course and turned toward a downhill ramp that was covered in sod. Convinced that

Henry would jump it, I leaned forward at the takeoff, but Henry touched down on the top of what he conceived to be a bank. He raised his head and neck and caught me right on the point of my chin, knocking me out. I woke up tumbling down the hill after the ramp. Fortunately, Henry stood patiently while I remounted and headed toward the finish line.

The U.S. Team results looked great in the record books. The cross-country course caused trouble for all the teams, but we held our own in the final placings, with our third silver Team medal in three Olympics. Henry jogged sound the morning after cross-country, and jumped clean that afternoon, but thirty-second place was not what I had been shooting for. I kept up as good a face as I could outwardly but knew I had let my team members down. It wasn't Jack's fault; he did what he thought was the best for the team, but I was the one in the saddle. I realized what had happened and promised myself I would never again let anybody tell me how my horse should go; I knew my horses.

Neil Ayer hosted a celebratory dinner in downtown Munich the night after our stadium jumping and invited 50 of his closest friends to recognize our team's accomplishments. After dinner, I drove with Gail and Mom to their hotel in the mountains. At breakfast the next morning I fell into casual conversation with the waiter. He asked what brought me to Germany, and I told him I was an athlete and planned on returning to the Olympic Village, while Gail and my mother were headed back to the United States. "Oh, sir," he said, "I don't think you will go there today. You should see the television."

Thus, I found out that terrorists had taken advantage of the relaxed security procedures at the Village and were involved in a deadly tragedy at the Munich airport. The IOC declared a 24-hour pause, then the Olympics resumed and I was able to return to the Village, which was now protected by armed guards. In years since, people have asked me about the attitude of the athletes who were close to this tragedy. (The bungalow for our team was only a few doors away from the Israelis.) I reply that Olympic athletes are talented, but not necessarily nice people. Usually, their first comment after learning of the terrorist attack would be something along the lines of, "Too bad for the Israelis; what does this do to my start time?" No matter what is going on around them, Olympic athletes maintain their focus. Having completed my competition, I had a little more time than some to consider this intrusion of a violent reality into the Olympic solstice, but most of the athletes were unmoved; they still had a job to do.

I Enter Show Business

——I did not have a job during the next week, as the eventers were to fly home at the same time as the dressage and show-jumping competitors. This allowed me to watch the other Teams compete. Historically, the show jumping was held on the final day of the Olympics and the presentation of the medals served as the closing ceremonies of the Games. That morning, I had an urgent message to meet someone at the ABC studios (ABC was the Olympic television channel at the time). When I went to their offices deep in the stadium, I was asked if I would be the color commentator for the live program covering the final day. Bill Steinkraus had been scheduled to do this, but his competitive schedule prevented it, and ABC needed a replacement—in a hurry. So now I suddenly did have a job.

With the show jumping over and safely taped, my job was to help the producer find the horses and riders he needed to show on the TV coverage, which would itself be taped. He needed it in a hurry; it was late afternoon now, and our show would go out live at midnight local time (prime time back home, due to the time change between Europe and the United States). All that day's performances had been preserved on huge "reel to reel" tape machines, as tall as two refrigerators. The producer had a list of horses and riders he wanted to include, but he could not navigate the order of go to locate particular riders on the tape. This was before the invention of digital video and finding footage of the required rider meant endless spinning back and forth through reels of 3-inch-wide tape. He was getting frustrated about the time this was taking him.

"Okay," my producer said (I never did find out his name). "Next, I want that gray horse that sprawled in the middle of the big oxer in the second round."

"That's the Argentinian you are looking for," I replied. "Run the tape fast forward until about halfway." The assistant did that while I watched flickering images on the small built-in monitor. "Okay, stop. Go slow motion. Okay, there he is." The producer led me through this process for another horse or two. Then, satisfied I understood what he wanted, he handed the list of horses for the TV coverage to his assistant and wandered off to prepare highlights reels from other sports, leaving it to us to get this segment ready.

The assistant and I assembled the show and presented it to the main editing suite on time. I was then told to grab a bite to eat and present myself at the voice-over booth half-an-hour before show time; we would do the final ABC Olympic games segment "live to tape." The tape had obviously been shot earlier in the day, but we would comment in real time while watching the tape with the viewer. This technique gave a "live" feel to a program even though the competition had happened hours before. It would be another quarter of a century before livestreaming became technologically possible, with competitive results instantaneously accessible.

Moving into the voice booth, I met Chris Schenkel; he would be the play-by-play voice, while I would do the "color commentary." Chris would set the stage for each horse: number, score to date, and so on. Then I would make comments on the performance we were watching along with our audience. I was lucky to have Chris, at that time the leading sports television commentator in the country. I had heard his voice on radio and television for years, so I was surprised when I met him in the flesh. He was thin and about an inch shorter than me, but he had a baritone voice like a pipe organ, effortlessly producing deep, mellifluous, and mesmerizing commentary. He had a photographic memory for athletic achievement, and easily rattled off my career, beginning in 1967, with side comments about my being the fastest round of the cross-country day and so on. On top of all this, I immediately knew I liked and trusted him.

We had a few minutes before the show went live, and I told Chris this was my first broadcasting effort and asked for some advice. "You know your sport, Jim," he replied, "so if someone makes a mistake, or does something especially noteworthy, just remember that kid's mother is listening. Say what you need to say, but don't run him down. Remember the viewer is seeing this for the first time, so react to things on screen right along with the viewer. Be careful not to be prescient; that's cheating the viewer. If the horse is going to slip on the next turn, don't act as if you saw it coming. It should surprise you as much as the viewer." I immediately got all that, and over the course of my years as a television commentator I have kept it in the back of my mind.

The actual show went easily. I had seen the tape, so my comments were half ready in the back of my mind. My back and forth with Chris seemed smooth; I don't recall either of us stepping on the other's lines. The producer was thrilled when we signed off, and Chris thanked me and said it had gone well. Then he asked, "Jim, how many people do you think just heard your voice?" I replied I had no idea. He said, "About 65 million." It didn't seem real. Chris and I had been in a small room with black foam pasted on the walls and ceilings, a single monitor on a table in front of us, each of us in shirt sleeves and wearing soup-can earphones—*65 million*. Huh. That gave me something to think about on my way back to the Village. Little did I know that new opportunities had just opened up for me; after this debut, I would spend the next 40 years as a "talking head" at equestrian events for various networks.

I had to pack because I was headed back to Virginia the next day—back to my new home south of Middleburg, back to my suddenly larger family, back to a growing working-student program...and back with my tail between my legs. I still felt I had let my teammates down, and I was having a hard time dealing with this. ■

_Still in Virginia, and Finally Home

Regret doesn't remind us that we did badly.
It reminds us that we know we can do better.

Kathryn Schulz
Journalist

I may have come home from Germany with my tail between my legs, but I had a tiger by the tail when I got back to Virginia. I already had a small working-student program when I left for England in July to go into training for the Munich Olympics and had left my young horses in work with the students. I put Kathy Newman (née Doyle) in charge. She managed the sale of a couple of horses but several still needed new homes. As part of helping to keep my horses in work, my working students had agreed to get instruction at the local horse shows from Kathy. These were teenagers who had started taking regular lessons from me, and they needed adult supervision. My plan with Kathy was that although I would be gone for most of the summer, I would get home as quickly as I could, check in the following morning at Colony Farm, and get ready to train for the few fall events available. (The facility, located east of Middleburg, is still there, although now called Fox Chase.)

I made good time driving from Gladstone, and—since I would go past Colony Farm on my way home—decided I might as well surprise everybody and stop by for evening stables. I had stalls all down the long side of the west end of the barn for the horses, and a tack room halfway down the aisle. There was no one around when I parked, but I heard loud radio music and raucous laughter coming from the tack room—and saw an empty beer can fly out of the tack room window to join a sizeable heap of beer cans, empty potato chip bags, and other evidence of a typical barn party. Just as I stepped around the corner and into the tack room, I heard the distinctive sound of a new can of beer opening.

Sticking my head into the tack room, I said, "Hi, guys."

Well. "Deer in the headlights" doesn't begin to describe the looks on the perpetrators' faces, especially two of them—with fresh cans of beer in their hands—I knew to be well below legal drinking age.

I made some remark about when the cat's away, the mice will play, but to make that work, you had to know where the cat was at all times. You never saw evening stables done in such record time, with the aisle swept, tack cleaned, and evidence of their misdeeds removed. I looked at the work list, said that would be fine and that I would see everyone at morning stables. Driving home, I had to laugh, but I also realized I was going to have to keep a close eye on these kids. As I've mentioned more than once, eventers of that era prided themselves on a work-hard, play-hard attitude, but I could already see I was going to have to emphasize that work-hard part a little more.

Gail, Hillary, and Jennifer arrived the next day, and we settled into a routine that was determined by horses and the demands of a young family. Without foreseeing it, I had started my working student program just in time to catch the wave of enthusiasm our silver medal at Munich had inspired. Along with Jack Le Goff's competitive success, Neil Ayer was the cause of much of this; he was tireless in his efforts to expand the sport at every level. Within two years, the USCTA had grown from several hundred members to more than a thousand, and Jack Le Goff was implementing a new "rider in residence" program at Gladstone. Eventing was starting to fire on all cylinders.

Beginnings... and an Ending

___ By October of 1973, Neil had organized the first truly international U.S. event at his Ledyard Farm, paving the way for foreign riders to fly their horses over to compete. It didn't hurt Neil's publicity efforts that Princess Anne and her fiancé, Captain Mark Phillips, were among the elite competitors. For the first time, U.S. eventers competed in front of a sizeable crowd.

My mother came back East for the event, as both Kilkenny and Foster were retiring before the final show jumping. I rode Henry while Jimmie Powers rode Foster. Waiting in the warmup ring, Jimmie and I figured once the announcer started his spiel, we would each canter around and jump a few fences on our own. When we could tell the announcer was getting to the end of his script, we would gallop from opposite back corners of the arena, turn down the center of the arena together at a high rate of speed, and jump the Myopia Hunt Club panel knee-to-knee in stride. We hit the panel on lovely flowing forward strides as planned and pulled up in front of the main grandstand to salute and dismount. Henry and Foster thought this was a great giggle and the crowd loved it, giving us a big hand as we led the horses out of the stadium. However, Jack (who hadn't been in on the plan) stopped us and said, "Well, that was very nice, boys…but I would not have been happy if it did not work."

After the festivities Sunday afternoon, we drove Mom and the girls home to Middleburg; Monday was a school day for Hillary, and our lives were increasingly circumscribed by what was best for her and Jennifer. Sometimes, horses had to play second fiddle. Gail threw a lovely party in early November to celebrate both Mom's visit and my twenty-ninth birthday. Mom stayed on for a few more days and flew home to Rimrock Farm in early November.

I never saw her alive again.

Later, I realized what Mom had done. When she set out to visit us for Ledyard, she had first stopped off to see each of my sister's five children in Kansas. Then she flew to England to see the "English Woffords," especially her three grandchildren there. She spent a few weeks in England, then returned to the United States to attend Ledyard. She had checked on each of her grandchildren and gone back to Kansas to die at home.

My sister, Dodie, said Mom was quite tired when she got home but continued to smoke and drink to excess, and it finally caught up with her. When they put her in the hospital in early December of 1973, Dodie called and said I had better come out, as Mom was fading fast. By the time I got to Junction City she had slipped into a coma, never to recover.

I was sad to lose Mom, but she had told me an interesting story while she was staying with us in Virginia. I came down one morning to find her sitting over her cup of coffee and a cigarette. When I remarked that she seemed to be in an especially good mood, she said she had dreamed of my father and it was the first time since he died 20 years earlier that in her dreams he was not suffering from the pain of colon cancer. They had been at a horse show with friends, having a good time. I said I was glad she had a good night's sleep, but the real import of what she said did not sink in for me until later. After the grand tour of her children and grandchildren, she'd decided it was time to go home and let go. She had been sad for more than 20 years, and now she wanted to be with Daddy, wherever that was. ∎

13

_Greengarden Road

You can't learn before you set out, can you?
You go along the road and learn as you go.

Pamela L. Travers
Creator of *Mary Poppins*

Gail and I dreamed of having our own farm from the time we moved to Virginia. We didn't have any money at the outset, but the real estate agents in the area viewed that as a minor problem and we spent hours driving the back roads, looking for a suitable place. We soon discovered that if Gail found a house that with "just a little work" would be perfect for a family of four, you could bet the stables were unsuitable. If I found a stables with real potential, Gail wouldn't even step inside the house for fear of the rats and the snakes. We laughed at this, sketched a house and barn that would suit us on the back of an envelope, put the drawings away, and went on with our daily lives.

Meanwhile, when Colony Farm was placed on the market in the fall of 1973 I moved our horses to Brookemeade, a famous old racing operation on the west side of Upperville. It did not have an indoor arena, but we made do with the quarter-mile enclosed jogging track around the shed row intended for two-year-olds. I put gymnastics on either side of the shed for jumping practice, and in mild weather we were able to school dressage on the extensive lawns. Between that and the limitless hacking available, Brookemeade was a good place to train Classic horses in the early 1970s.

With Mom's passing, however, our situation changed. The sale of Rimrock Farm left all four of her children with nice nest eggs, and Gail and I could afford to look for a building site. In early 1974 we purchased 100 acres of raw corn field on Greengarden Road and named it Fox Covert Farm.

Naturally, the stables and a cottage came first; we just pulled out the envelope with our drawings on it. Many of our decisions were made on the basis of mistakes I had already made and learned from. When I left Colony Farm a few years earlier, I left behind 36 horses in training; I knew I did not want to train that many Classic horses at once, which is why I planned a barn with 16 stalls.

For efficiency, I designed the stables on a "courtyard" plan with a center aisle—meaning stalls on both sides of an aisle wide enough to drive a tractor and spreader through. (I rode in two Olympics and one World Championships before I no longer mucked out my own horses. I knew what went on with the stable's work force—I *was* the work force.)

I connected the indoor arena to the stables, because I had trained at several different facilities by this time and knew a single building was more efficient. I built a small outdoor arena, but for two reasons did not build any cross-country schooling obstacles. First, I was out of money; second, the landowners surrounding me were all part of the Piedmont

Hunt country. They were generous about letting me hack over their land, and their hunt panels were well suited to training young Classic horses.

I moved us into the cottage on August 1, 1974. I say "I" moved us because Gail and the girls were visiting her parents in Colorado Springs; they enjoyed much better weather than in Virginia, where it was stinking hot. Fortunately, I had working students, and in a couple of days the move was done. I have hesitated to give the names of my working students throughout this narrative—in part from concern I might forget someone, and, in some cases, to protect the guilty. (When you have a barn full of young men such as Don Sachey, Derek di Grazia, Tad Zimmerman, Wash Bishop, Tom Glascock, and Jim Graham, there is a lot of guilt to protect.)

It is hard to explain the mystic hold that the Piedmont area of northern Virginia has on us, but after moving, as I've told you, 10 times in the first 10 years of our marriage, Gail and I both felt when we stood in that cottage that we had moved home.

We moved the horses into Fox Covert on December 7, 1974, by the simple expedient of riding one and leading two or three from Brookmeade. We went north up Trappe Hill Road, turned east on Millville Road then south on Greengarden Road, and about two hours later rode into our new home at Fox Covert. When the aisles were swept and the horses fed that first day, I had sixteen horses safely bedded down and contentedly napping after evening stables. My last international competitive effort had not turned out well, which left me with a feeling of failure; but I was so excited at finally having my own place that I couldn't wait for the next morning to start work at the stables. I was to feel like this for the next forty years.

I set up shop on Greengarden Road determined to build the best possible training and riding program I knew how to build. I am amazed at how brave I was then. I was starting a new business just before a major downturn in the overall economy, in an area that could hardly pronounce "eventing," where knowledgeable horsemen scoffed at the idea I would need an indoor arena, and I had no known or predicted potential client base. Talk about "build it and they will come"! But come they did: from this quiet, low-key beginning I built what was, for a time, one of the most successful eventing training facilities in the country.

In retrospect, 1974 went by me in a whirl. I purchased a farm, built a stables and house, and took the first of many Junior teams to Canada for the first FEI Junior Championships. (This competition would eventually become what we now refer to as the North American Junior and Young Rider Championships, the NAJYRC. I served Area II as the Junior and Young Rider coach off and on for the next four decades.) However, I missed out on riding at the 1974 World Championships. Everything I touched seemed to be at least somewhat successful—except when it came to my own riding efforts, where I was a failure. I rode an endless series of horses that were almost good enough, but "almost" doesn't win medals. I had always known that Henry was a special horse, and now I felt his loss ever more keenly. I did win a couple of point-to-points and enjoyed the thrill of riding at speed over fixed fences, but those experiences merely confirmed my belief that when racing, the fastest horse usually wins.

Daddy used to say that a jockey wasn't great because he won races he *should* have won, but rather because he won races he *shouldn't* have won. If I were to reclaim my self-image as a good rider, I needed to win a few competitions that I wasn't supposed to win. I wasn't fixated on the winning aspect of competition, exactly, but rather on the idea of excellence in competition. However, it's hard to be excellent without a horse, and I still didn't have a horse.

By spring of 1975, meanwhile, it had become obvious my program was so big I needed help. I could no longer be rider, coach, stable manager, and head traveling groom. I placed a blind advertisement in the *Chronicle of the Horse:* "Former USET rider requires stable manager/traveling groom. Apply Box M." I was sure it would evoke some responses and I was surprised the following week when I only got one. The young lady who answered my call gave me her current job description: she was the stable manager at Stephens College in Columbia, Missouri, where she and two young Amish men mucked out 60 stalls a day, plus she handled general managerial duties—ordering feed and hay, keeping the blacksmith busy, and so on.

She had worked as a traveling groom for several reputable hunter/ jumper trainers; she could braid and take care of all the other necessary details of presenting horses for competition. Assured that the salary and benefits were agreeable, I asked when she could start. "When do you need me?" she replied. She had already given notice before seeing my advertisement. Obviously, this young lady was ready to make a career change. It was now mid-week. Could she be here by Sunday? "I'll be there," she said.

Thus, Suzanne Schardein walked into my life and changed it forever. She had never been to an event, so she had a baptism under fire the following weekend when I took several students and four of my young horses to one. My horses were competing at different levels, and each needed specific tack for each phase. I went over each horse's equipment for each phase and she took careful notice. I figured this first outing would be a disaster, but that she would learn the routine after a few more experiences.

The event was spread over two days, which increased the difficulty of our schedules. Some horses did dressage and show jumping the first day, and cross-country the second day. Others did all three phases in one day. It took careful study of the schedule for me to know where I should be, at what time, and on which horse. I was so busy it was Saturday afternoon before I noticed that Suzanne had the correct tack on each horse, ready at the right time and place. In addition, each horse sparkled, and was sporting about 20 tiny little show braids for dressage.

I had not yet talked about turnout with Suzanne and now saw that was one lecture I could skip. I also skipped my lectures on how to bank a straw stall, how to sweep an aisle, how to wrap the leather and brass chain shanks around the halters that hung on each door (with the brass polished every Wednesday whether it needed it or not). I came to find that Suzanne had the same aversion to cobwebs and ghost turds that I had and, like me, despised dirty windows. Crooked blankets on a blanket rack were an affront to her sensibilities, as were dirty saddle pads.

It sounds as if I was only interested in appearances, and it is fair to say I placed a great deal of emphasis on how my horses and facility looked. The appearance of a stables and its horses is a visible manifestation of a horseman's commitment to excellence. In addition, Suzanne had already shown me the one essential trait I needed above all others: she was a good horsewoman. One of my horses, a lumbering Irish twerp, was a devil to catch in the paddock. "Squeaky" was a big bay, seven-eighths Thoroughbred with a high, hysterical whinny entirely out of keeping with his appearance—thus his stable name. He had figured out that coming to the rattle of grain in a bucket meant he would be captured and put back in his stall. Unable to catch him, I left him out overnight a few times. It was fortunate his paddock did not have water, or I might never have caught him again. Yet within a week, Suzanne would step to the paddock gate and call his name and Squeaky would lift his head and gallop to the gate, squealing with joy at the sound of her voice. It didn't take me long to form an opinion: this girl was a treasure.

However, she was a girl in an all-guy barn, and was being subjected to the FNG hazing typical of such situations. I tolerated this for a week, then called a barn meeting. With "all hands on deck" I told my boys that I needed Suzanne, but I had a waiting list for working-student positions. They could be replaced; she could not. They got the message, and things quieted down.

Without knowing it at the time, I was assembling the support team necessary for a successful competitive program. As with so many things, I did not have a role model to follow in setting up a successful system, so I was gradually, fumblingly, finding out how to develop one. With Suzanne in charge, I was assured of exemplary horse care. John Mayo was my veterinarian, and became my duck-hunting partner and lifelong friend. (John would later on be the Head FEI Veterinarian at the Los Angeles Olympics.) My farrier, Fred Cleveland, would eventually be voted into the Farrier's Hall of Fame, based partly on the work he did on the horses at Fox Covert. Gradually, I was putting the puzzle together; however, I still had a huge blank spot in the middle of the puzzle—I did not have a horse with talent to match my dreams.

This vacuum persisted throughout 1975 and all the way through 1977. I was more and more successful with my students, and worked harder and harder on my riding skills, but to no avail. Missing the Pan American Games was a sad occasion for me, and the 1976 US Olympic team won almost everything there was to win—all without me. It looked as if I were going have to get hit with a magic wand to get back to the level I aspired to, much less win anything. ■

__I Find Carawich...
or He Finds Me

The wand chooses the wizard, Mr. Potter.
It's not always clear why.

J.K. Rowling
Wand merchant Mr. Ollivander
in *Harry Potter and the Philosopher's Stone*

When it comes to horses, I think of myself as a fairly mechanical trainer. Squeeze your hands and the horse will slow down, close your legs and your horse will speed up—that sort of thing. However, there is more to it. Spend any amount of time around horses, and you become convinced there is a kind of communication between horses and humans that can't be measured. The worst among them sense our fears and take advantage of us, while the best among them sense our dreams and take us where we have always longed to go. For example, take Carawich....

Not many people get a chance to ride in the World Championships or Olympics. While you are involved in the training and selection process, you don't have time to think about anything else. If the stars align for you, then you are too busy riding to think about it. Only after the Games are over do you get a chance to think about your experiences, to wonder about the long, hard, winding path that brought you there and, especially, about how incredibly lucky you were to have a horse good enough to ride in the Olympics. If you have ever had such a horse, you can't help wondering if you will ever find one again.

I had ridden in the Olympics twice by the spring of 1977, but that experience was receding into the past. I had not been on a Team of any sort for five years—indeed, I had not won any competition above Preliminary level since 1972. I had not given up on my dreams yet, but I was beginning to wonder if one day soon I might have to exchange dreams for reality.

I was coaching at Badminton that spring and was standing in the courtyard of the Duke of Beaufort's hunter stables, waiting for the first veterinary examination to start. Lars Sederholm came up to me and we stood talking for a moment. Lars is a genius horseman and had a terrific influence on my riding; I always enjoy a chance to catch up with him. By now the horses had started to walk around the outside of the courtyard, and we moved up to the crowd-control barrier to watch the proceedings. Lars was distracted by someone, so I stood at the barrier alone for a moment, and watched all these wonderful creatures walk past.

I suddenly noticed a big, handsome, mealy-nosed, dark brown horse walking toward me. His enormous, flowing walk caught my eye immediately. Just as he got next to me he stopped and turned his head toward me. I had the sudden, eerie feeling that he was looking directly into my eyes— that I had been singled out and was being sized up. I stood, spellbound, while the hair literally stood up on the back of my neck. I can't say how long he stood like that because time stopped for me. I was not aware of crowd noise, or other people around me, or anything but this horse staring intently into my eyes.

The horse's groom tugged impatiently on his lead shank, yet he stood a moment longer, looking at me. Then he seemed to say, "Hmmm," to himself, turned his head forward, and went on with that powerful, athletic walk.

I grabbed Lars by the arm, interrupted his conversation, and asked him, "Who is THAT?" pointing at the horse's receding form.

"Oh, that's Carawich," Lars replied. "He is a wonderful horse, but you'll never buy him." The owners knew what they had in Carawich.

I said "Okay," to Lars but I was thinking, "What a strange experience I've just had." I watched Carawich go for the rest of the weekend, and he was indeed wonderful, but when I returned to the United States, I put the whole experience out of my mind.

By then it was early December of 1977, and I was starting to realize that I was not going to get a chance to ride in the 1978 World Championships, to be held at the new Kentucky Horse Park. All the good U.S. horses were already taken, and my search for horses in other countries had come up empty. I was 34 years old, fit, and at whatever peak of my abilities I was going to achieve. If I did not ride in the World Championships, I faced a long, dark three-year period of training, with little hope of making the Team for the 1980 Olympics. It made me sad, but that was just the way it was, and I might as well get used to it.

I did some buying and selling of English and Irish horses during that period of my life. I was looking for a horse for a client, and suddenly thought I might give Lars Sederholm a call, to see if he had anything for sale.

"Hello, Jimmy," Lars said, "What a coincidence. I have just now hung up with Carawich's owner. His rider is pregnant, and they have decided to put Carawich on the market."

"Well, call them back and tell them he is sold pending a vet exam," I said. We chatted for another few minutes about other horses, and then I hung up the phone. "Now what?" I thought. I did not have the money to pay for Carawich.

I wound up borrowing against my life insurance policy. It was the best business move I have ever made.

International rules in those days required that to be eligible to compete, the rider and the owner of a horse should be of the same nationality by January first of the year of the World Championships or Olympics. We got the deal done in time to have my name on the ownership papers before the first of the year, and I started a partnership with the best horse I would ever ride. I can remember to this instant that when I slid onto his back for the first time, I felt as if I were putting on a glove. I rode him for four years, and there was never a time when I did not feel that he could read my mind. If I tacked him up for some dressage work, he stood like a statue. But when I put his jumping saddle on, he would start to dance and fly-kick in the cross-ties—he knew the difference before I could even get on him.

He had a horrible, demeaning stable name when he arrived. I put a lot of store by a horse's stable name, but I am also very superstitious, and it is supposed to be bad luck to change it. "Well, my friend," I thought, "you are getting a new lease on life, and my riding life has definitely taken a turn for the better, so I am going to change your stable name and call you 'Pop.' You have a hell of a pop over a jump, and 'Pop' is what cowboys call the wisest and most experienced cowboy."

But now I had to "cowboy up," and prove to the world that I could still ride at an elite level. I had a brand-new partner, but no record to brag about with him. Examining our combination on paper, we were just a rider who used to be able to do it, riding a horse with a big win at Burghley as a seven-year-old, who had to prove that he still had it as a 10-year-old, even with a new sidekick. Together, we were going to try out for the 1978 World Championships. Every rider dreams of winning a big competition someday, but more than the winning, I wanted as flawless a performance as possible—to ride not well, but *really* well. The corollary, of course, is that I had to ride well to win. Good riding and success usually come hand in hand.

When riders ask me about trying out for a team, my answer is simple: "Winning everything just flat takes the politics out of Team selection." I'll talk about winning later on but want to set the scene as I experienced it in the spring and summer of 1978. Get this: by the end of the spring tryouts for the World Championship team, I had been first, second, and third at the three selection horse trials, and was riding under selectors' orders to go slowly at the Blue Ridge Spring Championships, which was run under the Classic format. This wasn't too bad a record, for someone whose coach had said he would never ride on his teams again. I just kept telling myself that we had to be so good the selectors couldn't ignore us.

Disappointment in Kentucky

——Pop and I had established ourselves as potential World Championship material, but rather than relaxing, I trained myself even harder. I became obsessed with my weight and fitness, while fiercely protecting Pop from too much work, training on hard ground, or any of the myriad of ways that horses can be injured. Pop was all I had, and I devoted myself to

him. However, I managed to over-train myself. When the World Championships rolled around, I had been named to the Team—and also weighed
137 pounds. The coach, selectors, and team doctors would be asking me
serious questions these days, but in those days, we all just shrugged and
said it was a long hot summer, and we needed to be as fit as our horses.
Riders were required to carry a minimum of 165 pounds (saddle and girth
usually weighed about 20 pounds) for a maximum length Classic; every
ounce over that was extra work for your horse.

The four combinations named to the Team at the beginning of August
were Mike Plumb with Lauriston, Tad Coffin on Bally Cor, Bruce Davidson
on Might Tango, and me on Carawich. We were to train in Unionville,
Pennsylvania, to take advantage of the turf available there for our conditioning gallops. Both Mike and I had active working-student programs
and brought students to continue working with them (and earning some
income) in the afternoons. One of my students, 18-year-old Desirée Smith,
had qualified for the World Championships as an individual. I trained
her for the event by following Jack's conditioning schedule closely, and
she went on to earn the distinction of being the second-youngest rider
to ever compete at the World Championships; the youngest, Mike Huber,
was younger than her by 30 days or so.

FEI rules at that time allowed each international team to bring a team
of four, plus two official individual horse-and-rider combinations. Our
two official individual combinations were Torrance Watkins, who would
ride Red's Door, and Mary Ann Tausky on her Olympic veteran Marcus
Aurelius, the "Bionic Pony." In addition to these six combinations, as
the host nation the United States could enter six individual horses and
riders. Jack would be responsible for supervising all 12 entrants to the
World Championships.

Jack had his hands full that summer. His relationship with his Team captain was solid: Mike Plumb and Lauriston were fresh off a big win at Ledyard '77 in deplorable weather conditions. Jack's latest star, Tad Coffin, seemed to be back on form with his Olympic gold-medal partner, Bally Cor, and Carawich and I had a record good enough to be in the final four. The only question mark on our list was Bruce Davidson, who would ride the seven-year-old Might Tango instead of Irish Cap, his gold-medal winner from the 1974 World Championships. One of Jack Le Goff's skills was his uncanny ability to know when a horse was "coming to hand" at the right time.

He had demonstrated that intuition in 1976, when Mike rode the seven-year-old Thoroughbred Better and Better instead of his ride at Burghley 1974, the Team's extremely experienced individual World Championship silver medalist, Good Mixture. You have to be sure of yourself to pick a seven-year-old instead of a medal winner for your team; you have to be proud of your system, when that seven-year-old matches the rider's 1974 World Championships results with an individual silver medal at the 1976 Olympics. By then, Jack knew his horses.

As we shipped into the brand-new Kentucky Horse Park in the heat of late summer 1978, Jack must have also known that to date his team was the most experienced and successful eventing team ever assembled—not just by the United States, but by any nation in the world. On paper, we were the favorites to win; we were the home team, the reigning Olympic champions, and two of our members were back with the same horses. In addition, I was back on the team with Pop, and we were obviously on form. And then there was Might Tango. He was inexperienced at this level, but his rider, Bruce Davidson, was an Olympic and World Championship gold-medal winner. I don't remember feeling complacent about our prospects; the course was too demanding and the conditions were brutal, but I thought we had as good a chance as anybody there.

Modern short-format eventing these days is designed for television; you rarely know who wins until the last few horses jump the show jumping course on the final day. But "Classic" events were usually decided by the speed and endurance test—and what a test the 1978 Championships were. In high heat and humidity, we asked horses to trot for 20 minutes to warm up, then gallop for five and a half minutes at steeplechase speed (690 mpm), followed by nearly an hour of trotting a second roads and tracks. Only after all this were we going to meet the cross-country course, which had an optimum time of 14 minutes, 12 seconds.

Suzanne led Pop down to the start of Phase A while my good Irish friend, John Harty, carried a spare pair of heavy riding boots for me. I had over-trained myself to make the weight and now was deathly afraid I would show up at the scales underweight, with no way to make up the few pounds' difference. Riding in a heavy saddle, I was relieved to see that I "weighed out" at 166 pounds; I would be allowed to use the bridle and girth, as well as my saddle, to "weigh in" at the completion of the cross-country.

John gave me a leg up while Suzanne held on to Pop, which took some doing. It was apparent Pop knew this was a big occasion, and he was ready for it. Classic riders were aware of how precious their horses' energy was and did everything to conserve it when they could. I mention this so you understand my dismay when the starter counted me down to the beginning of the first roads and tracks, said "Go"—and Pop bolted down the trot lane at a wide-open gallop. Not good.

I hadn't gone a hundred yards, yet both of us were sweating and puffing, and far from the Zen state that I tried to achieve while on roads and tracks. I wanted my Classic horses to jog quietly on loose reins, taking nothing out of themselves while I planned my next few steps ahead; walk here slightly uphill, trot on level ground, slow canter slightly downhill if the horse would allow it, all designed to save my horse's energy. But Pop was having none of that—he wanted to gallop forever, and he wanted to gallop now! I stood up in the stirrups, leaned down on a double-bridge, persuaded him to slow canter for a while, then drop to a trot, and finally we started to settle into what was proving to be an exciting morning.

Jack had given me my instructions the night before: Bruce would go first, with the intention of getting around clean, then come back and report to Jack about the subtleties of the course—where a turn was slippery, which fence did not ride as expected, how the horses dealt with the conditions, and so on. Remember, this event took place long before we had total coverage, as opposed to modern closed-circuit television near the start box and announcers describing the action. Teams depended on a "spy" system: knowledgeable volunteers ("runners") watched parts of the course that concerned the riders, then ran back to the 10-minute area, where they reported to the coordinator. The Kentucky cross-country course, which turned out to be a debacle, would have ridden differently for us if a "spy system" had been in place.

Our usual system was that the coordinator (in this case, Jack Burton) would correlate all the information gained, and send the runner back out to their area for more information. The coordinator would then brief the coach about what he had learned regarding how the course was riding, and when the next U.S. rider came into the box, the coach would then give the riders their final instructions. This briefing was supposed to happen during the ten minutes each rider had in the vet box before starting out on course.

Anyway, that's the way it was supposed to work. The reality was that at the last minute, due to record crowds of spectators, an extra layer of security had been added around the vet box, and Jack Burton did not have the correct pass to get in—therefore, he could not brief Jack LeGoff.

I came into the box a few minutes early, expecting Jack's usual detailed instructions. I was concerned about how the course was riding; based on what I could learn over the announcer's system, it was every bit as hard as we had thought. It was also obvious that "The Serpent" was the bogey fence. Any information I could get before starting would be invaluable.

Before the event that morning, Jack had warned all 12 U.S. riders to "listen to the engine." By this he meant that we should not worry about making the optimum time, but concentrate on getting around with whatever time faults the situation demanded. When we got to the box I said that I had tried to get Pop to listen, but we had exactly made the optimum time of 5 minutes, 30 seconds on steeplechase; Pop was taking an incredible grip on the bit and I had not wanted to fight with him, knowing that would waste more energy than would be saved by getting him to settle in a rhythm. I asked Jack for information about the course, and how he wanted me to ride it. Instead of his usual calm, detailed, explicit instructions, he burst out, "I can't find out a bloody [expletive deleted] thing. Listen to the engine." This meant I was to ride as efficiently as possible, go the various long or short routes we had planned, and make sure to see the finish line. Although more and more reports were coming back that The Serpent was a problem, Bruce had jumped the quick way; I stowed that information away, got a leg up, and headed for the start box.

Pop leapt onto the course with his usual enthusiasm and made nothing of the first few jumps. I got him settled in a rhythm but was too busy to check my watch; I knew I was jumping at a good working pace, and I got to the halfway point exactly at the required time of 7:06 (the total optimum time for the cross-country was 14:12). I was happy about this, as it meant Pop was jumping easily and I could afford to ease his speed back when he started to show signs of fatigue. I had a severe "peck" landing in the water at the Head of the Lake but survived it and headed out to where the Horse Park campgrounds are now.

I had not made up my mind about my route as we approached The Serpent, but Pop was still full of energy and Bruce had jumped the fast way, so I decided to save a precious few seconds and go the fast route as well. This involved a rail over a ditch, then a sharp right-hand turn to a zigzag set of post and rails at the back of a ditch with water running through it. The difficulty here was the tight turn placed the horse on an option stride; the second element could be jumped off a long stride or a short stride, but it was important to be decisive. I thought it might happen too quickly for the horse to read the question. So, I jumped into the distance well, made the turn—and told Pop the wrong thing. Instead of keeping him on a short, balanced stride, I asked him to leave a stride out and he responded correctly—but rather than leaving long from flat ground, at the last second Pop realized he couldn't leave long, and suddenly attempted to put in a short stride on the downside of the takeoff slope. This gave us the sensation of stepping off one more step in the dark; Pop stumbled into the top rail, went to his knees on the other side, and I hit the ground.

Although I fell off here, for the second time in my career I was the ironic beneficiary of a "frangible device." Just as at Puncheston in 1970, I jumped a rail that had already absorbed so much abuse it was propped up, but no longer fixed, so that hitting it caused minimal damage. I quickly remounted, jumped the rest of the course clear, and finished with a fall and some time faults. I had left my dreams of excellence behind me, however. Pop and I jumped a clear round on the final day and were part of our bronze medal-winning team, but I left Lexington once again knowing the sad price of regrets.

Another Badminton in My Sights

——I was too busy that autumn to sulk for long, as my students were actively competing, and for the most part doing well. The Radnor Three-Day Event in Malvern, Pennsylvania was the eventer's ultimate annual destination event for the entire North American continent at that time. Every autumn, you saw trucks with a trailer hitch and a bumper sticker that said "After Radnor," meaning everything else would have to wait until after that event. The community around Radnor had embraced eventing every bit as enthusiastically as that near Ledyard in Massachusetts, and riders planned all year for their week at Radnor.

I'd like to think that part of the enthusiasm was due to the challenging cross-country courses that were the heart of a Classic competition. I was proud of this, because I was now serving as the course advisor for Kate Jackson, who was the technical director for the event. However, a bigger attraction might have been the competitors' party, which was a real bash. As Denny Emerson later famously remarked, "The competitors' party at Radnor was like Woodstock; if you said you remembered it, you weren't really there." Work hard, play hard was still the unofficial motto of eventers.

I took some time off following Radnor after working hard all year. I had John Mayo, my vet, examine Pop carefully when he came home from Kentucky, and John found him absolutely sound, if slightly anemic.

He prescribed some supplements to bring Pop's blood back to normal, and in no time Pop was on his toes, obviously looking for work. However, I restrained myself, walked him under saddle from an hour to two hours every day, and did no technical training. Pop had time to just be a horse. I reported all this to Jack at Radnor; he replied that was good news, because the USET had decided to provide travel grants for horses and riders to attend Badminton in 1979, and Pop's name was at the head of the list. Most of the other horses named to the travel squad were already in training with me. The plan was for me to serve as rider-coach for the travel squad, while Jack would continue training his rider-in-residence program at South Hamilton. For our final preparation events, a few weeks ahead of Badminton in late April, Jack would come over and take charge.

This suited me, and in early March of 1979, the squad moved to England. We were lucky to be able to stable at Wylie, the estate of Lord and Lady Hugh and Rosemary Russell. This was at Jack's suggestion, as the 1974 team had trained there successfully. The final travel list was Karen O'Connor (née Lende), Ann Taylor (née Hardaway,) Karen Sachey, Wash Bishop, and Derek di Grazia. We didn't know it at the time, but the future of U.S. eventing had just arrived at Wylie. That future would see several members of that travel squad ride into the USEA Hall of Fame.

It took a surprising amount of work to make this trip happen, as I discovered while serving as not just coach, but travel agent, stable manager, and general coordinator. Somehow, I got it organized. We were all on tight budgets, and I had arranged for small house trailers (called "caravans" in England) to be parked at the stables, and for the estate workers' kitchen to provide three daily meals for my riders and grooms.

We spent the next six weeks in those claustrophobic surroundings during a wet, cold, muddy English spring. The heaters in the caravans were insufficient to warm us up and dry out our clothing, so we resorted to the dangerous practice of using the little propane stove in each unit for warmth. Fortunately, we remembered to turn them off before going to bed.

All this created problems, but I knew our biggest problem would be our landlady, Lady Rosemary Russell. "You know, Rosemary can be very difficult," Jack warned me before I left. I had heard stories already, so was forewarned for my first meeting with her. She had a long list of "dos and don'ts" concerning the stables, most of which were acceptable, if a bit onerous; a few we would just ignore. Then she got to the heart of the matter: the use of Wylie's famed cross-country schooling areas. She stated that she would drive me up there, tell me which jumps to jump, and then be there to supervise when we used it. I replied mildly that she could drive me up to the area and tell me which jumps *not* to jump. After that, I would tell my riders what I wanted them to jump. Her emphatic "humph" told me she wasn't pleased, but she got my point.

Rosemary was a Badminton-level rider before a spinal injury confined her to the motorized wheelchair, her Mini-Moke that she used to get around the estate. Obviously frustrated at not being able to ride, she devoted herself to helping others, and built the premier schooling area in England to practice her theories. Like all good horsemen, she was set in ways that worked for her and tried to control everything around her. She and I quickly came to a truce, but Jack had a different way of dealing with her. Jack was a master psychologist, and I had a glimpse of this the first morning he came down to the Wylie stables.

We were standing in the courtyard, quietly discussing our plans for the day, when we heard Rosemary's Mini-Moke on its way down the hill. It was her practice to arrive like a whirlwind, going off at her stable girls about imagined or actual failings of the staff. Jack turned from me, walked a few steps away, and suddenly kicked a water bucket out into Rosemary's path, spraying water and wet hay everywhere. Yanking a blanket off the rack, he hurled it into the middle of the courtyard, and launched into a screaming, red-faced and profane rage about how it was impossible to train with such unacceptable stable management, he could not work his genius under these conditions, he despaired of anyone being able to meet his standards, and so on at high volume. Rosemary had stopped her wheelchair at the sight of someone obviously throwing a violent fit. She blinked, listened for a few seconds, then meekly shifted into reverse and disappeared back up the hill to her house. Jack calmly walked back to me, lit another cigarette, and picked up our scheduling discussion as if nothing had happened. Rosemary handled Jack with kid gloves for the rest of our stay, and I saw that Jack wasn't just a genius with horses, he was good with people, too. He had convinced Rosemary he was crazier than she was, and she kept her distance.

Badminton, Again

——There is a great feeling of relief when you and your horse finally arrive at a Classic even after training for months, carefully preparing for what the FEI used to call "the complete test of horse and rider." I had not ridden at Badminton for 11 years, but I had been back several times, most recently in 1977 as coach for 18-year-old Bea di Grazia (née Perkins), one of the youngest riders to ever complete this event. All this made me comfortable with my situation. I had been here before and planned to ride better this time. Jack and I agreed that while we were interested in placing well, our true goal was using Badminton as an event leading up to the 1980 Moscow Olympics.

I would obviously try for the best dressage score available, and—if I got that far—to jump a clear show-jumping round on Sunday. But the heart of our plan was to have a speedy, efficient cross-country round, jumping the combinations where I felt most comfortable. "I want a clear round, between 10 and 15 seconds over the optimum time," Jack said. We both thought the Olympics were more important than our plans at Badminton, so this sounded exactly right to me. After I walked the course a couple of times, I was satisfied that Pop would handle it well. Because the horrible weather that spring had kept us from our full list of preparatory events, I decided to go the slow route at two combinations. We had not practiced the questions posed, and I was not under orders to make the time at all costs.

We often remark on riders' increasing confidence and competence when they return to a big event for another attempt. However, we some-times forget the horse goes through the same process. This would be Pop's second attempt; in 1977, with his previous rider, he had slipped going into the bounce at Badminton Lake and stopped with his chest against the rail, unable to jump. Horses have good memories, and I was quickly to find out that Pop had been thinking about Badminton as much as I had. His manners on the first roads and tracks phase of cross-country day were much improved; he broke off at a sharp gallop but came back to a slow canter, and soon dropped into a smooth, ground-covering trot. So far, so good. He took his usual fierce hold on the bit in the steeplechase phase, but I was fit and able to keep him at 690 mpm, the speed required to make the optimum time of four minutes. I could tell I was going to be a couple of seconds fast as I approached the finish line and stood in the stirrups, prepared for my usual wrestling match, convincing Pop that he was not allowed to gallop forever. Much to my amazement, he immediately dropped out of the bridle, and the next thing I knew, I was two seconds slow on Phase B—I had pulled up too soon.

This was so uncharacteristic of our former experiences that I worried myself sick all the way to the vet box. Once dismounted, I told Jack of my mistake. He watched Pop—who was already showing signs of complete recovery from his exertions—for a minute and told me my horse looked great and we would stick to our plan. This suited me; I got a leg up and headed into the start box. Pop was up to his usual pre-cross-country antics, but Suzanne was ready for him, and we got off to a clean start. After a few fences, I noticed that Pop was cruising along at exactly the pace I wanted, but he gave me the eerie feeling that he was dropped out of the bridle. He was jumping well, and we were hitting our minute markers spot on, but he was…different.

This sensation continued all the way to the Lake, which was about halfway around the course. The bounce into water was the same obstacle where Pop had slipped two years before, and I intended to avoid it. I swung wide and went for the alternate route; it was much easier and didn't take all that much more time. We jumped in well, galloped across the water, jumped the bounce bank onto dry land, and got a roar of approval from the huge crowd that always gathers at the Badminton Lake. With that, Pop grabbed the bit and took off up the hill in front of Badminton House, pulling like all hell. I was too busy to think about it clearly, but I suddenly realized he had been worried about the water because he had embarrassed himself there two years ago; once he was past that, he was back on top of his game.

We took one more planned long route and finished the course 12 seconds over the optimum time. Considering Jack had given me a target of 10 to 15 seconds slow, I was pleased, at least until Jack came up to me in the vet box and grumbled something about how I "could have been a little bit quicker." I'd been yelled at by competitive coaches before, so gave a mild reply and turned away. Coaches are never happy.

But as I flew home with Pop the following week, I was happy. I had jumped a clear round on the final day at Badminton and finished in fifth place. Because I was the highest-placed owner-rider, I received the Jubilee Plate from HM The Queen, which was a great thrill for me, and I had the satisfaction of watching my wonderful horse jig back to the stables at the end of the victory gallop, sound as a bell of brass. Life was good, especially considering how far I had come in a little more than a year—from not having been on a team for six years to a good finish at Badminton, with a World Championship team bronze medal to boot. I knew there were improvements that Pop and I could make, and after he had some time off I was eager to get started all over again. This time my goal was the 1980 Moscow Olympics.

I returned to a full barn of students at Fox Covert and plunged into the preparation of those horses, while teaching every weekend clinic I could book. My Badminton trip had ended successfully, but the prize money I won only went a little way toward getting rid of the red ink that covered my checkbook; I had to get back into the scuffle, if I were to keep Fox Covert solvent. Most of the USET travel squad now graduated from my program. Their success was the best sort of advertising and I had a waiting list for stalls. I didn't know it, but I would still have a waiting list 20 years later. All that was well into the future. In the meantime, the Olympics started to occupy a greater and greater place in my thinking.

I had planned a working vacation for Pop after Badminton, walking on the hills around my farm, but no technical training until late in the summer, when I would start preparing him for the fall U.S. National Championships. However, Jack and the selection committee soon changed that plan; they wanted to put Pop and me on the long-list for the Olympics, and to skip the fall season entirely. I was to bring him to the Nationals in late September and do a combined test for the selectors: dressage and show jumping, but no cross-country. This would show that Pop was sound and in work.

This proposal went over like a lead balloon with me, and Jack and I had a polite disagreement about Pop's future. But then Jack, who was always thinking, did a smart thing. He called in reinforcements. Mike Plumb, our team captain, called me to say that in his opinion the selectors were right, and that I should act according to the team's best interests, not my own competitive desires. I wasn't happy, but when both your coach and your team captain tell you to do something, you'd better do it. Pop and I spent the fall "on the bench" while others were busy competing. However, I had plenty of horses and students to train, and clinics to give, so the time passed quickly.

Preparing for the Olympics That Wasn't

___ The next thing I knew, it was January of 1980, the beginning of another Olympic year. This meant Pop and I went back into training, and that I went back on my diet. At this stage of my career, I accepted that I was a little older, and that I had to use my experience to make up for a few extra pounds. I set a goal of 155 pounds and lived on about a thousand calories a day until I got to it. I wasn't a kind, sensitive, caring human being during the process, but the intense demands of an Olympic cycle required intense efforts from the athletes concerned.

The team offered tune-up sessions with Jack at the training facility in South Hamilton, Massachusetts in January and February. I always profited from these sessions, especially because Pop, like most serious Classic horses, didn't think dressage was all that important. This sort of session, early in the training cycle, was perfectly suited to my plans for him. Jack had the answers to my problems. Moreover, I had learned to join up with Jack as soon as possible before a big competition. His mood just after the first of the year was pretty good, but he would become more irascible as the season wore on. Thus, in mid-January, I found myself training in Massachusetts with Torrance Watkins, Kim Walnes, and Ralph Hill.

Remember that "work hard, play hard" motto I mentioned earlier? That was Ralph and me. If you have ever seen two Jack Russell terriers run around in circles, then suddenly touch noses, and vanish—not to be heard from for long periods of time—that was us. We knew Jack would take care of the "work hard" part, so Ralph and I took it upon ourselves to serve as unofficial social chairmen, taking care of the "play hard" part. For example, on our first Sunday, I organized a horse-drawn hay wagon ride for all the grooms, supporters, families, and anybody else interested in spending a crisp New England afternoon burrowed under fresh straw, covered with heavy woolen horse blankets, and fortified by copious amounts of hot chocolate generously laced with peppermint schnapps. Those who didn't go to sleep enjoyed the ride. It might have been my finest hour as a social chairman.

Naturally, this was too tame for Ralph; the last weekend of our session, riders and grooms followed him to a sports bar that was advertised as a "roller disco." Read that sentence again, to understand Ralph's genius. Everybody rented roller skates, bought a drink from the "baristas" or "roll-eristas"—good-looking waiters and waitresses who circled the dance floor, making sure your Harvey Wallbanger didn't need a refill. What could go wrong, right? Every 10 minutes the DJ changed the direction of the circle around the floor, which allowed these new roller-skating divas and rock

64. __ Packy McGaughan was the complete package, equally adept as an international competitor, coach, and author. He combined talent with a keen intellect and a passion for the improvement of the sport, and his untimely passing left a hole in the horse world it will be hard to fill. ■ *© Brant Gamma Photos*

65. __ There are some things in the horse world we cannot measure. Jil Walton has an unusual attribute: horses love to jump for her. Shown here at Galway Downs, Jil's horse My Sedona is jumping for fun. I expect Olympic veterans such as Jil to ride well, but there are other dimensions in riding that I can only watch and wonder at. ■ *© Rick Patterson*

66. ___ David O'Conner and Custom Made at the 1996 Atlanta Olympics. While David usually looks cool and composed in the saddle, I chose a photo that reveals his inner drive and determination, qualities that would contribute to his individual gold medal four years later at the 2000 Sydney Olympics.
■ © Brant Gamma Photos

67. ___ Kim Severson, shown here on Over the Limit, has an unusual skill: she rarely repeats a mistake. Once she learned something from me, she applied it consistently. This allowed her to appear on the eventing scene like a shooting star and win a handful of Olympic and World Championship medals, culminating in her individual silver medal at the 2004 Athens Olympics. ■ © Brant Gamma Photos

68. ___ Although we tried, John Williams and I could never make Sloopy's dressage marks match his superlative jumping results. John would have to labor in obscurity until he found Carrick, who immediately put him onto the USET's teams throughout the early 2000s. ■ *© Brant Gamma Photos*

69. ___ Linden Weisman obviously knew how to jump a big drop well, and Anderoo appreciated it. However, Anderoo was surprisingly fragile mentally. It took Linden's subtle understanding and horsemanship to produce him for the bronze medal Team at the 2000 Sydney Olympics. ■ *© Brant Gamma Photos*

70. — Gina Miles and McKinleigh were an unlikely pair to go to the 2008 Beijing Olympics and win an individual silver medal. McKinleigh was 18 hands and Gina is no bigger than a New York minute, but the partnership worked, even when Gina was impressing McKinleigh with the urgency of the situation. ■ *© Michelle C Dunn*

71. — Nina Fout has made a career of riding "racetrack rejects," and Three Magic Beans was her most difficult challenge. Her horsemanship skills put her on the 2000 Sydney Olympic Team, where she won a team bronze medal. In addition to eventing, Nina wins at point-to-points, horse shows, and side-saddle classes—she is a classic all-around horseman. ■ *© Brant Gamma Photos*

72. ___ Lynn Symansky worked determinedly for years, trying to get to the top of the sport, but suffered an endless succession of horses who were "almost good enough." Once she found her unicorn horse, she and Donner have been USET stalwarts ever since. ■ *© Brant Gamma Photos*

73. ___ Sharon White is an unusual blend of talent, equine intuition, and determination. When you combine her with her beloved Cooley On Show ("Louie"), she is a threat to win every time out. It helps that Louie is one of the best jumpers in the world today.

■ *© Pete Landon/Brant Gamma Photos*

74. ___ When you are at a dude ranch, you can ride into the mountains on quiet cow ponies. If the Seymour and Wofford girls are together, there is a fair amount of giggling involved. From left, this is Catherine Seymour, Hillary Wofford, Elizabeth Seymour, and Jennifer Wofford at the A Bar A, Saratoga, Wyoming. ∎

75. ___ Although the Wofford family is horse crazy, we have dealt with other animals as well. Daphne Dillon and Jennifer Wofford are obviously getting ready for the local 4-H show. Fortunately, Jennifer chose horses over cattle. ∎

76. ___ As my daughters got older and school allowed, I took them with me to events. Hillary was always a delight and was handy to have as an extra helper in the 10-minute vet box at major three-day events. My stable colors are green and white; it must have been cross-country day, with both of us wearing cross-country green. ∎

77. ___ Henry was a wonderful horse. He went to three Olympic Games, then retired and hunted another six years with the Piedmont Fox Hounds. Henry loved his hunting but wasn't exactly a lady's ride. Gail solved this by riding in front with the Master. No matter how long or hard the hunt, Henry would be there at the end. ∎

78. ___ I am with Jud Glascock, Tim Dudley, Sandy Young, Doc Saffer, and Lewis Wiley in Smileyburg, Kansas, on a riotous expedition disguised as a quail hunt. Six close friends, plus wives, have escaped the pressure of work and children for a vacation in comfortable surroundings. After a few trips like this in the fall, I would be ready to go back into training on the first of the year. ∎

79. ___ My mother and Gail are shown here with a homebred I thought would never turn out, Dr. Fugi, who has just finished winning every class in his division. Gail saw something in him and was second in the country at the end of the year. Fort Sill, Oklahoma, was a good show for us—Gail and I won every class in the entire division. Shows like that make up for the hard times. ∎ *© Gloria Axt*

80. —— If you are going to get attacked by a wild hog, you want to be in good company. Dale Elrod is ready for further trouble, while Big Al Martin is showing off his new "Quailmobile." They're two of my best friends, and the three of us walked, drove, and rode over most of southeast Texas, looking for quail, drinking beer, and having fun. ∎

81. —— A man who is too busy to fish is not truly a success. Jim Wolf, Pete Howell, and I firmly believe that. Good fishing partners are hard to find, and we treasure our times together. Besides, hangovers don't hurt as much when you are going to fish the Yellowstone River during a Caddis fly hatch. ∎

82. ___ Gary and I are dressed for success in Alaska's bear country. We are all smiles in this photo, but a little later in the day there was a moment when we thought we might need the ultimate bear repellant. I wasn't too worried; I figured I could outrun Gary. ▪

83. ___ Knowing I would be stressed after coaching at the 2004 Athens Olympics, Gary Johnson invited me to the Goodnews River in Alaska. When I got there, he asked what I wanted to do. I said, "Lets drive upriver until we run out of water, and fish our way back to the lodge." We are about to start upriver, with glorious uncertainty waiting for us. ▪

84. ___ My daughter Jennifer Wofford Ince's and my work schedules led us to Alaska at the same time for a couple of days on the Kenai River. From the bend in her rod, she has hooked something sizeable. We both look like the dog who caught the car: "What do we do now?" ■ © *Gary Johnson*

85. ___ You can hope for something special to happen, but you have to take what the river gives you. As it turned out, on the last cast of the last day, Jennifer caught a gorgeous Dolly Varden and has the photo to prove it. Sometimes a plan comes together.
■ © *Gary Johnson*

86. ___ Hillary Wofford Jones and Plenty of Sweets in the middle of a terrific foxhunt. Mr. Stewart's Cheshire Fox Hounds are in full cry, and Hillary is determined to stay in touch with the hounds. "Sweets" obviously could not care less, and Hillary has him under considerable pressure to catch up. A peach doesn't fall far from the tree. ■ © Jim Graham

87. ___ When I first retired, I did some amateur stewarding work at local point-to-points. This explains my more formal attire, and the smile tells you how much I enjoyed my new career as a race official. However, my clinic business was expanding, and I sadly gave up officiating. ■ © Doug Lees

88. ___ I made it to my fiftieth birthday and decided to throw a black tie dinner dance to celebrate. I never thought I'd make it this far, and figured, "What the hell, it's a chance to show off my wife and daughters." My girls are having a blast, and I'm slightly stunned at my good luck in having such a family. ■

89. ___ Carr-Hughes brought eventing to prime time television. Considering their outstanding track record, I was flattered they chose me to be their color commentator at Kentucky for a decade. Here I am surrounded by two of the brightest television minds in the business. Eventing is lucky that Jim Carr and Bob Hughes took an interest in the sport. ■ *© Michelle C Dunn*

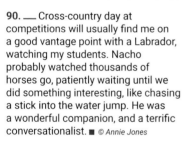

90. ___ Cross-country day at competitions will usually find me on a good vantage point with a Labrador, watching my students. Nacho probably watched thousands of horses go, patiently waiting until we did something interesting, like chasing a stick into the water jump. He was a wonderful companion, and a terrific conversationalist. ■ *© Annie Jones*

91. ___ Duck hunting in flooded timber is a lovely experience. No, I didn't shoot them all myself, but I was happy to hold them while the other guns went to get the boat. Although Tiger swam out and fetched most of them, he is still watching the sky, hoping for one more duck. ■ *© Carol Stephens*

92. ___ While I was president of the AHSA, I had to do a fair amount of "ribbon snipping." Understandably, I was all smiles when I escorted HRH The Princess Royal, as well as the royalty of the show jumping world for the prize-giving at the 1989 Tampa World Cup. Big Ben and Ian Millar were no strangers to the winner's circle, and Bill Steinkraus, on Ian's left, was a winner in every endeavour. ■ © www.photogyllensten.com

93. ___ At one point in my career in horse politics, I was president of the AHSA (what would become USEF) while Bill Steinkraus was president of the USET. By this time, Bill had gone from hero to role model to mentor to, finally, good friend. We would both have rather been hunting, or fooling with horses, but we felt a debt to the sport, and worked closely together to improve it. ■ © Brant Gamma Photos

94. ___ I'm shown here accepting the U.S. Equestrian Federation's Lifetime Achievement Award. While I was enormously pleased to get the award, you can see a slight bittersweet look in my eyes. I'm realizing this is the last time I will ever stand on the national stage and am sorry there is not enough room on the stage for all the horses who put me there. ■ *© Nancy Jaffer*

95. ___ I am never happier than when I am bent over the withers of a good horse at the gallop, but hunting with Tiger, the best Labrador I've ever had, is a pretty good substitute. Standing hip-deep in cold water with your four-legged friend is a wonderful way to spend a morning. ■ *© C.Martin Wood*

stars to quench their thirst before setting out in the opposite direction. After a couple of turns in both directions, and a couple of Harvey Wall-bangers, I had that lovely thought that I was kinda getting the hang of this new skill. At that instant, I barely avoided a three-disco-diva pile-up on the far turn and sobered up enough to realize I was having way too much fun, and I'd better slink away before I broke something. Ralph was a big boy, had his own truck, and was obviously taken with the raciest model of the rolleristas. What happens in South Hamilton, stays in South Hamilton. When Pop, Suzanne, and I drove home the next day, I was sore in places I didn't even know I had places, and happy to be returning to Fox Covert to start my spring training.

My daily schedule looked like this during my spring season: At six in the morning I went to the Middleburg Training Center and galloped four sets of young racehorses for Lewis Wiley. By the time I got back to Fox Covert, Suzanne would have walked Pop for two hours while leading Alex, and I would ride them according to their daily training schedule. Alex was a USET horse that Jack had sent home with me as a second upper-level ride, to make sure I was fit enough and stayed competition-sharp. This was a thrill for me, as I had always loved Alex, but until now never had the chance to ride him. Used as a sort of upper-level schoolhorse for the riders in residence at the USET, he had been around most of the cross-country courses on the East Coast (and had riders miss their distance to most of the jumps on him) and evinced a dull "been-there, done-that" attitude. I was sure that a different atmosphere would bring out the qualities I saw in him.

Once I was through with my upper-level horses (I had gotten out of the young horse end of the business by now), I trained the other horses and riders at Fox Covert. Then in the late afternoon, three days a week, I drove to a local gymnasium that had a complete set of Nautilus machines and worked out for an hour. By then it was time for evening stables, and after that I went home to dinner. Once Gail and I had discussed our day, and I helped tuck the girls into bed, I never had to worry about falling asleep; my head barely touched the pillow before I was out cold.

I had followed a similar schedule for several years, so was comfortable with it and knew where I was in terms of my own and my horses' fitness. Because there were far fewer spring competitions in those days, my students and I were able to stay on this schedule for weeks at a time. I don't remember my results from the spring selection trials, as my instructions from Jack were to get the best possible dressage score, show jump clean, get my horses settled into a good rhythm cross-country and not worry about the time. We knew what Pop and I were capable of by now; the only thing we had to prove was that we were fit and sound.

This plan was working perfectly so far, due to the intensity of my concentration, and our performance at the spring Classic was good enough to be named to the team. However, this intensity meant I never read a newspaper or listened to the news, which is why the announcement that the United States would boycott the 1980 Moscow Olympics hit me like a thunderbolt. Just like that, thousands of U.S. athletes were robbed of the chance to represent their country on their sports' biggest stage. Jack was as stunned as I was, but soon called with the news that the FEI had decided to host Alternate Olympics in each of the three Olympic equestrian disciplines, and eventers were to compete in France, at Fontainebleau. We would ship 12 horses in mid-July, a month ahead of the Alternate Olympics, to Compiégne, north of Paris. Jack had found some lovely stabling, the surrounding area had miles of sandy trails for hacking and cantering, and we had access to some dressage arenas and show-jumping facilities.

The event at Fontainebleau was to be run under World Championship rules: the dressage, cross-country, and show jumping would use Olympic specifications, and each nation could enter a team of four plus two official individuals. Our team was Mike Huber on Gold Chip, Torrance Watkins on Poltroon, Mike Plumb on Lauriston, and me on Carawich, with Wash Bishop on Taxi and Karen Stives on The Saint as the individuals. The six other U.S. horses and riders would go on to compete at Luhmühlen a week later.

A Wild and Wonderful Ride

—— Pop gave me my greatest thrill on horseback at the Alternate Olympics in 1980—he ran away with me around a formidable cross-country course. But it didn't start out that way on cross-country day. I had left a few dressage points on the table but was generally happy with his attitude so far—until the Phase A starter said "Go." This was usually a signal for Pop to play the fool at a flat-out gallop, but not this time. He trotted out of the start box on a loose rein, obviously switched off and whistling a carefree tune to himself. I was suddenly gripped with fear. Was something wrong? Was he colicking, getting a fever? These two worries persisted to the start of steeplechase, with me tormented by doubt, and with Pop as "happy as Larry." (Whoever Larry was, he was a happy dude.)

The pattern repeated itself at the Start of Phase B. Pop broke off sharply, but then settled on a soft rein into a galloping rhythm that was quick enough to bring us to the end just under the time allowed. In addition, he quickly figured out that the steeplechase fences were lightly stuffed with brush but presented no kind of serious obstacle. By the third fence, Pop was stepping through (as opposed to jumping over) the filling, and I could feel the tops of the brush with my feet. He was displaying economical jumping at its finest. This year I timed the change in my galloping stance at, rather than before, the finish line, in order to avoid the time faults that had plagued me at Badminton last year.

Pop's new attitude immediately resurfaced on Phase C; he walked quietly for two minutes, then resumed a relaxed, ground-covering trot. He was on the buckle and totally laid back. I, on the other hand, was even more worried. Pop had never acted like this before; he had to be sick or hurt. I trotted the last hundred meters at the end of Phase C so that Jack and our vet, the incomparable Marty Simensen, could watch him for unsoundness. He was obviously sound, and Suzanne and the USET "pit crew" took over while Jack, Marty, and I conferred. Marty said Pop's temperature, pulse, and respiration were the best of the day, and his vitals were almost back to normal after Phase C. I reiterated my concerns to Jack and Marty, but we all mentally shrugged. It was the Olympics, we could find nothing wrong, and under the circumstances I would do the best possible job I could. Getting on Pop there was always a struggle, as he would be ready to strike off at the gallop even if we had not gotten into the start box yet. But this time, uncharacteristically, Pop stood like a statue as Jack gave me a leg up.

And then, and then, ladies and gentlemen, and then...the minute I gathered my reins, Pop went crazy. One second I was sitting quietly; the next thing I knew, he was slinging Suzanne around like the tail of a kite, running sideways, knocking over water buckets, spilling tack boxes and grooming kits everywhere, while grooms and officials scrambled over the crowd barrier fencing to escape being trampled. Suzanne got him barely under control and headed for the start box, while I sat up there and started to laugh. I suddenly realized that Pop had learned to save himself for the cross-country, and now he was ready for his favorite part of the whole event. I was still smiling as we went under starter's orders, but I had not caught up with Pop's thinking, which was basically, "Sit still, Woff. I got this." Finally understanding the rhythm of the entire speed and endurance test, and sensing the importance of the occasion, Pop took over.

He bolted toward the first fence much faster than I would have liked. However, I quickly got the same sensation as I had on steeplechase: I was going faster than I wanted, but only a little bit faster, and Pop was locked in the reins. I couldn't get him to slow down, and if I didn't keep a firm hold he would increase his speed. So—a balancing act on my part: keep enough pressure on the reins and Pop would not keep increasing his speed, but if I softened my hands, we sped up. Needless to say, I had a tight grip on the reins. There was a very big but straightforward combination early in the course: rails up onto a square bank, several strides across the bank, then a big set of rails with a drop behind. My plan was to slow down slightly for this combination, but Pop was having none of that. Never slackening his pace, he skipped up onto the bank, left out several strides and launched himself over the rails, landing like a feather and leaning into the next turn.

John Harty had come over from Ireland for the event, and he and Gail were watching the combination. Gail later told me that as I went by, she gripped John's arm and said, "My God, John, isn't he going too fast?" In his lovely Irish brogue, John replied, "Sure now, he's a great lepper, and they'll be all right." Then Gail said he added, under his breath, "...if he doesn't fall."

Most of the course took place in a pine forest with lovely sand footing. The track became more and more twisty as we went along, so I expected the first part of the course would probably be the quickest. I noticed I had no trouble guiding Pop through the turns and bends; all I had to do was step into my new inside stirrup, look in the direction I wanted to turn, and he would take me there. This system was working well until I rounded a turn at 600 mpm to find a lady with a baby carriage in the middle of the path. I squalled at her and she pushed the baby carriage into the poison ivy and leapt after it as we whizzed past. There was no contact, so I guess all's well that ends well. I was too busy to stop and ask.

This wasn't my only brush with near disaster that day. The far end of the course was flagged using old-fashioned gas station tape, with a 180-degree turn to start horse and rider back toward the finish line. The problem was, I only completed about 179 degrees of the turn before Pop left the track, broke through the flagging, and started creating his own path through the poison ivy and sumac that lined the galloping lane. Ducking branches and leaves, we broke through the tape again and were back on the galloping lane, headed toward a huge, old-fashioned maximum open ditch. There was now a flapping, clattering noise behind us with every stride and looking back, I saw yards of tape snagged in Pop's off-hind galloping boot. The noise was caused by his dragging it with him as he careened down the hill. Pop took this as an incentive to go faster; by the time we got to the open ditch, we must have been doing 800 mpm.

I knew I would have no luck trying to pull up, get off, get rid of the tape, and remount. It would take too much time and anyway, Pop wasn't going to pull up for anything. So I mentally shrugged, jumped the ditch, and left the gas station tape behind. No harm, no foul, right? Thinking about my experiences later on, the analogy occurred to me that Pop went through the course like a child at Christmas. He hurried toward each new obstacle like a Christmas present, ripped it open, inspected its contents, and immediately lost interest and turned his attention to the next present.

He was still pulling like a demon when we arrived at the final combination on the course, a difficult water complex. There was a longer way through it, and several alternate routes once you were in the water.

Some instinct had made me walk one alternate route out with special care; this was a good thing. When Pop pecked on landing in the water, I quickly turned to the long way, being careful not to cross my tracks while turning back to jump out. The next jump was a large set of rails with a formidable, maximum drop behind them. As we took off, I reminded myself to slip my reins. This was a worthy suggestion, but as we landed I found myself up around Pop's ears. Fortunately, I righted myself, we jumped the last few fences, and went through the finish line with the fastest time of the day. I pulled up by the scales and received permission to dismount. But when I got down, I found my hands were cramped on the reins. Pop had been pulling so hard all the way around the course that my hands had literally frozen closed, which explained my serious bobble at the last big drop; I had been snatched out of the saddle by my short reins. I peeled my fingers open one at a time, and handed Pop to Suzanne while I "weighed in."

As I stepped off the scales, Gail came around the corner and burst out laughing. "You should see yourself," she said. Taking my helmet off, I realized I was decorated with leaves and branches stuck in the button on top of my helmet from my off-road excursion, while my arms were covered with minor scrapes and cuts from the branches and thorns we had burst through. I just smiled and went looking for a beer.

We threw a party that night, but it wasn't too wild; we would not finish as a team. Mike Huber's horse had a fall and would not be presented for the final vet check. Mike Plumb's horse took a dislike to the final cross-country water and did not complete. Overnight, this left Torrance Watkins, with her lovely pinto mare, Poltroon, in third place, and Pop in second place—and that's how we finished. The party was a little more exuberant the night after show jumping, but it didn't go on too late. Jack was leaving early in the morning for Luhmühlen with six horses and riders, and Gail and I were headed home, where I had a busy program waiting for me.

On the flight home I thought back over my results and was strangely satisfied. I had not won the individual gold, but I had come close—and most important, I had ridden well. One thing I could say for myself is that I had enough sense to sit quietly and let Pop "run his race." We had finished with the fastest round of the day and an individual silver medal. Is it any wonder that I loved him above all horses?

The Education of Alex

——Other horses at home now took the majority of my attention. My students were doing well and waiting for me to come home so we could put the final polish on their performances before the fall U.S. Championships at Chesterland, in Unionville, Pennsylvania. In addition, Jack had allowed me to keep Alex for the fall season, and I was excited about that. By now, Alex had nine months of good Virginia grass, as well as a different feeding and training regimen, under his belt. Tom Glascock, my senior working student, had done a good job of conditioning while I was gone. I'm almost as proud of the job I did with Alex as I am of Pop's performance at the Alternate Olympics. Without Jack noticing it, Alex had developed a bit of a schoolhorse attitude as a result of having been used as a high-level schoolmaster; he was bored with life. At Fox Covert he spent at least 12 hours a day turned out with Pop. Suzanne led him when she hacked Pop out, so Alex's back was spared the weight of a rider except for the three days a week that I either jumped him to keep his jumping muscles tuned up or practiced his dressage movements. After I'd built a solid aerobic base on him, I trailered him to a local training center and galloped him with racehorses there. For his final work before the fall championships, I "open-galloped" him a mile at probably 600 mpm, then worked him head-and-head for a quarter mile with a Stakes winner, and he held his own. Alex thought he had died and gone to heaven, he was having so much fun.

We won the Nationals that fall, but there is a backstory. As a school horse for the Team, he had become used to a rider worried about remembering the dressage test, not getting lost on roads and tracks, and jumping the cross-country according to Jack's last minute cross-country advice: "Not too slow, not too fast, but just right." This sort of advice tended to produce time faults but clear rounds, which was Jack's secret intention, and Alex was complicit in the strategy. His rider would typically lie awake Saturday night after leaving the competitor's party early, hoping to not miss their stride in Sunday's show jumping too many times.

At the Championships, Alex was in for a shock. I showed up ready to have my horse go well, by which I meant I would get as close as possible to the standard requirements of each phase of the competition. I wouldn't win the dressage, but by riding an accurate, forward test, I could get close to the leaders. It was easy to ride accurately on Alex but that forward part escaped him entirely, so I wore the biggest, longest, sharpest spurs I had ever used on an event horse. They worked when I applied them vigorously, and Alex turned in a nice score, much to people's amazement. He had spent years with riders who were satisfied with average, but he was starting to realize there was a new sheriff in town.

The real surprise for Alex, however, waited for him at the start of Phase B, the steeplechase. His manners on roads and tracks were lovely as he trotted quietly, taking nothing out of himself on Phase A. (This was a welcome change after my experiences reminding Pop that he had confused Phase A with a jumping and galloping phase.) When the starter said "Go," Alex and I burst out of the start box and were at 700 mpm within a few strides (the required speed was 690 mpm). Michael Page had taught me that horses were never fitter than at the start and the jumps were never easier, so the first quarter of the course was the place to get a jump on the clock.

Alex galloped happily enough, but slowed slightly before the first brush fence, waiting for me to take the reins and start "looking for a spot." I had trusted his experience and had not bothered to ride a school at home, so this was the first steeplechase we had jumped together. A brusque application of the spurs and a sharp reminder with my stick produced the sort of effort I was looking for; taking the first in stride, Alex brushed through the top of the soft cedar stuffing in the fence. It didn't take him long to figure out that the fences were stuffed improperly, and there was nothing substantial about them. (I have pictures from Chesterland that year of Alex, looking slightly bored, stepping completely through the lowest part of the steeplechase fence with cedar sticking up to the brown tops of my boots.) The rest of the steeplechase was easy for Alex, on the basis that he was galloping at the required speed but doing very little jumping.

Pulling up on Phase C, he walked for a couple of minutes and his breathing came back to nearly normal. The rest passed uneventfully, and I had plenty of time in the vet box with Jack, who advised me about the cross-country. Once again, we burst out of the start box, and went whizzing down to the first fence. In the final approach, I had time to think, "Gee, I hope he remembers to jump over the solid rails and not try to push through it like the steeplechase fences." But Alex was nobody's fool and jumped it well enough, given that he was going probably 100 mpm more than he was used to.

He probably thought I'd settle down in a moment and he would canter the rest of the course quietly and go home to a warm bath and a carrot.

I explained to him that nothing less than his best effort would be on display today, and backed up my argument with my stick at the next couple of fences. I can honestly say I have never put as much pressure on any other horse around a cross-country course. Alex had been around this course a few times and he knew exactly where the stabling was. He galloped freely when going toward the barn, but immediately started to whine if the course turned away from home. I had a few more teachable moments going away from the barn and managed a clear round just inside the optimum time. He cooled out quickly, and while he didn't jig on the way home with Suzanne, he did walk with his ears up, looking for dinner. I was proud of him because he had answered my call, and I was proud of the adjustments I had made in my normal training schedule to produce him in such good condition that a fifteen-mile Classic was just a stroll in the park.

We jumped a clear show-jumping round to win the Nationals, and accepting the trophy was a satisfying moment for me. The accolades that go with the title are nice. It was the third time I had won, but even sweeter was the feeling that I had ridden well over all three days, and after months of planning and preparation I had produced a horse in peak condition. However, driving back to Virginia was bittersweet for me. The loan of Alex was over, and he was loaded on the Team van that would return him to South Hamilton. I thanked Jack, and mentioned that whenever he retired Alex, I would have a home for him.

Success at Last

——In the meantime, I had a large group of horses at home in training for Radnor, and Pop's recuperation from his exertions in France to supervise. My competitive season was over, and what a season it had been! Three years of riding Carawich had brought me back to the top end of the sport, and the view was a lot better from there than from the six years I had spent on the bench, wondering if I would ever get another chance to compete at top-level events, much less be successful.

I had other considerations while I was headed home. Some friends of mine from Radnor, Dick and Vita Thompson, had reached out to me the previous spring. They had an Advanced horse in training with another rider who had lost interest, and would I take the ride? I had agreed and brought the horse to Fox Covert on trial. After a month or so, I called the Thompsons, and said I didn't think the horse was suitable for eventing. They agreed and asked me to buy them a couple of young horses while I was in France for the Alternate Olympics, as they enjoyed their connection with the sport as owners and organizers at Radnor. I'd made a quick side trip to England and Ireland before flying home and purchased two young horses for the Thompsons: one was "Mutley," a team 'chaser that Lars Sederholm had for sale. He was a five-year-old, 17-hand bay gelding Irish Sport Horse with extravagant paces and a powerful jump; the other was "Vulgan's Heir," a four-year-old, Irish, 16.2-hand chestnut gelding Thoroughbred bred to be a 4-mile steeplechaser. (They immediately became Mutt and Jeff, after the cartoon characters.) They had settled in well, and I made plans to start them in some local events in the spring.

As if this weren't enough on my plate, Jack had announced plans to take a squad to Luhmühlen, Germany in the summer. Luhmühlen would be the site for the 1982 World Championships, so our trip would give us a chance to get comfortable in those surroundings. With this in mind, I started the year with a training session at South Hamilton, Massachusetts. Jack was always at his best early in the year, and his comments served to guide my work. I took Pop and Mutley, and Jack loaned me Blue Stone, a nice Irish gray gelding, as a third ride.

As 1981 progressed, it shaped up to be an exciting year for me. The United States Olympic Committee (USOC) named me as Equestrian's first athlete representative. (This position was appointed at the time; later on it became an elected position.) I had also been nominated as vice president of the National Federation at the annual meeting of the AHSA. This was not a big job in itself; you basically stood around waiting for the serving president to retire. However, behind the scenes I would be expected to handle hot-potato issues that came up and develop solutions for them. I had already been involved in horse politics, but this was taking it to a new level. I've forgotten the exact date, but around this time I was also named to the USET Executive Committee, which meant in addition to my riding and training, I was subjected to an endless avalanche of memos and conference calls.

This was my fourth year riding Pop and I knew him intimately; that was the good news. The bad news was that Pop wasn't training as well as he had the year before. I was running him at the same prep events and he was placing well, but he wasn't quite as sharp. I discussed this with Jack, who asked if he was sound. I replied that Dr. Mayo had done a complete vet scan—blood tests, the works. Nothing. Jack just shrugged and told me to keep working. However, I knew something was slightly out of kilter.

To top off my confusion, despite my misgivings Pop won Kentucky 1981, one of the few events I ever won going "wire-to-wire." I'd had my problems that spring, having lost Mutley to a broken leg at an early spring competition; a win at Kentucky was a great lift to my spirits. In addition, the Thompsons offered to replace the loss of Mutt with a horse that was currently competing at a higher level, and in Ireland I found Rockingham, an eight-year-old dark bay, 16.1-hand Irish/Thoroughbred gelding. He had enough experience for me to aim him toward our fall National Championships at Chesterland. The Thompsons were becoming friends as well as owners, which is the best possible relationship for a rider to have. In addition, the more they experienced the life of horse owners, the more they enjoyed it, and the more supportive they became.

Obviously, things were working well for me, but I was still secretly unsettled. Something was missing in Pop's preparation, and I couldn't track it down. In addition, I was starting to think about my future. I was now in my late thirties. My physical nerve was still good (a major factor for a Classic rider); I had some nagging injuries, but they were manageable, tolerable, and most importantly, concealable from the selectors. I was preparing for my competitions with a growing sense of competence. But I was starting to envision a future beyond riding. I was more and more deeply involved in horse politics, but—again—I did not view that as lasting forever. I felt an obligation to pay back to the sport by volunteering my time to various organizations, but that obligation was not open-ended. I did not intend to spend the rest of my life sitting in committee meetings or listening to interminable conference calls.

I did not have to decide right away, but I could feel that decision time would soon arrive. In the meantime, I had to get Pop ready for our trip to Luhmühlen. Jack and I had determined our plan during my winter training sessions. It was the same as we had used at Badminton two years earlier: We weren't going there to necessarily win, but to keep Pop sharp without any needless stress on his system. I was comfortable with this. Our goal was to win the World Championships the following year, and I knew Pop was a favorite to win a medal in 12 months.

I maintained a busy schedule of clinics in between competitions that spring, as I (once more) needed to restore my financial situation to solvency. I had sacrificed a lot of income in 1980 in order to stay home and train for the Olympics.

During my travels to and from clinics throughout that summer, the mystery of Pop's condition continued to plague me. Teaching clinics meant a lot of time on airplanes, and I took my training records from the spring of 1980 with me. Once aloft, I matched them with this spring's records. I compared them day by day for the two months before Kentucky, but this meticulous inspection only produced more mystery. Pop had done exactly the same amount of work, on the same day before the competition, on the same terrain. To an eerie degree, the two training schedules were identical, yet Pop felt different—I just couldn't figure out *why* he felt different.

Flying home late one night, I looked over my two schedules one more time, still didn't find anything, and gave up. Reclining in my seat, I thought how lucky I was to have Suzanne, who could keep Pop in work for me while I was gone, including many of his conditioning gallops. She loved to tease me that Pop was a perfect gentleman with her, and never pulled during his gallops, although he leaned on me unmercifully from first to last.

Eureka!

The mystery was solved. Although Pop had worked the same amount, over the same terrain, at the same speed, for the same amount of time, he actually had done less work with Suzanne than he had with me; he didn't pull when Suzanne rode him. Satisfied that I had figured out the mystery, and learned a little more about conditioning horses, I closed my eyes and slept like a baby all the way to Dulles Airport. I had horses and riders waiting for me back at Fox Covert, and a program to run.

The Highs Are High, but the Lows Are Low

——Soon enough I was back at Dulles headed for Luhmühlen, Germany. The Team was coming over for this one event in order to check out the course and conditions for the 1982 World Championships. Pop was training well, and I was happy with our preparation. Once I had solved the mystery of Pop's seeming lack of conditioning, I made sure that I was in the saddle for his last month of his training. As expected, he did his best to run away with me, and his last few gallops were right on the mark. We were as prepared as we were going to get that year. This was hugely encouraging. I had my eyes on the 1982 World Championships, and I felt I had a real chance to win it—everything I did between now and then was dedicated to that one goal. I wanted to produce Pop at his absolute best, to give him one more chance to show the world what a superlative animal he was.

Of course, that was not the whole story. I had been rated number three in the world after the Alternate Olympics in 1980. Naturally, I felt I should have been number two, behind only Nils Haagensen of Denmark, who had won the individual gold medal, instead of Lucinda Green of Great Britain. I still had something to prove, and I had the horse to do it with. Luhmühlen in 1981 was only a step toward that goal.

We shipped into Luhmühlen safely and Pop settled in like the pro that he was, taking a nap in his stall and then on his toes when we hacked out. After our dressage test I was quietly confident; while we were not winning, we were close. Jack and I had agreed our goal this year was not to win but to prepare to win at the 1982 World Championships.

The 1981 cross-country course was big, but plain vanilla; course designer Wolfgang Feldt was not "showing his cards" for his plans for 1982. Pop settled into his easy rhythm on the cross-country course that day and was jumping effortlessly. About three-quarters of the way around we had to make a 90-degree left turn, jump onto a big square bank, take one short stride on top, jump off, turn 90 degrees right, and jump a small thatched-roof house. Pop threw a prodigious leap onto the bank, took a shuffle stride, jumped off...and landed three-legged lame. We staggered over the small house and I cantered on for a few more strides, hoping Pop had just stung himself, but he was lame, and I pulled him up. Then I jumped down, ran up my stirrups, and took one of the longest walks I have ever endured, leaving all my dreams of a World Championship title behind me.

Pop walked home on what we found out that night was a broken pedal bone. Our team vet, Marty Simensen, looked at the X-rays and said Pop would need about six months' stall rest, and would probably never be truly sound again. As if that weren't bad enough, there was a good chance that the stress of standing three-legged for months would cause him to break down in front. If that happened, we would have to put him down. I had to decide whether to ship him home or find a convalescent facility in Germany and leave him overseas for a year. I knew that if we could get him home, we would care for him better than anyone else in the world, so I pulled out my secret weapon—Suzanne—and on the following Monday shipped him home with the rest of the Team horses, knowing that Suzanne would take the best possible care of him.

I had to fly home myself the same day, as I had a large contingent of horses and riders waiting for me. The Fall National Championships were only a month away, and in addition to my training and coaching duties, I had a ride in the Championships on Vita and Dick Thompson's new horse, Rockingham. I had ridden Rocky in a few horse trials in the spring, but he had "tied up" (suffered a bout of azoturia) on arriving at Kentucky, and I had missed the chance to ride him over a big course under pressure.

The Championships at Chesterland would be my next chance to find out if Rocky had the makings of a Team horse at that level. Unfortunately, I discovered that Rocky panicked under pressure, and I could not count on him over a big course. For a year that had started out with a wire-to-wire win at Kentucky and with Pop and me at the top of the heap, 1981 had sure gone downhill. During the fall and winter of that year, I had to do some serious thinking.

I had been considering retirement before Pop came along in the late 1970s, and now here I was, five years later, back on the Team bench. Although retirement was always in the back of my mind, I felt an obligation to Vita and Dick, and agreed to continue riding Rocky as long as they were interested. I had shared my misgivings with them; they knew I was doubtful that he could ever be truly competitive at the upper levels. My hunting and fishing diary says that I was not totally distracted and depressed, as I did my fair share of hunting that fall. I had a full barn, my teaching program continued to be successful, and 1982 promised to be busy, if not as successful for me. ■

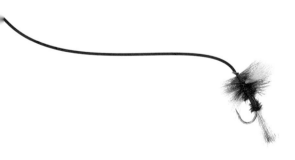

CHAPTER

15

Los Angeles Olympics—Maybe

Ya wanna be real nice to people on the way up...
'cause you're gonna meet 'em again on the way back down.

Anonymous
(Country and Western artists' saying)

By this time, my first rodeo was far behind me; completing two Olympics and two World Championships will turn you into a pretty good imitation of a veteran. But even after all that experience I was still unsatisfied. I wanted to be the best event rider in the world before I retired. Pop's injury made it look as if I would have to give up on that dream. But I still had a full barn, and two upper-level rides: Rocky and Blue Stone (a 17-hand, gray Irish Sport Horse gelding owned by the USET). I think Jack felt sorry for me. I had done a good job with Alex, so he sent "Blue" as an additional ride early in 1982. I now had two Advanced horses to get to know, and to get ready for Kentucky.

I was finding out that Rocky was blazingly fast cross-country, but at some point his feet would get going faster than his brain and he would panic. All that spring, I worked on keeping him from getting what we "scientifically" termed "gerbil brain." We got some good ribbons, but he popped a splint before Kentucky, so once again I missed the chance to ride him over a big course, where his speed could make up for his typically Irish disdain for dressage.

Blue presented a different set of problems. A terrible cribber, he wore a cribbing strap whenever he was not under tack. Jack never turned horses out, as he was convinced they would hurt themselves playing—or, in Blue's case, jumping out of whatever enclosure he was in. Jack had a 20-foot round pen with sand footing enclosed by 6-foot chain link, and he would turn horses out in there for a short time. Blue took one look at the green grass on the other side, popped over the 6-foot fence from a walk, and immediately started to graze. Jack panicked at this and refused to allow Blue to be turned out at all, so when he got to me he had either been under tack or in his stall for the past six months. He was cribbing violently regardless of the strap, was a picky eater, and took no interest in his work.

After 1978, Jack and I formed a closer partnership, and over the next few years, we rarely disagreed. However, turnout was one of the few areas we did, and so Blue went out the next morning following his new paddock buddy, one of my old hunters. Blue was in such a hurry to get to the grass he never thought of jumping out. I can't remember him ever taking the trouble to jump out, when all that lovely Virginia grass was available. He continued to crib, so I purchased a spray that contained peppers, capsaicin, and other distasteful substances. Every time I found a place in his stall that showed signs he was cribbing, I sprayed it liberally and he did not return to it. By the time he shipped to Kentucky he no longer wore a strap, and his cribbing was almost cured.

However, by then it was obvious that Blue and I were not a good match. He had been ridden by several different Team riders before me. Show jumping was easy for him, but dressage was a problem; Blue was basically lazy, and it was difficult to motivate him. General Chamberlin once said a trained horse should respond to the wind from the rider's heels; in Blue's case, that wind had to be a hurricane to get a response. I was used to horses who were insanely brave and needed no encouragement to go to their fences. Blue, on the other hand, did exactly what you told him to do, and no more. Not having figured this out yet, at the final preparation horse trials I managed to be the only rider in history who had a cross-country refusal with Blue. I forgot to tell him to jump, so he didn't jump.

He was a bit green around the Kentucky cross-country course but jumped clean and finished fairly well. Jack and I talked about it after the event, and I told him I didn't suit Blue, and that Mike Plumb needed a horse. Jack agreed and Blue went back to the training center in South Hamilton, Massachusetts. In the meantime, I returned to Fox Covert; I had to nurse Rocky back to soundness and train my students for more competitions.

It was a sign of the growth in the sport that we were developing more "destination" events. At first, we only had Kentucky and Radnor to look forward to, and if you wanted to be successful, you only had a couple of chances every year to prove it. Now, however, we had spring championships for Juniors and for Intermediate horses. On the East Coast, our big destination event was the Essex Horse Trials, held annually at the USET training headquarters in Gladstone.

I did not have a ride at Essex; Rocky had been aimed at Kentucky, and "Jeff," aka Vulgan's Heir, was not successful for the Thompsons. Because Jeff was an evergreen they had decided to sell him and look for a replacement.

I had plenty of students to worry about, and various committee meetings over the week, so I wasn't bored as I walked toward the official briefing.

The Rainbow Reappears

——Little did I know that once again, incredible as it seems, I had just stepped into the shadow of the rainbow. Walking toward me was one of the foreign judges for the event, Judy Bradwell, a famous English rider and judge. I should say instead I saw her limping badly toward me; Judy had suffered a crashing fall with a young horse the year previously, and at the time was lucky not to lose her leg entirely. As she healed, doctors told her she would never walk again, so she had proved them wrong, Then they told her she would never ride again, and to prove them wrong again, Judy had taken up dressage, because she could not stand the shock of landing after a jump.

After a brief catch-up session, Judy explained she wanted to sell her best horse, Castlewellan, whom I knew she loved above all other horses. "Jimmy," she said, "I've got to sell him abroad, as I couldn't bear to watch him being ridden by someone else." She went on to explain that she knew "Paddy" would have a good home with me and asked if I were interested in buying him. Basically, I said, "I'll be right back." Both Dick and Vita Thompson were at Essex, and I found them before the briefing started and explained the situation to them. All three of us knew about Castlewellan, as he was already very successful in both the U.K. and Western Europe; he had won Luhmühlen two years ago as a seven-year-old. People had been trying to buy him for years, but Judy knew this was her horse of a lifetime and wouldn't sell. Only a tragic accident had changed her mind, and I was the recipient of a chance at buying a horse who could put me back "into the scuffle" at the top end of the sport. To make a long story short, by nightfall Paddy had a new owner in the Thompsons, and a new rider—yours truly.

Judy told me a great deal about him before she left Essex: likes and dislikes, feeding and conditioning schedules, and so on. However, she warned me that he was not as easy to ride as he made it appear. She told me that he could throw a fit out of nowhere, and she had learned there was no dealing with him when he was in that sort of mood. The best thing to do was take him for a walk and try again the next day. I thanked her for the inside information, but like any upper-level rider, thought to myself, "I'll fix that, no problem." No matter how good the other rider was, I thought I was just that little bit better. Of course, those other riders had never met Paddy.

By the end of June 1982, Paddy had settled in well at Fox Covert and my dream of riding at the 1984 Los Angeles Olympics, 52 years after my father rode there, was back on track. By early fall, he had thrown several uncontrollable fits with me where he would resist his dressage work violently; like Judy, I had learned to shrug and take him for a walk. The next day, he would come out of his stall in a totally different mood, and ready to work at whatever I had planned for him.

Naturally, Jack had been taking an interest in Paddy's progress with me, and I had shared these experiences with him. He had no better answer than I had, but we agreed that a full-scale fall event was not in my best interests, and I aimed him for Radnor at Intermediate level instead of the Fall U.S. Advanced Championships. I only had about 90 days to get to know him, and that wasn't enough time to predict his responses; if I got it wrong, I wanted to be at an event where I had a wider margin of error. Both Jack and I knew Paddy gave me a real chance at making the 1984 Olympic team, but I had to form a much better partnership to make that dream a reality. As it turned out, I was needlessly cautious, and we won the Championships at Radnor that fall.

Paddy, a bright bay 16.1-hand Irish/Thoroughbred gelding with a star and a snip, was a dream to ride. Judy was a terrific dressage rider and had trained him very well. He had three lovely paces; judges took one look at him and fell in love. He was the only horse I ever rode that gave me a chance to win the dressage every time I rode down the centerline. He was also one of the few horses of that era that I believe would be equally successful today. He had no quirks on cross-country, and his Thoroughbred breeding gave him the speed and the stamina to deal with a full-scale Classic event. He had a wicked rightward drift when show jumping, but he was a careful jumper; I learned to compensate for the drift.

People ask me what differences I notice between those Classic events and modern short-format events, what was the stage of the sport in the 1970s and '80s, and so on. Certainly the change in formats has revolutionized the sport, and riders are much better technically than we were in that era. Eventers draw larger crowds these days, jump for more prize money, and are in a much more professional environment than in years past. But an overlooked aspect of modern eventing is a near-miraculous technological advance in diagnosing equine ailments. Half a century ago, when a horse like Paddy threw a fit, horsemen simply trained around that lost day. Nowadays, a full-scale veterinary workup would almost certainly pinpoint the underlying physical problem that produced "one of his fits." I am convinced Paddy had an undiagnosed neurological condition, one that produced occasional intense pain and caused him to react violently. It speaks to his temperament that he would return to work the next day without carrying a grudge.

When the fall season was over, Jack announced to his riders that the 1983 Pan American Games would not include eventing, and those of us with Olympic aspirations should get in touch individually about our plans for the coming year. I called Vita and Dick, who suggested I work up a plan and tell them about it. They were the most wonderful owners and friends, and were behind my efforts 100 percent. Jack and I agreed I should aim Paddy and Rocky for Kentucky in the spring and then train in England that summer. Paddy would go to Burghley and Rocky to Wylie. Fortunately for me, Mark Phillips heard of my plans and offered stabling at Gatcombe Park, plus lodging for both Suzanne and me. Once again, I had a chance at competing with the best in the world, on a horse that was up to the challenge. I had always dreamed of riding in the Los Angeles Olympics, to follow in my father's footsteps, and it looked like I had a good chance to make that dream a reality. Now it was up to me to produce Paddy and Rocky in top form. I was getting to know them and was confident that next year I could produce both horses ready to be competitive.

As usual, I took some time off during the winter. This gave me time to both look backward—to think about my results—and look ahead, to make sure my plans went as well as possible. In addition, regardless of what happened over the next two years, I had to plan for life after the Olympics. I could feel a lessening of my drive; I still did good work in the saddle, but I knew my career as an international competitor was winding down. I determined 1983 and 1984 would be my last years as a rider. I would make them as successful as possible, but I had to think about making a living. Hillary and Jennifer were growing up, and they would need schools and so on. The sport was not yet completely professionalized; no matter how hard I worked, it was usually enough to break even, but I couldn't seem to get ahead.

The IOC rule regarding amateurs was still in effect, if much ignored. This tied my hands a bit because, for example, the Thompsons could not pay me a salary, but the real answer was that my business model wasn't effective. It was an enormous help to have owners paying for all the expenses on their horses, but I still had to teach lessons, give clinics, and generally hustle to make ends meet. I knew I had to retire in order to improve my financial situation, but for the short term I was dedicated to my Olympic efforts.

I had a full barn and plenty of outside lessons, but I warned all my clients that I was going abroad in the summer of 1983 and would not be back in time to do any coaching in the fall. I said I would understand if they moved on to other coaches. My increased focus on my own horses paid off; at Kentucky, I placed fourth with Paddy and thirteenth with Rocky. Although not satisfied, I was pleased with their efforts so far, and Jack and the selectors seemed equally pleased. Paddy's outbursts of insane behavior were few and far between, and seemed to have no effect on his overall training. Dressage judges still fell in love with him, and the cross-country and show-jumping courses felt easy for him. Rocky was maturing and becoming a little easier to ride to his jumps. His dressage, a typical Irish work in progress, left a lot to be desired. His speed across country made up for that at bigger competitions where the courses were longer and harder. It was up to me to make sure that he jumped clean as well as fast. All in all, I'd had a good spring, and Suzanne and I packed the horses up and left for England with high expectations.

Mark Phillips promised he had all the requirements for training eventers when he invited me to stay with him, and he was as good as his word. Excellent stabling, plenty of turnout, good footing, and miles of rolling hillsides for hacking and galloping: Gatcombe Park had it all. We settled in easily, and after a couple of weeks of training I thought, "I don't want to jinx myself, but I'm riding well, and my horses are going well." I rode Paddy first, as he liked to go straight to work and get it over with for the day. I then hacked Paddy out, usually for two hours, while leading Rocky. (I learned right away that I couldn't lead Paddy and ride Rocky; Paddy was spooky and would pull away from me and run back to the barn.) Once I got back from our long hack, we tacked up Rocky and I rode him for a while.

I started with Paddy right after eight every morning and finished with Rocky about noon; I was spending four hours a day focused entirely on my two horses. I finally realized that the reason my training program was going well was that I did not have any time constraints. I took whatever amount of time it took to train each horse, because I did not have students and *their* horses to worry about. I could devote myself entirely to my horses, and myself. I had to watch my weight carefully, so most days I had cereal for breakfast, then an apple and some cheese for lunch. After a short nap, I went for a run on the Gatcombe Park hills. I knew both my horses and I had to be fit if things were to go well for us at events, and that meant putting in the time and effort now. (I now realize my diet wasn't the best for an athlete, but starvation was how I had always gotten my weight down. Besides, at the time I wasn't getting nutritional advice from the Olympic Committee—or anyone else, for that matter.)

Gatcombe hosted the British National Championships for the first time in 1983, and I was using that event as part of my training for Burghley and Wylie. I knew once I'd walked the Gatcombe cross-country course that I would use the event as a combined test, meaning I would ride only the dressage and show jumping; the ground was hard, and the cross-country was a legitimate Championship course. I had not been able to manage a cross-country school, and I knew this course was too much, too soon for my horses.

I won the dressage with Paddy, was well placed with Rocky, and— much to my surprise—was in the lead after dressage and show jumping.

Somewhat regretfully, I scratched before cross-country. I had a plan for my two destination events, and I was sticking to it.

I planned several more horse trials for both horses, using the first couple of events as cross-country schools rather than as competitions, then tried to be more competitive at Castle Ashby and Thirleston. The ground remained hard and I was worried about Rocky's splint, so I was judicious in how fast I galloped the cross-country. I needed to use some speed for my last few gallops in order to get both horses fit for the steeplechase phase in their target competitions. Fortunately, I was able to use a famous steeplechase trainer's gallops. David Nicholson had a lovely uphill, all-weather track, and I had some useful sharp works before Burghley.

I drew a sigh of relief once we shipped safely to Burghley. I had been trying to ride at Burghley since the 1966 World Championships, and after seventeen years I had finally made it. When I picked up Gail, Hillary, and Jennifer at Heathrow on the Monday before the event, I had my family with me for the first time in a couple of months and suddenly realized how much I had missed them. They were a good-luck charm for me, as all three days at Burghley went well. I "left a few points on the table" in the dressage and had a couple of near-misses on cross-country, but my fitness program had worked well and Paddy jumped clear on the final day, to finish in fourth place. Between finishing fourth at both Kentucky and Burghley, I had had a good year. Burghley was the biggest cross-country course Paddy had ever jumped, and I had learned a lot about him. I could look forward to the spring of 1984 with confidence, armed with my deepening understanding of how to ride him in all three disciplines. It looked as if my dream of riding at Los Angeles was getting closer to coming true.

I put Gail and the girls on the bus to Heathrow early the Monday following Burghley. The girls had to get back to school, and Gail needed to be home to supervise the farm in my absence. Hillary and Jennifer waved goodbye from the windows as the bus pulled away, and I was suddenly overcome with a wave of homesickness. I already missed my family terribly, missed my own home, missed my Labrador, and was sad at the prospect of another month alone in England. I had been living on the road for almost 20 years, devoted to my competitive career and my horses, so focused that I had not realized I was homesick. I decided I was ready to retire; I couldn't face another long stint on the road.

Back at Gatcombe, I dedicated myself to Rocky and his upcoming efforts at Wylie. I had maintained throughout my life on the road that I was never bored or lonely if I had a good book to read. I put that to the test during the next month. After a week off following Burghley, Paddy and I would lead Rocky out. Then I would train him—especially in dressage, but I also had to practice show jumping and ship him to David Nicholson's gallops. (I had trained at Wylie in 1979 and knew the terrain well: although a shorter distance, it was much hillier than Burghley.) Fitness would be at a premium, and I knew that no matter how hard I worked on Rocky's dressage, I would start on cross-country day with a lot of catching up to do.

The drought finally broke at the beginning of September and we got the sort of weather one associates with England in the fall: cold and wet with soft footing. Thus the hard asphalt jog strip at Wylie was nearly my undoing. After nursing Rocky carefully through the summer, always choosing the best possible footing and not letting him gallop too fast in his horse trial tune-ups, I thought his splint was a thing of the past. The jog before the start of the competition was a reintroduction to reality, as he jogged out slightly uneven—and off to the holding area we went. The vet came, examined him, reported to the Ground Jury, and after a moment I jogged him again. There are a few adjustments that make a horse look better while jogging in hand. I did everything I could, then waited for the news. After a nerve-wracking pause while the jury talked it over again, I was given the thumbs-up signal. Just like that, we had ducked an ignominious elimination for lameness after months of preparation.

Although I was relieved, my mood did not immediately improve. The president of the Ground Jury came over and delivered a well-deserved warning after the jog was finished. He basically said that a rider of my experience and reputation should know better than to present a horse that was not fit and sound in every particular, and I could not expect the jury to be so lenient over the next few days. I mumbled my apologies and promised to do everything I could to make sure Rocky was completely acceptable to the jury over the rest of the competition. Poor Rocky and poor Suzanne; while he spent the next few days either in ice or poultice, she practically lived at the barn.

The eventing gods then smiled on me: it rained steadily for the rest of the event, which softened the ground appreciably. Being Irish, Rocky thought he had come home to Ireland again, loved galloping in the mud, and finished cross-country full of run on his dressage score. He was in third place overnight, and at the Sunday morning jog was sounder than he had been before the event. As if my luck had not already improved enough, I suddenly realized that one of the horses ahead of me had not been presented to the final vet check. I was now in second, less than a rail from first.

However, it was a little early to pop the champagne. Show jumping with Rocky was a bit of a coin toss: put enough bit in his mouth to control him and he would sulk, might even stop, but if I didn't have enough bit, I was guaranteed to run through the tops of a couple of fences. I decided if I was going to have trouble show jumping, it would be from going forward, not holding back. I had forgotten to factor in the subduing effect on Rocky of having galloped a full-scale Classic speed and endurance phase the day before, and he was surprisingly rideable. We had a few hair-raising near misses but jumped a clear round. The rider going last was as unlucky as I had been lucky, and Rocky and I won Wylie 1983, finishing on our dressage score.

It is a thrill any time you win an international event, but it is even more meaningful when they play the "Star-Spangled Banner" in a foreign country. That is a goose-bump moment. Vita and Dick Thompson were busy organizing Radnor for the following weekend and had not come over for Wylie. My phone call to them was one of the nicest calls I have ever made, and when they calmed down a bit they promised to throw a heck of a party on Saturday night at Radnor to celebrate Rocky's victory.

Gail and I didn't stay to party at Wylie after the show jumping. Suzanne had already left for Gatcombe, as the horses would ship back to the United States on Tuesday, and we had to get back there in order to pack for our flight home. This had been my last training session abroad, but it was by far the most successful. I had a lot to look forward to over the coming year, and my Olympic dreams were clearly in view.

A Model Patient

_____ For the past few years, my "time off" during the winter had not been the period of total relaxation I would have liked. I got away to do as much duck hunting as I could, but more and more of my time was taken up by my administrative duties with what Gail and I now referred to as "the alphabets." After the 1980 Alternate Olympics, I was appointed as the USET equestrian athlete representative to the USOC. This was a new program, one that took some time to organize. It put me in close contact with the other athletes and the USOC bureaucracy. I also joined the FEI Event Committee; this was a big job, as the committee made the rules for the sport worldwide. This position was gratifying, as my father had been on the Bureau of the FEI 30 years ago, and I felt I was following in his footsteps once again.

In addition to all this, I was now an officer in all three associations responsible for my sport—the USET, the USCTA, and the AHSA. I had been elected vice president of the AHSA in 1981, which meant that at some point in the future I would move up and become president. The current president was in no hurry to retire, and I was in no hurry to succeed him; I had plenty of administrative projects to keep me occupied. For the next few months, however, I planned to be busy with my competitive career; the alphabets would have to stay in second place for now.

Paddy had come back well from his exertions at Burghley and Rocky's splint had cooled out. In addition, I was excited to be able to put Pop back in training for the spring season. We had shipped him home after he broke his pedal bone in Germany and started his prescribed period of complete stall rest and then carefully controlled hand walks. I had turned his rehabilitation over to Suzanne, and she made a real project out of him over the next couple of years. My vet had warned me that the two dangers in rehabilitating a broken bone were (1) that he would break down in his left front, due to resting on it too much in order to take the load off his injured foot; or (2) that Pop would get laminitis, due to his total lack of exercise.

Suzanne regulated his food carefully, and "strapped" him for 30 minutes every day. This is an old-fashioned massage that stimulates the horse's blood supply and maintains muscle tone. She kept his weight light, and Pop turned out to be the model patient. He loved his daily massages, calmly walked out in hand, and after a few weeks of stall rest we noticed that he could lie down to take a nap. Pop's hindquarters were so strong he could get up using only his left hind. This was a real benefit, as it meant his other three legs were getting a rest, thus lessening the risk of his breaking down.

After this period of rehabilitation we got permission from Marty Simensen, the Team vet, to begin walking him out under saddle. Starting with short periods of walking indoors under tack, Suzanne gradually increased his walk exercise until she was using Pop to lead out other horses on long hacks. By the spring of 1983, Pop had started some light dressage training, and the end result of all this effort was that Pop went into training for the Olympic selection trials along with Paddy and Rocky in January of 1984.

I went into training along with my horses. To start my day, I galloped four sets of racehorses at the Middleburg Training Center. By the time I got back to Fox Covert, Suzanne would have hacked out my three horses, and I schooled them in show jumping or dressage according to their training schedules.

I had discussed Pop's progress with Jack, and he was delighted to see an old friend come back into my plan. We agreed that he would not be considered to be my best chance to make the team, but he was another ride for me at the spring selection trials. If we had to use him, he was a pretty fancy back-up reserve horse.

It was a sign of the times that I had several horses to ride in the selection trials. Other experienced riders were in the same situation, which made a big change from when I first showed up on the eventing scene. Although previously the Team took every qualified horse in the country when we left for a big competition, it would not be the case this year. The 1978 World Championships at Kentucky had broadened the available pool of experienced riders; the chance to ride in the Olympics was becoming a goal for more people, and this year the competition for a place on the Team would be more intense than ever.

The Team selectors recognized the changing circumstances and planned a series of trials throughout the spring—including a special section at Kentucky—culminating in a final trial at Ledyard in July. Although I wanted to do as well as possible in the selection trials, I had a different plan for each of my three horses. They all did the same conditioning gallops, but my approach to their technical work was much more customized. My work with Rocky was aimed at relaxation and calmness. I knew he was not going to win any of the trials; I wanted to produce clear jumping rounds, while accepting some cross-country time faults in an effort to prevent "gerbil brain" on his part.

I knew Pop as well as any horse I have ever ridden and worked on bringing his dressage work back up to international level. His show-jumping work was aimed at strengthening and sharpening him after a three-year layoff. I hoped to produce him back on form, but knew he was a long shot to reach that level again. I was resolved to not persevere if I felt he was no longer up to it.

...and Then There Were None

———It was no secret that if I made the Team, it would be on Paddy; he was one of the best horses in the world, and by now I was experienced enough to take advantage of his abilities. But from the start of the season, I could feel him slipping away from me. His tantrums were becoming more frequent, and I was not always certain I could win the dressage phase as I turned down the centerline to start my test. I now realize that whatever neurological problems he had were becoming more serious; lacking modern diagnostic capabilities, I was perplexed.

Paddy was sound when jogged in hand, but less and less comfortable practicing dressage. In addition, some sort of fever or disease he had suffered over the winter had affected his feet; the periople of his hoof walls dried out, the surface of his hooves became dry and cracked, and he lost shoes on a weekly basis. This meant lost training time—with a horse who was already not training well. I discussed all this with Jack, but there was little long-distance advice he could offer except to do my best and keep training.

To add to my distress, I was coming to realize that Pop was not the same. He jumped everything well, but I could tell that he was doing it to please me, not because he loved the sport and couldn't wait to get to the next obstacle. He went well at the first selection trial, and jogged sound the week after, so I thought I would keep going for one more competition, but during a show-jumping school at home, Pop "tied up" for the first time in his life. Azoturia attacks the muscle fibers and it takes a long time for a horse to recover completely. Pop had absolutely no history of tying up, and it scared me. I called Jack and told him I was withdrawing Pop from the selection process and planned to retire him at the Kentucky event. At first, Jack attempted to talk me out of it, as he wanted me to keep my options open for as long as possible. I replied that Pop didn't owe us anything, and it was time. Jack wasn't happy, but at the end of our conversation, he finally agreed, telling me, "Okay, Jimmy, you are right, don't squeeze the lemon until it's dry."

At this point, I still had two horses to try for the Team—at least, I had two until the next selection trial at Master's Cave in Glyndon, Maryland, where I had a stop cross-country with Rocky. This was a black mark against him in the selectors' minds. I knew Rocky stopped when he panicked, but I thought I had trained him well enough so it was a thing of the past. And just like that, I went from having three rides to having one—and Paddy had just placed his own black mark in the selectors' book. I had tried a double bridle the week before the event because he had started coming above the bit in his dressage work. He seemed to accept it, and it seemed to help. However, for the first time since I started riding him, he threw one of his temper tantrums during the dressage test. It is hard to get a competitive dressage score when your horse is rearing, spinning, or running backward. This sort of performance quite rightly concerns the selectors, because one of the traits they prize above all others is dependability: will the horse and rider go the same way under pressure that they are going now? For a horse like Paddy, who had been a threat to win every dressage class he went into, this was a startling loss of form, and was bound to lurk in the selectors' minds.

Naturally, Jack was unhappy, and I spent an uncomfortable few moments with him later on that day. I had described Paddy's episodes to him, so Paddy's behavior was not exactly a surprise to him, but he had not realized how violent these outbursts were, or how uncontrollable Paddy was while he was misbehaving. Jack and I were close friends by this time, but I knew he was more interested in winning than he was in friendship. He would pick the four riders who gave him the best chance at the Olympics, and it was up to me to produce Paddy so well that Jack and the selectors had no option but to put me on the Team. At the end of our discussions, we just shrugged; Jack knew I was totally dedicated to making the Team, was still in the scuffle, and would do my best throughout the process.

Things were looking up for me by the time we got to Kentucky. Paddy had settled into his work, and I had him back in a snaffle for all three disciplines. I found that he went better if I gave him frequent periods of rest during his dressage work. Without realizing it, and with no veterinary diagnosis, my intuition was leading me to understand Paddy and his problems. His fits were caused by pain, and compressing his body produced pain, so I worked him for shorter and shorter intervals. This prevented the fits, but meant my test lacked the polish I had been able to produce before my troubles with him began. I was willing to leave a few points on the table, if it meant I could get through his tests without obvious disobedience. All this was enough of an improvement for us to finish fourth in the selection trials, only a few points behind the leaders. We were still in contention for a spot on the team, and my dream of riding at Los Angeles was still alive.

Rocky was Rocky, and I had to keep him as calm as possible throughout his training, as his performance was directly related to his attitude. In effect, I had to improve his competitive results by not trying to be competitive. This attitude worked fairly well; Rocky was thirteenth and jogged out sound after his exertions, so I returned home in a slightly better mood.

I was still shaking my head at one Kentucky cross-country moment with Rocky. Neil Ayer, the course designer for the L.A. Olympics, was starting to experiment with combinations, puzzle fences, and related distances. In effect, he was starting a trend that continues to this day. There was a combination part way around the course, on top of the hill above the stabling, which required a very accurate line over several elements. Rocky was not always the straightest of horses, and I was worried about the combination. He came back into control nicely and stayed straight when he jumped through, but jumped the last couple of elements on his forehand. I softened the reins after the last element, bent over his withers, and let him accelerate down the hill into the Draft Horse Field.

We had a long run before the next obstacle, a maximum table. The only time I am ever completely comfortable on a horse is when I am out of the saddle at the gallop; that feels right to me, and I relax and enjoy it. As Rocky accelerated away from the combination, I let him gallop along on a soft rein. Midway across the field, I suddenly realized that I was mentally planning the sort of gymnastic exercise I would build in order to teach Rocky to keep his shoulders in front of himself while jumping through combinations. I woke up about 10 strides away from a maximum table that we were approaching at a wide-open gallop, and told myself to pay attention—these jumps were too big to be approached while mentally distracted. We jumped the table well, but I landed telling myself that if I no longer brought intense concentration to every stride, it really was time to retire. If I didn't pay attention, I could get myself hurt—or, even worse, get my horse hurt. We had plenty of time to practice gymnastics when we got back to Virginia.

I gave the horses a little break after Kentucky but went back into training quickly. The Team would be named soon, at Ledyard, and I had to be as ready as possible. This was a nightmare, as Rocky was getting too fit and his dressage and show jumping were deteriorating. I took as much pressure off him as I could, because I knew that he would not be one of the finalists. If we had to use him in Los Angeles, putting him on the Team would be the least of our worries.

At the same time, Paddy was more and more difficult to keep in training, and I had a growing awareness that my Olympic dreams were slipping away. I had one of the best horses in the world, but I could not produce him in winning form. His show jumping and cross-country were still dependable, but his dressage was almost— not quite—good enough. Several horse-and-rider combinations were producing admirable results in the extremely competitive Olympic environment that year, and I was not able to do more than finish close behind them. I knew by now that if I didn't win the final trial, I wouldn't make it. It made me sick to my stomach to think of missing out on riding in my final Olympics, but the scoreboard never lies.

The week before the final trials, the USET held a fundraiser in North Salem, New York, where Team candidates did a combined test before shipping on to Massachusetts. There was a lot of razzle-dazzle involved with the event. We had to attend sponsor meetings, cocktail parties, and generally be on display in order to raise money for the Team. This was part of being a Team rider and I went to all the required activities, but my heart wasn't in it. I expected my results after the combined test: not quite good enough. I finished on my dressage score, no faults in show jumping, with my final score just behind the leaders. Glumly packing the horse van, Suzanne and I headed for Ledyard.

Ledyard, the culmination of the spring season, was where a team of four riders and one reserve would be named. Those five riders would go into final training at the USET center in South Hamilton, Massachusetts. Once I got Paddy settled into the stabling, I arranged a dressage lesson with Jack for the next day. Jack had not held any training sessions over the winter, as there was not enough interest from riders to make it worthwhile. I had wondered at this at the time but stayed in touch with Jack as closely as possible. I had not realized what a poisoned atmosphere surrounded the Team riders until Jack came back to me late that afternoon and told me he would not be able to work with me the next day. Somewhat startled, I asked him why. He replied that other riders had complained to the selectors that I would be given an "unfair advantage" if I got a lesson from the Team coach.

That's how insane the situation had become. The Team coach, whom the Team paid, and who was available to all the riders, wasn't actually allowed to coach, because someone would gain an "unfair advantage" from that coaching. Other riders did not want to use his services, which was all right, but they did not want me to use him either. Crazy. Jack and I discussed it, agreed that "it is what it is," and stuck to our jobs over the weekend. By now, my results sounded like a broken record. I was fifth or sixth after dressage and finished on that score. It was good, but not good enough.

On Monday morning after the event, the selectors announced the Team and reserve riders. Mike Plumb, Bruce Davidson, Torrance Fleishmann, and Karen Stives were named to the Team. I would go with them as non-riding reserve. It was ironic; I had begun my career with the team in 1966, as the non-riding reserve, and 18 years later, I would close out my career as the non-riding reserve. I felt as if I had been kicked in the stomach but resolved to get through the next few weeks.

Just when I thought it couldn't get any crazier, it did. After a few days, we had our first gallop at Ledyard. The next morning, I got a call from Jack Fritz, vice president of the USET. He said the other riders had decided they wanted to train in Unionville, where they felt they would find better footing, and didn't want Jack's services anyway. Jack Fritz said he had made reservations at local motels near Unionville, and we were to ship down that day. Stunned, I went looking for Jack and discussed the situation with him. He was not moving to Unionville and was unsure if he would attend the Games. I said I was happy to stay in South Hamilton and stay in training with him. Jack said I had to follow the Team, which had agreed to the riders' demands, and by late morning Suzanne, Paddy, and I were headed for Unionville.

I trained by myself for the next couple of weeks, and got Paddy going as well as I could. If anything happened to one of the four Team horses, I had to be ready to go. However, even this fell apart. The day before we were to put the horses on the plane for L.A., Paddy was lame at the final jog. All those pulled shoes had finally caught up with him. I immediately called Marty Simensen. He was already at Santa Anita, where all the Olympic horses would be stabled. He said there was nothing we could do by long distance, so we put Paddy on the plane with the rest of the Team, and off to Los Angeles we went.

Once we landed, we had to pick up our credentials and Team uniforms before going to the stables. There, Jack, Marty, and I jogged Paddy, who by this time was hopping lame. Marty diagnosed an abscess and opened it up, which gave Paddy immediate relief but meant whatever last-minute scenarios I had considered were no longer reality. I would be a spectator at the Olympics. I cheered on our dressage rides, served as the head of our "spy system" on cross-country day at Fairbanks Ranch, and stood at attention while they played the "Star-Spangled Banner" to honor our gold medal eventing team. Remember that old joke about "mixed emotions"? Mixed emotions are watching your mother-in-law drive your new Mercedes off a cliff. I had mixed emotions about our success.

My entire family had come out for the Games, and we stayed the whole two weeks. The Monday following the closing ceremonies, I loaded up my in-laws' station wagon, and we drove back to Colorado Springs by way of the Grand Canyon. I was finally spending some time with my family, and now had time to think about the next chapter of my life, a life that would not revolve around competitions. I wasn't sure what it would look like, but I knew it was time for me to do something different. ∎

_Learning My Political ABCs

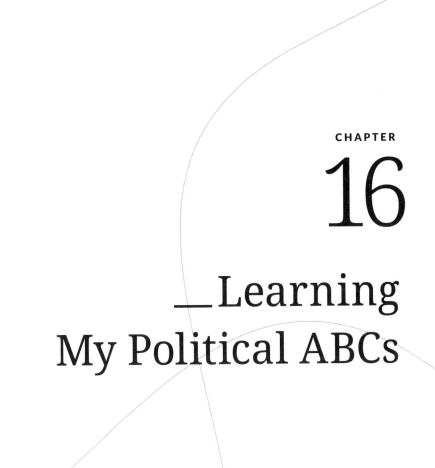

All political careers end in defeat.

Enoch Powell
British politician

As I mentioned, "the alphabets" was my family's term for the various equestrian organizations that I worked with from 1970 until 2004. (Notice the time frame. This long-term involvement was a backdrop for many of the other events I describe in this book.) Whenever the phone rang at dinner time, one of my young daughters would leap on it to answer, then turn to me with a mildly disgusted look and say, "Daddy, it's the alphabets." Sure enough, it would be someone calling from (and here I'll remind you of all the organizations and their acronyms) either the United States Combined Training Association (USCTA, the original version of our modern-day United

States Eventing Association), the United States Equestrian Team (USET), the American Horse Shows Association (AHSA, now the United States Equestrian Federation—USEF), the United States Olympic Committee (USOC, now the United States Olympic and Paralympic Committee— USOPC), or the Fédération Equestre Internationale (FEI). Luckily, I did not hear from the International Olympic Committee (IOC); I never did any work for them.

It's all right to skip this section if you are bored; talking about meetings and politics bores me too, these days. But there was a time when I was immersed in that part of the horse world, and some interesting things happened to me then. Yogi Berra said, "If it's so, it ain't bragging," and I happened on the scene as some significant changes were occurring. Keep in mind that this section is not so much about my role in the coming changes (some referred to them as revolutions) as it is about *the changes themselves*. The horse world you inhabit now is not the way it has always been, and I want to make an unofficial record of things before I forget it all.

While the alphabets are an enormous jumble of acronyms, they pro- duced an enormous amount of effort, most of it aimed at the betterment of equestrian sport. Each had a different mission statement (often badly presented) and many overlapped. Thus, the possibilities for confusion were endless, and turf wars were a constant problem. That was the world of "horse politics" in the fall of 1970, when Jack Fritz called and asked me to be the secretary of the USCTA.

Remember, I was 26 at the time, and had no experience working on committees. I had only recently moved to the East Coast, and even more recently achieved some success. Besides my young age, my competitive success was the main part of my resumé. Kilkenny, my horse at the time, was so wonderful that he covered up my shortcomings and convinced people I actually knew what I was doing. Eventing had been administered by middle-aged men up to this point, and due to our small numbers—we had fewer than a thousand members until 1973—this wasn't a big job. Eventers were a small group, with a cult-like devotion to this crazy sport we called "combined training." U.S. events were unrecognized by the AHSA in their early days, and the combined-training rulebook consisted of 26 mimeographed pages that had been drawn up by Jack Fritz and Jack Burton.

But Jack Fritz had a vision and, skilled administrator that he was, went looking for young talent to staff the organization he had in mind. In short order, besides myself, he had signed up Roger Haller, Denis Glaccum, Trish Gilbert, and Denny Emerson to sit on various committees. Major General Jonathon R. Burton ("Jack" to his innumerable friends), Stuart Treviranus, and Alexander Mackay-Smith had been hard at work for a while, and they were still involved as the pace of change increased. During this time (early 1970s), Jack Fritz's most important achievement was convincing Neil Ayer to become president of the USCTA. Neil is *the* seminal figure in the history of our sport. By the time he accepted the USCTA presidency he had already been president of the U.S. Polo Association, and in a few years he would also be president of the Masters of Foxhounds organization.

Neil wasted no time establishing an office, and soon thereafter hired Eileen Thomas to be the executive director. This gave the sport a knowledgeable voice at the other end of the telephone line. With Jack Fritz's guidance, Neil successfully lobbied the AHSA to form a new Eventing Committee, and to include a section of rules for combined training in the AHSA rulebook. By the time I joined the leadership structure, we had a chapter of rules in the AHSA rulebook and a discipline committee—almost like a real sport.

However, eventing was still a small, disorganized group of people who wanted to gallop at speed over solid obstacles and then party like hell that night. I went to the meetings, and spoke up when I felt the urge, but the energy for growth and improvement was all coming from Neil. I had the good sense to realize I was just a spear carrier in his opera and left the day-to-day stuff to him, a role I would play for the next 12 years.

Of the various issues that faced the USCTA during my tenure, I am proudest of my early involvement with the Junior program (the Young Rider level was added years later). Roger Haller called me in early 1973 to tell about a new program for Juniors: Joker's Hill, a facility outside Toronto, Canada, was hosting an international Classic event for Juniors. It would be open to teams of riders from the United States and Canada, as well as other teams from North America—for example, Puerto Rico and Bermuda. Roger and I (both of us running teaching and training programs at the time) decided we would both take teams to Canada.

The event was supposed to be run at the Preliminary level, but when we got to Joker's Hill, our teams were confronted with an enormous course, were not up to the challenge, and did not finish. Our results would improve as years went by; I coached Young Rider teams off and on from 1973 until 2000, when my team riders went first, second, third, and fifth, and swept the medals. I thought that was a suitable time for me to retire from coaching the Area teams, and bowed out gracefully.

My involvement with the AHSA followed a different path. The national federation, as its name implied, was then an association of *horse shows*, not of individual riders and owners. The AHSA had become the national federation by default when the Army horse-show team was disbanded in 1949 and the U.S. Cavalry Association (the national federation at the time) simply handed the title over to the AHSA. There was no USET in

1949; that came a year or so later, when my father and numerous other good-hearted souls founded it. This civilian association was ostensibly an "umbrella" organization, but in reality it was all about the hunter-jumper universe. It usually ignored its few breed and discipline affiliates such as the International Arabian Horse Association, the American Quarter Horse Show Association (IAHA and AQHA, more alphabets), and the USCTA.

The AHSA board of directors at the time was mostly East Coast, white-bread, middle-aged, in comfortable circumstances, and guided in too great a degree by the few professional show managers on the board. When I joined in 1971, I had missed the January meeting; the May meeting, held during the Devon Horse Show in Pennsylvania, was my first experience—and it was a doozie. That meeting was a good illustration of the issues facing the AHSA, issues of which the board was either ignorant or negligent. These included a scandalous drug culture (one that still exists today, and for the same reasons: people will cheat to win). Of the several challenges facing the AHSA, this was the main one that confronted me as I joined the board.

Let's set the scene. The AHSA May meeting was traditionally held at "Ardrossan," Hope Scott's Bryn Mawr estate. (Hope's life inspired the 1940 romantic comedy, *The Philadelphia Story*.) The schedule: a Bloody Mary reception on arrival, an 11 o'clock meeting, lunch at noon, then a quick return to the nearby Devon show grounds, since most of the board members had horses competing.

I drove to the front of the main house, handed my keys to the parking valet, walked up the front steps, took the Bloody Mary that was offered, and stepped into the midst of an organization coming to grips with an existential problem. I quickly learned that our Drugs and Medication Committee (D&M—more alphabets) had issued charges against 20 AHSA members for using a tranquilizer (Reserpine) about which many veterinarians had (until now) assured their clients, "They don't have a test for it…" The vets forgot to add, "…yet." D&M had frozen samples, waited until a legally defensible test for Reserpine was developed, tested the samples, and then issued the charges.

Drugging performance horses had become a widely recognized problem by the late 1960s. In response, the AHSA strengthened its drug rules, formed the D&M Committee, and—probably most importantly—hired good lawyers while it braced for inevitable legal challenges. Thus, I was introduced to Ira Finkelstein and Bill Roos, attorneys for AHSA who would be a part of my political life for the next 20 years, and who became my good friends. Another of our attorneys, Ned Bonnie, became one of my closest friends.

It wasn't exactly news when the D&M committee issued charges. However, it *was* big news when it emerged that the best-known riders and trainers in the hunter-jumper world had been charged. Many were members of the board, and several were at the May meeting. Once the Bloody Marys kicked in at the reception, there were some candid exchanges of view, several red-faced confrontations, and a few hasty departures by board members. All this before lunch—awkward.

Driving away from Ardrossan after the meeting, I reflected that I had arrived at the AHSA at an interesting time. I didn't know the half of it. As time went by, I found myself more and more involved with issues facing the association. At first I voted in support of policies I believed in, such as the D&M program. However, I was just another board member; others were doing the work and, especially, dealing with the pushback. Most notably, then AHSA president Dick McDevitt had his stables burned down because of his staunch support of the association's anti-drugging effort.

Over the next few years, I became more involved in the workings of the Association, and was appointed to numerous committees. I had already become close friends with Ned Bonnie before this time; we met while we were both riding timber races at various point-to-points. We had wives and families of similar ages, and shared a similar outlook about AHSA affairs. The better I came to know Ned, the more I admired him. He had a prodigious appetite for work and applied himself to whatever litigation or political issue engaged him at the moment. He had an unerring instinct for the salient fact or case law in any legal issue, and once he determined the major premise of his argument, he was indefatigable in pursuing minor premises that would support his argument. I quickly found that his moral compass always pointed true north, and he was always an advocate for the "little guy." He and I would be forces for change within the AHSA for the next decade, and our first issue might have been our biggest.

During my time in England in the late 1960s and early '70s, I had joined the British Horse Society (BHS…I know…sigh) in order to ride in local competitions. The BHS was an "umbrella" organization and did a good job for its members, whether dressage, jumping, eventing, hunters—indeed, whatever discipline or breed was covered under the umbrella of the BHS. I shared with Ned my conviction that the AHSA could be much more effective if it were a membership organization rather than an association of horse shows. For example, until we developed a true membership category, exhibitors had a very limited influence on the rules. I believed that our first step on the road to improvement would have to be a change in our structure.

I've heard it said that the art of political leadership is to find a parade and step in front of it. Thus, I found myself leading an effort that had actually been bubbling around under the radar in the AHSA for a while, and had my first experience as a change agent. I'm hogging the spotlight by saying this, as if I did it all myself. There were others whose involvement and efforts were the main reason our vision of an individual membership body prevailed. They did most of the work, but in reality were happy for me to stand in front as a target for the outraged "slings and arrows" from board members who did not want such a revolutionary change. My efforts did not go unnoticed; unbeknownst to me, Ned Bonnie decided I had a future in the leadership structure and—thanks to his efforts as my political "goombah"—in 1981 I was elected vice president.

Ned and I were involved in various scuffles and had a pretty good political success rate. In the early 1980s, it became impossible for people in the horse business to obtain liability insurance that would cover their operations. Sensing a need in our membership, we came up with the concept of a wholly owned insurance company that would service the horse industry. We called this concept Equisure. A fellow board member from Denver, Preston Smith, became enamored with Equisure, and Ned and I increasingly turned over the details to Preston, while we tended to the political process of getting board approval.

This took a lot of doing and was hugely controversial. Niccolò Machiavelli said, "He who innovates will have for his enemies all those who are well off under the existing order of things, and only lukewarm supporters in those who might be better off under the new…" I think something like that was at work here, possibly because it was the first time the AHSA had actually created value for its members. Some viewed Equisure as a threat to our 501c3 status (although our tax attorneys gave complete approval), while others were suspicious of *any* change to begin with. While we were successful, resentments continued under the surface. Naturally, as soon as it started to show a profit, it was greeted with howls of dismay from those interests on the board "that we were going into business"; after I retired, Equisure was spun off to private interests. Sigh.

For the next few years, I chaired several committees and led innumerable "ad hoc" committees formed to deal with various issues. Ad hoc committees can be a sign of a prescient leadership structure, proactively dealing with serious topics of concern, or they can be a sign of ineptitude at the board level, which then shove off issues to some subsidiary group to deal with, rather than facing unpleasant truths.

Professor Frederick A. Lindemann, World War II scientific advisor to Winston Churchill, remarked that "a committee is a cul de sac down which good ideas are lured and quietly strangled." I agree with Professor Lindemann for the most part but do think committee chairs have a great deal of influence if they choose to use it. Once I became vice president, there were so many issues needing attention that I hardly knew where to turn next. Dick McDevitt solved this dilemma for me, quietly putting me in charge of dealing with several pressing issues. First, I became the point man for discipline and breed affiliates' concerns. Similar efforts in the recent past had failed; the AQHA had tired of being ignored by the Park Avenue board members and had left the AHSA. This was unfortunate; despite considerable efforts, I was never able to get the AQHA to reconsider.

We continued to recognize Western classes, so when the Stock Seat Committee told me their Equitation Medal entries were down, I helped them write a rule that opened the division to more potential competitors. We passed the rule at the next meeting under the elastic "emergency rule" provision in use at the time, and our entries in that program exploded. Successful efforts such as this improved my standing with non-English affiliates, who were assured of a receptive audience when they presented their complaints.

Originally, my influence was based on most board members' knowing me as "Dot and Gyp Wofford's cute little red-haired boy. He's one of us, don'cha know." Membership on the board was nearly a lifetime tenure, and several members had served on the board with my father. Between my status as a legacy member, and my efforts on behalf of the non-English affiliates, I was able to produce a majority of the board's votes on most issues. Once my efforts to change the AHSA to an individual membership organization were successful, I was going to need that ability to command a majority when Dick McDevitt handed me the next hot potato.

Now that we were an individual members' organization, how were the members to be represented on the board? Were the directors to serve in perpetuity, as now, or would the association members be able to vote on who filled the board seats? There were innumerable issues such as this to deal with, all deriving from the quiet revolution of empowering the members to take charge of their association. In my mind, the crux of the problem was the structure of the leadership positions. It was not unusual for officers to retain their positions for 10 to 15 years, or until they literally died in office. The AHSA had only three presidents since the early 1950s. I knew them all and they were without fail public-spirited gentlemen who sincerely loved horses and wanted the best for the horse world. But they liked things just the way they used to be. Change was not in their lexicon, even though the association needed to join the late twentieth century.

As with so many things in life, the answer was simple, but effecting the answer was complicated. My proposal for change—the association needed term limits for officers and board members—was controversial. In order to bring about this change, we needed to rewrite our bylaws. Once the decision was taken to change the bylaws, and to make me the point man on the effort, I realized that (1) drawing up the new bylaws was an enormous task; and (2) the politics of convincing board members to vote for the new bylaws, once they were drawn up, were difficult.

To my surprise, the majority of the board agreed that we needed a new structure and were prepared to vote for it. That solved half of my problem. For the actual new bylaws, I turned to attorneys Bill Roos and, especially, Ned Bonnie. Bill, the AHSA counsel, had an encyclopedic memory of New York administrative case law (the AHSA was incorporated in New York); whatever we came up with would be legal, and defensible. (The AHSA's experiences defending our D&M program, led by Ira Finkelstein against sustained and expensive litigation, made us keenly aware that whatever we wrote would most likely be challenged in court, and Bill made sure whatever we wrote would be legally defensible.)

At the same time, I leaned heavily on Ned Bonnie, who produced a set of new bylaws for consideration in record time. Remember that the bylaws set out how the association is organized, how the board is selected, how the officers and executive committee are elected, and so on in great detail. Ned and I shared a dislike for board members' serving in perpetuity, and a distaste for associations with "interlocking directorates." We developed term limits for officers and directors, which would take a little salesmanship to obtain approval. Board members with 20 years of service would have to vote themselves out of office.

While we were at it, I paid close attention to the composition of the nominating committee; these control the future of any organization, which means the mechanism for appointing them is important. It was becoming apparent by this time that in a few years I would be the next president; I wanted as much influence as possible on this committee, in order to influence the future of the association.

We presented the new bylaws with some trepidation, but they passed with little comment. Our "politicking" efforts had been successful. Hugely relieved, I remarked to Ned as we walked out of the fateful meeting that the board members had in effect voted to end their tenure on the board. We had indeed gotten turkeys to vote for Thanksgiving.

I want to make the point again that I was not alone in these efforts. In addition to Ned and Bill are dozens—hundreds—of people who helped with, followed, and from time to time led this movement for change in the association. Just as with my students, I am reluctant to start naming people, not because I don't want to share the spotlight, but rather because I am afraid I will leave out someone who worked tirelessly.

And speaking of working, my goodness, how I worked during this period! In the *Federalist Papers*, Alexander Hamilton speaks of energy in the executive. I must have had a lot of it, as I was balancing my duties as vice president with running the largest teaching and training business for eventing in the country at Fox Covert. Because I would soon be elected to succeed Dick McDevitt as AHSA president, in preparation I read (for the second time) both the *Federalist Papers* and the *Anti-Federalist Papers*. Admittedly, a copiously annotated CliffsNotes got me through my first reading in Civics 201, but this time I waded through it on my own.

In a microcosm, the AHSA had many of the problems that faced the Founding Fathers, and I could learn from their approach to various topics of self-governance. I was aware of most of the issues facing us but felt they were manageable. The change to a membership association had helped our bottom line by increasing the membership numbers, but our staff was underpaid and under-motivated. Our receptionists started out at $16 an hour in 1985, and commuted as much as two hours each way to get to the office. Our executive directors had tended to come and go while I was there. Dr. John Lengel, who ran the D&M labs and testing, was brought in for a while to run the New York offices. He did a wonderful job, but the strain of filling both positions caused him to return to the labs in Ohio, and the next executive director was promoted from within. Meanwhile, I was equally concerned with external issues. Our flawed relationship with the AQHA had caused them to leave us, and the Arabian breed division (the IAHA) was making the same noises. If we weren't careful, we could lose 30 percent of our membership all at once.

At the same time, I led the effort to either save or disaffiliate the Tennessee Walking Horse Association (TWHA). I had been in negotiations with certain members of their board, explaining that their "soring" practices were barbaric from the perspective of modern equine welfare standards, and they would have to eliminate it or be dropped from the AHSA. The Tennessee Walking Horse has lovely gaits without the soring that produces exaggerated movement, and some members of their board and I agreed that in place of the "Big Lick" classes we could create a division more suited to pleasure riders on a plantation type of horse, comfortable and easy to ride.

The TWHA board met the night before one of our AHSA board meetings, and my liaison called to tell me we were going to lose the vote—by one member. The old-time "Big Lick" trainers, who were the perpetrators of the soring so prevalent in the breed shows, had come down out of the hills and convinced just enough board members to continue soring. I was sad about this but explained to my TWHA liaison that I would move to disaffiliate the next morning, which I did. I knew we had done everything possible to retain the division, but convinced we had to stand against cruel training practices. We were right and for the right reasons. The lesson I took from this experience was that if an organization wants to be respected, it must be respectable.

There were other dissatisfied AHSA breed affiliates as well. For example, I attended innumerable meetings with the IAHA, and felt their concerns were manageable, given time, attention, and—most importantly—*action* by the board to address their concerns. This last part was difficult because Dick and many long-term members were about to vacate their positions, which would result in a period of slack energy during the transition.

When I was elected AHSA president in January of 1988, I became responsible for about 50,000 members, an expensive and unwieldy office on 42nd Street in New York City, and issues galore. This was in addition to my attempts to make a living riding and training, and would swiftly prove to be harder than I had expected. (As an aside, and just to brag, it was an interesting time to be a member of the Wofford family. My sister-in-law, Dawn, was chairman—their version of president—of the British Pony Clubs, and my brother Warren, also living in England, was chairman of the British Riding Clubs. Among us, we were responsible for about 150,000 riders, and our discussions around the table when we poured the second bottle of wine were something special.)

I settled comfortably into my new role. I had run unopposed and had a working majority of the board for any of the issues we faced. On the other hand, my negotiations with the IAHA continued and, if anything, worsened. There is a kind of centrifugal force in an umbrella organization, and at the AHSA I watched a continual attempted sloughing-off of breeds and disciplines—sometimes successful, sometimes not; sometimes necessary, most times not. Two ways to deal with complaints were to provide excellent member service, and to deal with complaints in a timely fashion. To improve communication with the affiliates, I instituted a system of "discipline directors." These were young ladies already involved with their breed or discipline, which flattened their learning curve. They were the contact point for members with questions and complaints; for example, if you had a hunter-jumper problem, you called Joanie Molony, Leah Danner for Arabians, and so on. These discipline directors attended all meetings of their committee and served as recording secretary.

I had other means of finding out what was on people's minds. One of our large affiliates decided they would be better off outside the umbrella and started making noises about leaving the AHSA. The "leave" movement was run by a small cabal inside their executive committee. I quickly made confidential contacts with others of that group, and before long I was getting a copy of their president's fax from the secretary involved—before he had a chance to initial his latest memo and fax it to me officially. (Yes, we used fax to transfer documents then, so quaint.) It wasn't exactly fair, but it was an important issue, and I used every advantage I could get.

Fortunately, that president lost the confidence of his board, and they voted to stay with us.

With the breed and discipline directors responsible for the day-to-day interaction between us and their breed or discipline, I started first with our largest committees, hunter-jumper and Arabian, but soon had a contact point for every one of our 35 breeds and disciplines. The discipline directors kept the minutes of each meeting their committee held and provided me with a copy of the minutes. Thus, I kept my finger on the pulse of that group even if I was not in attendance. Although it meant I had a lot of reading to do, in this way I knew what the association was up to behind the scenes. In addition, the discipline directors were smart enough to bring me word of "off-topic" problems that had either been discussed in executive session, or not discussed at all. This type of intelligence was invaluable, and I encouraged it.

At that time the president as the CEO had extensive executive powers, could select the national nominating committee, name all several hundred committee members each year, and hire the executive director on a series of one-year contracts. This was a system designed for either a placeholder or a benevolent dictator; I chose the second approach. I wanted to make as big an impact on the AHSA as possible, but I knew I wouldn't be there forever; I literally couldn't afford to stay long-term. At the same time, I had to deal with the operation of our staff in the short- and mid-term, and one of the most distasteful tasks I had was to replace our executive director. She had been counseled several times, with no appreciable change in her performance, and I asked her to resign. This was wrenching for me, as I understood the effect on that employee, but I felt the affairs of the AHSA could no longer wait.

Many of my duties took me to meetings and "ribbon-snipping" occasions on weekends, which were also the prime times for me to teach a clinic somewhere and make some money. However, I invariably felt a responsibility to the AHSA, and cancelled or rescheduled the clinic while I tended to AHSA affairs on an unpaid basis. This wasn't a successful business model.

I had expected to find member services a challenge, and it certainly was, but the problems were soluble. In addition, the Drugs & Medications committee usually had one or two hot potatoes for the hearing committee to adjudicate, but we had a well-established body of precedent built into N.Y. state administrative law to support our D&M hearings and we were usually successful at "setting down," or at least fining, individuals who had run afoul of our regulations. On the other hand, the unexpected issue that occupied much of my presidency was the Ted Stephens Amateur Act, which empowered the USOC to oversee all Olympic national federations and, in this case, determined how athlete grievances were to be adjudicated.

I soon got on a first-name basis with the Stephens act, and as president found myself involved in athletes' grievances. This immediately became a lawyer-intensive activity, as in the spring of 1988 a contender for the Olympics in Seoul, Korea, filed a grievance. In my view this grievance was based on a simple issue. Athletes were expected to attend a mandatory final selection. This athlete had broken a leg at the trials and was unable to complete. Pre-injury, the athlete was a shoo-in to go to the Olympics, but the selection procedures were clear—no completion, no participation. We couldn't change the rules after the selection. Fortunately, the USOC hearing panel agreed with me, and upheld our selection procedures.

As president of the National Federation, I was responsible for defending our selection procedures, but I made sure to include the USET in the discussions. After all, we were defending procedures the USET had drawn up. Bill Steinkraus, in his capacity as USET president, sat at the table with me, and we were successful at beating back any turf wars that attempted to spring up between the AHSA and the USET. This came in handy before the 1990 World Championships in Stockholm, Sweden, when we once again faced a grievance by an athlete who felt wrongly left off a team. The USOC "findings" were that the selectors, a panel of expert horsemen, had met and decided which horses gave us the best chance of winning a medal. The issue came down to the selectors' opinion against the athlete's, and the selectors won. However, the decision was closer than it should have been; the USOC only reluctantly upheld our procedures, feeling our criteria were too subjective.

This led to a 10-year experiment using strictly objective show-jumping selection procedures, which condemned us to failure until the USET figured out the right balance of objective and subjective criteria. Bill and I saw eye to eye on this and many other issues, and he was a major source of support and advice for years. There was continual sniping and whining behind the scenes, as many of our directors and staff felt they could do the other side's job better. While Bill and I kept our thumb on these turf wars, years later they would devolve into a bitter feud, which some referred to as a "seven-years' war." In the final analysis, the USOC arbitration to decide which body—the USET or the AHSA—would be the national federation wound up costing all three organizations a million dollars—each—in legal fees, only to arrive at a conclusion that should have been worked out in a morning's discussion. (Fortunately for me, this happened after I was long gone from horse politics.)

My presidential tenure at the AHSA was for three years, with a possible three-year second term available. However, after two years I told the nominating committee that I was happy to remain if we could work out some form of salary. The nominating committee discussed this with the board, but my proposal was too big a change in tradition. They thanked me for my service, and in the spring of 1991 I went back full-time to horses. I was sad to leave the organization, but financially, I had no choice. ■

_Conclusion and Commencement

Conclusion: *the end or finish of an event or process.*
Commencement: *the beginning or start.*

This next part is hard to explain. How did someone as horse-crazy as me show up in a nine-to-five job? If I wanted to skip over it, I would just say, "For the next few years, I put on a coat and tie and drove to work five days a week."

That's true enough, but as with any event that happened in the past, you need context to understand it. Context in this case will require (you guessed it) a digression.

In the fall of 1984, after Los Angeles, the IOC "opened the Games." This meant that going forward, one did not have to be an amateur (or even a shamateur) in order to compete at the Olympics. This was very important in the horse world.

First let's look at the concept of "amateur." (As you know by now, when I say "digression," I'm serious.) In an August 10, 2009, *Time* magazine piece, the essayist Kurt Anderson remarked that in the past the adjective "amateur" was entirely positive. "An amateur pursuit meant something that one pursued—a field of study, an artistic enterprise, a craft—not unseriously, but out of love rather than merely to earn a living." This was true in the world at large, and especially true in the world of Olympic athletes. If you wanted to compete in the Olympics, you had to be an amateur; to be a professional was a disqualifying condition. This was the world in which I was raised. Add to this my upbringing around cavalry officers, who were officers and gentlemen by the grace of God and act of Congress, and you have someone who is unconsciously set against becoming a professional.

I had already vaguely noticed that when cavalry officers retired, they did not open up boarding and training facilities, or begin teaching lessons and clinics. It just wasn't done in polite society. Foreign cavalry officers who came over after World War II and hung out a shingle here were greeted with understanding; the same society that subconsciously looked down its nose at home-grown professionals made allowances for people like Bert de Némethy and Jack Le Goff. There wasn't much left of society in Europe after World War II (the thinking went, as I imagine); in order to earn a living, men turned their hand to any skill they had. All this is to explain the obvious when one watches old films and studies old photos of horses and riders both here and abroad; those riders weren't very good, and the horses weren't very well trained, by our modern standards.

Anderson's definition of amateurism is true, but Webster's dictionary also describes an amateur as someone who is incompetent or inept. We certainly loved our horses and our sport, but we were equally incompetent and inept. Looking back, it is clear to me that the raw material was there, but we had to hustle to make a living in the "real world," in order to be able to train and compete as amateurs. Those of us who were shamateurs were obviously living a compromise that gave us the worst of both sides—not very good at riding, and not making much of a living in the outside world. Thus, U.S. horse sports were stuck in a sort of Catch-22: we couldn't make a living with horses as a profession, so there were no professionals. Because there were so few professionals, each generation was bound to repeat the mistakes of their predecessors. The opportunities that we take for granted in the horse world today simply did not exist in eventing in 1984.

This explains why I retired from competition after the 1984 Olympics and took a job with Collier Cobb, a mid-sized commercial bond and insurance firm. The owner of Collier Cobb, Fitzgerald (Gerry) Hudson, was a long-time client of mine and we had become friends. He shared my interest in hunting, and we went on hunting trips together once my competitive season was over. On one of these trips, knowing I had announced my retirement, Gerry asked me what I was going to do next. I replied that I didn't know, but it would definitely involve regular hours and a regular paycheck. One thing led to another, and I left the horse world behind and went to work for Collier Cobb.

Karen (née Lende) O'Connor took over both my barn and the ride on Castlewellan; she was quite successful with him, winning the 1985 Fall U.S. National Championships by a huge margin. She quickly developed a business model based on working students and filled the stables at Fox Covert Farm.

Meanwhile, for the next several years I drove into McLean, Virginia, put in my time from 8:30 to 4:30 five days a week, and spent the weekends at home. This had a lot of advantages, especially at first. I caught up on my duties as a father. I saw plenty of soccer matches, track meets, and school plays, and enjoyed watching Hillary and Jennifer grow up. My hours were regular, and the paycheck was nice. And as it turned out, although I *thought* I had retired from competition—man proposes, God disposes—there was one more major event in my future.

Me, the Optimist

——Although I had turned the Fox Covert stable operation over to Karen Lende, I was still riding and teaching on the weekends. The Thompsons had offered Karen the ride on Rockingham along with Castlewellan when I retired, but Rocky was a notoriously difficult ride, so Karen said, in the nicest possible way, "Not on your life." Vita and Dick then loaned Rocky to me as a foxhunter, and I hunted him with the Piedmont Fox Hounds for several seasons. He remained difficult, but Erskine Bedford, our MFH, was a good horseman and recognized my problems. He didn't mind my circling behind him at a high rate of speed, as long as I was keen to hunt. Between the hunting and the teaching, although I may have been retired from international competition and was working, I was riding fit and still involved with horses.

Then I got a call from Diana and Bert Firestone in the fall of 1985. Karen was named to the 1986 World Championship team that would compete in Australia. Because the seasons below the equator are reversed, the Championship would take place in the spring, which meant Karen could not ride their horse, The Optimist, at Kentucky. Would I like the ride? With a recent Bill Steinkraus comment about getting better after retirement in the back of my mind, I didn't give it much thought before I said, "Yes"—I would ride him for expenses and 10 percent of the prize money. The Firestones thought this was a fair deal, and that's how The Optimist ("Bill") came into my life.

Purchased by the Firestones as a ride for their son, Matthew, Bill had turned out to be spectacularly unsuitable in that role. Matt was quite strong, but fairly short, and Bill was an enormous bull of a horse. I had been watching him go for a year or so and had always secretly liked him, even as I watched him run away with a succession of riders. I have a soft spot in my heart for 16.3-hand mealy-nosed brown geldings from Ireland, but at first glance it was hard to have a soft spot for Bill. He was unattractive: plain bay with no markings, slightly lop-eared, Roman-nosed, and pig-eyed, with a dull expression. He had a thick neck, massive shoulders, and powerful hindquarters. At first glance, in other words, he was the epitome of a thug.

The Firestones had several additional horses in training with Karen at Fox Covert, and I was fortunate that Bill's groom, Janice Hilton, came with him. Janice was extremely knowledgeable, having worked for Lorna Sutherland Clarke in England before emigrating. She told me that if we got to Kentucky, it would be the one-hundredth Classic event she had worked at. (She didn't tell me until much later that in all that time, she had never groomed a winner.)

Much to my surprise, within a couple of weeks of starting to ride Bill in January, I was thoroughly demoralized. No matter what I tried, we were not on the same wavelength, and I could tell we would not be successful if this trend continued. He resisted my efforts to get him on the bit and charged every obstacle in his path with a frighteningly powerful rush. After I had ridden him early one Saturday morning, once again with a signal lack of progress, I handed him over to Janice and went to teach some lessons in my indoor arena.

Bill, I See You!

____Bill's stall was next to the arena, and I had already noticed that he would hang over his stall webbing and watch my lessons. He focused his attention on the activity, and if I raised my voice he lifted his head and pricked his outsized ears until the arena settled down. On this day, Janice returned him to his stall, and he audited the rest of my lesson until I finished. Then he turned his attention to his hay.

I didn't realize it at that moment, but when I stepped from the arena into the barn aisle that day, I was stepping into the shadow of the rainbow once again. Bill heard my footstep outside his stall, and when he raised his head and looked at me, he looked directly into my eyes. His ears were up, his visage was attentive, and his eyes glowed with recognition and intelligence. Startled, I looked back at him—but suddenly it was as if his face were melting. In a flash his eyes were dull, his ears at half-mast, and he had assumed his normal lack of expression.

Laughing, I pointed at him and said, "Too late, Bill, I saw you!"

I suddenly realized that I had completely misunderstood Bill. He didn't misbehave because he was stupid; he misbehaved because he was *smart*. (I did tell you he was Irish, didn't I?) Bill did not need his rider to tell him what to do, or even worse, *to try to make him do it*. Bill knew his job; he wanted his rider to remember the test or the course—and leave the rest to Bill. If the rider tried to make Bill do something, he was just as happy fighting with the rider as fighting with the course. After all, as strong and athletic as Bill was, the jumping was not a challenge—and anyway, he didn't care about dressage one way or another. But if a rider challenged Bill by leaving it up to him, Bill would respond.

Armed with new insight, I changed my approach, and Bill changed his way of going. I don't mean that things were perfect after that, but we showed regular improvement. However, Bill wasn't done teaching me new things. I'd already had my nose rubbed into the mistake of judging a horse by appearance. Now Bill taught me not to get tunnel vision when training event horses.

You can imagine that my morale improved after we won our first competition together, a nice Intermediate warm-up event in North Carolina. I had always done as little competing as possible when training Classic horses. Our cross-country and show jumping were nowhere near as technical then as in events today. I used my Classic preparatory events as a general fitness checkup and made sure my technical work was showing improvement. With only one more horse trials left before Kentucky, at Ship's Quarters in Maryland, I felt pretty good about our chances. Our dressage work needed continual improvement, but that was no surprise. However, at our initial outing, it was apparent that our show jumping needed work. I had been lucky to leave the fences up. Even though the course had been slightly small and relatively easy, Bill had towed me around at a high rate of speed. This would not suit a big-time event.

While my conditioning plan was working, and my dressage improvement was slight but steady, I changed my show-jumping approach. I did a lot of jump-and-walk, jump-and-stop exercises, and worked on combinations with tight distances. Because I set these new problems and left them for Bill to solve, I thought I was happy with things by the time we got to our last "prep" events; it just goes to show you how wrong a fellow can be.

At Ship's Quarters, traditionally the last event before Kentucky, everything was maximum but straightforward, not technical. It was just the right type of challenge to set horses and riders up for a Classic. I was already patting myself on the back halfway through my show-jumping course, thinking about how much better Bill was going. Then I turned into the triple combination. Set at maximum heights and spreads, it was a vertical, one stride to a maximum oxer, then two strides to another maximum oxer. I cantered quietly to the first element, Bill jumped it off a nice stride, and when I landed, what do you think I said to myself?

"Uh oh."

I suddenly realized that I had practiced *shortening* Bill's stride, but to the exclusion of *increasing* his stride. Long story short, I couldn't get there from here. The only thing good to come from that particular in-and-out is that I learned not to have tunnel vision when training horses. Putting in two strides in a one-stride, three strides in a two-stride, and crashing through two maximum oxers will get a trainer's attention. Bill's courage and strength got me out of that scrape, but only just. Unlike my first outing with Bill, where I had won easily, I drove home in a bad mood with a lot on my mind.

My training from then until Kentucky emphasized flexibility, not just long or short. It must have worked, as I wound up winning Kentucky for the second time. Bill was not too far out of the lead after dressage, jumped clean and fast cross-country, and was in second place, less than a rail out of first, going into the show jumping. This was nerve-racking, as Bill was notorious for his casual attitude toward painted rails. However, I persuaded him to leave all the rails up, and once the rider ahead of me knocked down a rail they could not afford, I wound up a winner at my final Classic. After the disappointing finish to my Olympic aspirations two years earlier, this time I could retire on top. When I walked out of the arena following the victory gallop, I felt as if the eventing gods had reached down, patted me on the head, and said, "There, there. You were hugely disappointed not to go to Los Angeles. Now we gave you a big win, but it's time you retired again, this time for good. Don't push your luck." That was good advice, and I took it.

Alphabet Soup

——By the time I rode Bill at Kentucky in 1986, I had been immersed in horse politics for a decade and a half. I've shared details of my adventures in the Byzantine corridors of equine sport administration in another chapter, but for now I'll just say that I sat down at my kitchen table in the summer of 1987 and looked at my life. I had developed a steady sideline in weekend clinics since 1984, and because I did not have horses and riders of my own to worry about, I could schedule my clinics around family and school activities. My reputation as an instructor was growing. It came as a shock when I suddenly realized I was making as much on weekend clinics as I was earning in business during the week. Winning Kentucky certainly gave my reputation as a rider and trainer a boost.

In addition, I had been approached by the chair of the AHSA nominating committee. Would I accept the nomination as president of the National Federation? I said yes readily enough. My nomination had been generally understood for the past few years, and this only made official what I had thought was coming for a while. It was a big job, but I was up to speed on the various issues facing the AHSA and had a clear picture of where I wanted to lead the organization. I felt an obligation to give back to the sport, and this was a way to pay my debt to society. I gave notice to Collier Cobb in the fall of 1987 and was elected president of the AHSA for a three-year term in January of 1988. I was returning to the horse world as the elected leader of a growing industry, and as a professional in an increasingly professionalized sport.

I stayed busy teaching clinics on weekends and flying to New York every other week for meetings at the AHSA offices on 42nd Street, and attending other meetings of the five organizations (AHSA, USET, USCTA, USOC, and FEI) with which I was involved.

I soon realized, however, that I had not anticipated the rapacious demands on my time from those entities. All five were 501c3 not-for-profit organizations, which was admirable. The problem was that many of their meetings, competitions, and other activities were held on weekends.

Abraham Lincoln remarked that a lawyer's time was his "stock in trade." He could have added that the same is true for equestrian coaches.

So it was that in January of 1991, I stepped back into the shadow of the rainbow, when (as I mentioned earlier) I declined a second unpaid term as AHSA president. From this point, I could devote myself more and more to horses. I had some committee assignments in the various organizations, but was gradually cutting back, quietly resigning from them as the opportunity arose. When my term with the USOC Active Athletes Committee concluded, I did not stand for reelection, feeling that the president of a national federation could not satisfy the requirements of both positions. I resigned as secretary of the USCTA, having spent 15 years there. (USCTA president Neil Ayer protested to me, but I replied it was all I could do to attend the meetings, much less take part. He replied that if I resigned, he might be encumbered with someone who actually "wanted to do something." I smiled, and said that might not be all bad, but it was his problem now.) My two statutory terms on the FEI Events Committee had now finished. I was still doing a fair amount of *ad hoc* work for the FEI on various study committees and so on, but knew these activities would dissipate with time.

I had warned Karen Lende that I might be returning to Fox Covert if the AHSA did not accept my proposal for a paid position, so she was not surprised when I told her that she would need a different facility. Naturally, she took all the horses and riders with her when she moved out, and the stables were strangely quiet for a few months, but Fox Covert was full once again by the end of the spring season and would stay that way for the next decade. Although several other facilities were now offering professional training, I had an advantage from my shamateur days, when I taught and trained on a regular basis. The few students I had at first were successful, and this increased the demand for my services.

I was relieved that I finally had a business model that would work, so when the USET asked me in the fall of 1991 if I would be interested in taking over coaching the Eventing Team, I immediately asked about the salary. When they told me, I replied I was already making that amount and to get back to me with another offer.

I never heard from them again. That fall my good friend Mark Phillips was hired and led the Team to medals at almost every major competition from 1992 until 2012. Although I was sad at my missed opportunity, I was happy for him, and for the Team. The Event Team's 20 years of success with Mark reaffirmed my own belief that a team needed a strong leader in order to provide continued success. I well recalled how, following the Team mutiny in 1984, the team riders had taken charge of their own programs but had produced no Olympic medal and only one World Championship medal over the next two Olympic cycles. Considering the success Jack Le Goff had provided, those few years without a team leader seemed like a lifetime of failure.

Oh, Canada!

____ I had always wanted to coach at the Olympic level, and in the fall of 2000 it seemed I might have another chance. Wendy Dell was in charge of Canada's eventing program at that time. She called me and asked if I would be interested in doing some clinics for them. I replied that I did clinics for a living and would be happy to work with the Canadians.

Their Team had not qualified for the Olympics since 1984, and after a few clinics, I was eventually brought on board to help them rebuild their program. This was going to be a challenge, as there were very few qualified horse-and-rider combinations in Canada. Part of my job was to serve in the Canadian committee structure—the events committee, the instructor certification committee, and so on. I knew I needed to have a voice there but held many of the same positions in the United States. Feeling it was a conflict of interest to work for two different countries at the same time, I took the opportunity to resign from all my U.S. positions.

This allowed me to devote as much time as possible to my Canadian duties. However, my time there was limited, because the Canadian Olympic Committee (COC) did not provide much financial support. Their support system was based on international results; if a Team did well, the money flowed. However, if a Team did not do well in international competition, it could go into a death spiral. Fewer results, followed by less support, followed by even less success, was a recipe for a program to become moribund. However, I knew this going into the Olympic cycle, and was in it for the challenge, not for the results. We were able to field a team of four plus two official individuals at the 2002 World Equestrian Games (WEG) in Jerez, Spain. We had little success, but it was a good shake-down cruise for the support staff. It allowed me to identify strengths and weaknesses, as well as giving our riders some much-needed international exposure.

By the 2003 Pan American Games (to be held at Fair Hill, Maryland), I felt better about our program. Several of the WEG riders were back, and some of the riders who had been taking my clinics in Canada were ready for their international debuts. I had no illusions that our "A" team could beat the U.S. "B" team that usually shows up at the Pan Ams. The only real news to come out of the Pan Am event would be if the United States did not win the Team medal. However, our silver medal was a shot in the arm for our team morale and increased the funding levels from the COC. This was good news, as we would need all the help we could get to field a team at the 2004 Athens Olympics. This would be the first Olympic Games to use a short format, and there was a great deal of concern about fitness levels. I prepared the team using my own methods. I had to be careful with the soundness of the horses; we did not have any spares.

When I first started training horses for other people, I was keenly aware that each rider only had one horse. If I broke that horse, the rider would go home. Thus, my methods were historically designed to produce a sound, fit horse at the end of the process. I had been training event horses for 30 years by now, and I was confident that I could produce a team ready for the level. I had been training the Young Rider Teams from my U.S. area throughout the past three decades and was comfortable with the FEI rules and schedules.

When I got the Canadian team to Athens, however, I suddenly realized just how green my Team was. I had an official complement of about 25 riders, grooms, vets, blacksmiths, and support staff. Out of those 25 people, only three of us had ever been to an Olympics before, in any capacity. There was a certain amount of "deer in the headlights" at first, but they settled down and rode well enough given their experience. We had brought five horse-and-rider combinations and were allowed to start a team of four plus an individual. The Canadians and the Americans were the only Teams that finished all five combinations, which would stand the Canadian Team in good stead going forward. However, I felt I had done my job, and it was time for them to find a younger coach to stay with them for a longer period of time. In the fall of 2004, I turned in my resignation to the Canadian Federation, gave up all my Canadian committee positions, and turned my full-time attention to my program at Fox Covert. And that's where my attention has focused from 2004 until now. I train horses and riders, give clinics, write books and articles, fish in the summer, duck hunt in the winter, and enjoy watching my grandsons grow up. Living the dream is working for me. ■

__Standing in the Shadow of the Rainbow

I was recently asked, "Jim, why do you ride?" Simple question; complicated answer. My immediate smart-aleck answer might have been, "Because I can't stop myself," but I bit my tongue; the question was asked in seriousness and deserved a serious reply. After all, this is my life we are talking about here. That's when I realized I could not verbalize the answer to my satisfaction. When I am not sure how to say what I want to say, I turn to others. Famous jurist and novelist Robert Travers was, like me, a devoted fly fisherman. He once said that he fished, "...not because I regard fishing as being so terribly important but because I suspect that so many of the other concerns of men are equally unimportant—and not nearly as much fun." If you substitute "riding" for "fishing" in his quote, you will start to understand why I ride.

Although I have had several other careers in my life, I've always been irresistibly drawn back to horses. When Daddy died, I stopped going to the barn for two years, until Jonas Irbinskas pulled me out of the artificial world I was creating for myself while lost in my mind. I went to Culver Military Academy because I could ride every day. I was a college student for a while, but that was more to stay out of the Vietnam War than any desire for higher education. My three years in the Army were an extension of my desire to ride as much as an avoidance of my patriotic duty. The commercial insurance bond industry did not fill some unexplained void in my life, but it filled my pockets while I figured out how to make a living with horses. A career as an author wasn't on my mind, but I started writing about horses 30 years ago, and I haven't stopped yet. My excursions into "horse politics" and "the alphabets" were to pay my debt to society by serving in the political trenches of the equestrian world, but horse politics never defined me. It took horses to do that.

Bill Steinkraus said, "No throne can compare with the back of a horse, and there is no way in which man can come closer to nature than by becoming one with the horse." I know how he felt. I would give almost anything to be young again, and brave; young again, I'd strike off at a fast gallop on Kilkenny, aim him at a big, solid fence, and feel once more the sense of boundless energy and endless possibilities he gave me. Or, I would give almost anything to once more lean forward over Carawich's withers as a slightly older, more cerebral rider, knowing we faced a cross-country course both huge and technical, and feeling, no matter the speed or the circumstance, that peaceful sense of certitude he gave me.

Those pleasures are now denied to me, but they remain crystal clear in my memory. I realize now that I have spent my life in the shadow of the rainbow, and how extraordinarily fortunate I was to be there. And when I stood there, I was on the back of a horse, complete. ■

ACKNOWLEDGMENTS

I never meant to be an author, it just happened. At first I thought I was quietly going crazy. After I retired in the mid-1980s, I started hearing voices in my head. I don't mean "Lead my people out of Egypt" sort of voices—rather, random snippets of text, spoken in my mind. The scary part was that some of it was in iambic pentameter and blank verse. This last little bit really worried me, as this can be one of the signs of schizophrenia; there is some mental illness in my family. At the time, I just figured I was the next apple to fall off the family tree.

And then along came Bill Steinkraus with a book proposal. I had thought about writing a book, but I had thought about ending world hunger, too. Neither one of them seemed likely, but Bill explained he would hold my hand through the writing process, bring me a contract, get me a sizeable advance, edit the content, and make sure it got published by Doubleday. He was the senior sporting book editor and could make all this happen. It came to pass, and *Training the Three-Day Event Horse and Rider* was a resounding success, selling out a first printing of 10,000, and it is well into its second printing. "Bill's book" (I wrote it, but he translated it into English) went on to sell more copies than there are members of my discipline's association. That's called market penetration.

Turns out, those little snippets were sentences and paragraphs, churning up out of my subconscious, ready for the printed page. Quite a few printed pages have followed, totaling seven books—so far. Behind every book there stands an editor. When editors are good, you don't notice them. Although they were indeed good at their craft, and you would not otherwise know about them. I need to mention that Steve Price, Nancy Jaffer, Sara Lieser, Sandy Oliynyk, and Mandy Lorraine all at one time or another kept me on the rails, cured my many grammatical and syntactical errors, and helped me say what I meant to say in the first place. I had no intention of writing an autobiography until Martha Cook, Rebecca Didier, and Caroline Robbins of Trafalgar Square Books appeared, took me to the mountaintop, and showed me their concept. You now hold it in your hands, and I am blessed they picked me out. If you ever want to publish a book, Trafalgar Square Books is the ticket.

In the modern world, the printed page starts out in a computer, which means I had to learn how to operate a laptop, which means I found ever more new and interesting ways to hit "delete" when I meant to hit "save." Merrilyn Crosgrove Saint has talked me off the internet ledge more times that I can remember; without her, these books would have been lost in some inaccessible computer purgatory. Naturally, a good book needs good photos to illustrate the text; Stacey Wigmore has an uncanny ability to find photos that match my text, for which, many thanks. Brant Gamma once again produced exactly the photo I needed when I needed it, and I am grateful for her extraordinary efforts. Also, thanks to Marty Bauman—founder of Classic Communications, eminence of the press tent, and author of *Kentucky Three-Day Event, a 25-Year Retrospective*—who was his usual invaluable help with the photos in this book.

Over the past decade and more, I have been fortunate to have the same editor, who has gone from a professional associate to a good friend. There

I was, standing in the shadow of the rainbow with nothing to do, when Sandra Cooke appeared. Next thing I knew, I had a monthly column in *Practical Horseman* magazine for her to oversee and several books to add to our resumés. Mark Twain said, "The difference between the almost-right word and the right word is the difference between the lightning bug and the lightning." I have been blessed with an editor who knows the difference, and her contributions to my texts have been invaluable. Thank you, Sandra, I literally couldn't have done it without you.

And speaking of "thank you," for various reasons I have a long list of people I need to thank, both in the horse world and in the real world. Much of what I learned about horses comes from my teachers in that world. My father, Jonas Irbinskas, Bill Bilwin, Bert de Némethy, Lars Sederholm, and Jack Le Goff were invaluable in putting me on the path to understanding how to ride and train horses.

I spent a few years in the "real world" at Collier Cobb and need to thank Fitzgerald Hudson, as well as Lee and Clyde Harper for the kind understanding I received from them while I wrestled with the arcane worlds of construction bonds and insurance. It wasn't for me, but it seemed like a good idea at the time.

I made a slight detour from riding and training into the world of equestrian politics. None of my efforts there could have been successful without the help and support of innumerable people, so I am taking a risk in naming several people, yet forgetting to mention others. In the USCTA (later USEA) world, Eileen Thomas was the power behind the throne, and whenever I had questions or problems was an invaluable resource for me. Behind the scenes at the USET, Jack Fritz was the driving administrative force and an endless source of ideas for the improvement of the horse world. Bill Steinkraus filled so many roles it is hard to know where to begin to thank him for his advice, support, informed comment, and most importantly, his friendship.

The AHSA (later USEF) took up a great deal of my time, and I formed many fast friendships while I was there. It tells you how rocky my tenure was when I start out by thanking the attorneys involved in our daily AHSA affairs, Bill Roos and Ira Finkelstein. They defended our mission when it was under attack by powerful financial interests attempting to make it legal to cheat using medications. Their efforts produced the organization we have today; it wouldn't exist in its present form without them.

Involved in these efforts, and many more, was one of my best friends, Ned Bonnie; I mourn his loss every day. An attorney, Ned was dedicated to the well-being of horses and to providing a level playing field for all competitors, from the largest stables to the "little guy" with a tagalong horse trailer and a dream.

I made many other good friends at the AHSA, and I think we made major improvements while we were there. In no particular order, John Lengle, Chrys Tauber, Alan Balch, Al Martin, Jane Clark, Linda Allen, Tatiana Doughty, both Jean and Lisa Blackstone, Dick McDevitt, Frank Chapot, Don Burt, Marge McDonald, Steve Hawkins, all made invaluable contributions, along with many whose names are not mentioned. I'm sure I've left people off who should be on this list, and I plead senility rather than bad manners.

Finally, I must thank my family, including my two daughters, my four tall, handsome grandsons, and most especially my wife, Gail, for their patience in dealing with this absent-minded creature called an author, who goes bumbling through their lives with a faraway look in his eyes. They will testify I have been in that condition for so long they now view it as a permanent state. This book is a testimonial to their patience with me, and I am endlessly grateful to them. Every time I see them, my heart swells with love and pride. ∎

INDEX